THE PEOPLE'S LAWYERS

MARLISE JAMES

THE PEOPLE'S LAWYERS

HOLT, RINEHART AND WINSTON

New York   Chicago   San Francisco

Library of Congress Cataloging in Publication Data

James, Marlise.
      The people's lawyers.

      CONTENTS: Rights lawyers: Roger Baldwin and the
early years of the American Civil Liberties Union.
Leonard Boudin and the National Emergency Civil Liberties
Committee.   Mel Wulf and the new ACLU.   Anthony
Amsterdam: a practicing civil libertarian law professor.
Poverty rights lawyers.   Consumer rights lawyers.   [etc.].
      1.   Lawyers—United States.   I.   Title.
KF298.J34   340'.0973   74–182761
ISBN 0–03–001041–1

First Edition

Designer: Andrea Clark
Printed in the United States of America

To

ANNE ROBERTS AND BERNARD EUGENE JAMES
whose love for each other
created the author

and to

THOSE LAWYERS whose love for people
created the book

Contents

Author's Note

This book began as a modest project to write about those left lawyers who were, because of the cases they had handled or the organizations with which they were connected, already nationally known.

As I began to research and interview, however, and was referred from one person or organization to another, I came to realize that there was a large group of equally dedicated, hard-working, and interesting left lawyers who, for various reasons, were virtually unknown to the public. The history and scope of what I call the people's law movement increasingly interested me. I followed up the referrals I had been given and discovered that my original idea, to be fair and even partially inclusive, had to be expanded greatly.

This book is the story, then, of some of the people's lawyers living today, and of the tides of history and organizations that have allowed them to be such. While the book is comprehensive, it is far from being all-inclusive. To cover all of the people included in the movement would take several volumes.

Organizational and general history is covered from the point of view of persons or people who took part in that history. While there are sections of explanation about organizations, firms, or collectives, there are no sections that deal exclusively with them. I feel that history is highly personal and such a thing as objective history cannot exist in our time. Nor do I believe in objective reporting. My bias throughout has been strongly in favor of people's lawyers.

One purpose of this book is to shatter the rather stodgy, touch-me-not image that most people in this country seem to have of lawyers, radical or otherwise. Presenting everything from the personal viewpoint of the people involved helps, I trust, to achieve this purpose. Unfortunately, this approach tends to underrate the influence, diversity of views, and scope that organizations have, apart from the people who describe them.

With one exception, all of the people included in this book were interviewed in person. During these interviews I asked the interviewees to place themselves at center stage, to tell me about their pasts, presents, and futures. I also asked questions to elicit, in the strongest possible words, their views of the country, the court system, the people's law movement, and their personal philosophies. To avoid repetition, I have edited my questions out of the final manuscript. Consequently, the people in the book sound very strong, self-centered, and often arrogant. After interviewing over one hundred lawyers I think that, as a rule, they are strong and, generally, egotistical people. If they were not, they would not be good lawyers. However, they are not quite as egocentric and arrogant as they will probably sound to the reader.

In the course of my research I have spoken with people from most of the legal collectives in the country and many of these collectives are included in the book. In these sections, I have not attributed quotes. One of the basic ideas of the collective is that the people who belong to it are unified, through struggle, in their ideology. Another is that no one person should be singled out for special attention. I believe that, by not attributing quotes, I both honor and illustrate those parts of the collective idea. In these sections, I have also tried to use each separate collective to bring out a different aspect of the collective ideology. For example, with the New York Commune, I have explained the basic collective idea and written about the problems that go with it; with the People's Law Office I have shown some of the necessary changes that a collective that stays together must go through; with the Bar Sinister I have shown the backgrounds of some people who have been attracted to collectives; with the Venice Collective I have shown the philosophy of a collective that has a countercultural as well as political orientation; with the Community Law Firm I have shown how the collective firm works in a community setting; with the Gainesville Collective, how a collective fares in the South.

The third section of the book is "Second Nation Lawyers." I've chosen to call it this rather than "Third World Lawyers" because the latter term connotes an international movement and I've included only American lawyers working within the boundaries of the U.S. I believe the former was first used in the Kerner report, which described poor and minority people as "a second nation in our midst." I have purposely kept myself out of these chapters as much as possible. I feel that the people I interviewed can explain their own problems and views much more accurately than I can. One attorney, Kenneth Cockrel, could easily have been in this section. However, without the explanation of his views preceding those of his white radical comrades, the Detroit chapter of section II would have been confusing.

Several white radical attorneys are also included in this section because they serve as primary defense counsel for second nation groups.

I want to thank all of the lawyers who are included for reading, revising, and commenting upon the sections of the book that concern them. I especially want to thank Anthony Amsterdam, Jim Lorenz, Carol and Bob Lefcourt, and Haywood Burns for reading and commenting upon entire sections of the book.

For their help and support while the book was in progress, I would like to thank Robert James, Pat and Barbara Patterson, Richard Negretti, Helen Hess, Vicki Schultz, Ed Marcotte, Gene

Bloom, William Girdner, Nick Impenna, Sig Moglen, Erna Akuginow, Oscar Collier, Sun Bear, Morning Star, Coco, Che, and, especially, Barbara Sautter.

M. J.

August 1972

Introduction

Most white Americans grow up believing in the myth of the lawyer as demigod. Perhaps because we have no overt aristocracy we have taken the people in certain professions—mainly the medical and legal—and put them into the place that aristocracy has occupied. We've crowned them with mantles of wisdom, and expect them always to be brave, honest, upright, true, kindly, concerned—pillars of the community.

While there have probably always been scattered members of the legal profession who have possessed traits that the myth attributed to them, they have always been the distinct minority. What the legal profession has always been about is money, influence, power, and status. While one cannot deny the fact that many of the leaders of the original American revolution were lawyers, one can look at what that revolution really accomplished—an entrenchment of the monied, land-owning, white male middle class in power —and question how concerned and kindly those lawyers actually were. The legal profession in the United States, as in all other countries, has always been the handmaiden of people with power.

Down through our history there have been exceptions, lawyers who were willing to risk their reputations, and their incomes, by defending unpopular clients or causes. But, until recently, these exceptions have been few.

It was not until the beginning of the twentieth century that this situation began to show any marked change. Before America's entry into World War I, a group of concerned citizens responded to the government's repression of individual rights with wartime restrictions on free speech and freedom of the press by forming a group that later became the American Civil Liberties Union (ACLU). Some of these concerned people were lawyers, and their participation in the ACLU really marks the beginning of the people's law movement. With the founding of the ACLU, the convictions of the few extant people's lawyers became institutionalized, and their convictions became a more powerful influence because of the unity and strength they were able to find in numbers.

Although these lawyers were not radical by the standards of today, they were quite advanced for that time. They declared that people from any class should be accorded the same rights that were previously accorded only those who possessed the power to exercise them.

In 1925, an organization was formed that paved the way for another input into the people's law movement. It was then that the National Bar Association (NBA) came into being to serve the needs of the Black bar. At that time and until 1945, Black lawyers were not allowed to become members of the American Bar Association (ABA).

During the New Deal, radical lawyers, generally with a labor orientation, began to surface, thus providing the final input into today's people's law movement. By 1937 there were enough of them to form an organization, the National Lawyers Guild (NLG), which provided another alternative to the ABA, which, since its founding, had been on the side of the established powers. The NLG came into being partially as a protest against the anti-Roosevelt sentiments of the ABA, partially in protest against its policy of segregation. The NLG was composed of lawyers who considered themselves more interested in human rights than property rights.

With three different organizational inputs feeding it, the people's law movement was quite strong in the late 1930s. However, in 1939, when the Nazi-Soviet nonaggression pact was signed, the movement began to weaken. At that time, as later, any person with a left or labor orientation was considered somewhat suspect, and the people's law movement suffered generally because of these suspicions.

In 1940, two events occurred that later would have very profound effect on the people's law movement. First, the legal department of the National Association for the Advancement of Colored People (NAACP) became a separate entity, the NAACP Legal Defense and Educational Fund, Inc. (Inc. Fund), and began strongly to serve the civil rights needs of second nation people in much the same way that the ACLU served the civil liberties needs of white—and some minority—people. Second, as a herald of coming harm to just about every liberal-to-radical organization in the country, Congress passed the Alien Registration Act. The second part of this act, commonly known as the Smith Act, forbade the advocacy of the overthrow of the government by force or violence, and conspiracies to bring about such overthrow. It was really from the passage of this act that what later became known as "the witch hunt" commenced.

Many liberal organizations, the ACLU included, responded to the atmosphere of those times by passing resolutions barring Communists from their memberships. Elizabeth Gurley Flynn, one of the Union's founders and a member of its board of directors, was ousted from the board because she had publicly declared that she was a Communist.

When the United States entered World War II, the people's law movement dropped to a low point. Civil rights, civil liberties, and radical rights were mostly forgotten during the war. More than one hundred thousand Japanese-Americans were placed in concentration camps with hardly a murmur from any lawyer or legal group.

Following the war, with Russia as our new-found ally, it appeared that people's lawyers might be able to get on with their business. Then, the cold war began, the government resurrected the Smith Act, and the witch hunt that had begun eight years before intensified. During this time, anyone who smelled like a fellow traveler, or even a sympathizer, was in trouble.

The rights lawyers in the ACLU fell over each other in the rush to proclaim their patriotism. They were not willing, either in court or in front of congressional committees, to defend the victims of what is commonly called McCarthyism.

Individual members of the NLG were kept busy defending the rights of their labor and radical clients. They did their work so strenuously that they were accused, as an organization, of being the Communist party's legal arm in this country. While some members of the Guild were, in fact, members of the Party, the majority were not. When the attorney general threatened to place the NLG on his list of subversive organizations, some of the more timid members left the Guild, and many of those who remained spent a good deal of their time fighting the threat of the attorney general. Eventually, they won.

During these dim days for the then-existing people's law organizations, a new one came into being. The National Emergency Civil Liberties Committee (NECLC) was formed by rights lawyers disillusioned with the ACLU, and by non-Communist liberals who were not afraid of being labeled Communist.

For the next few years, swimming against the rising tide of anticommunism, the NLG and the NECLC did what they could to remind Americans of the Bill of Rights. Often, they could not do enough. The tide did not begin to turn until 1957 when, in the Yates case, the Supreme Court ruled that the Smith Act was meant only to stop action-inciting advocacy, and not advocacy of abstract doctrines.

Ironically, it was during these generally bad days for the people's law movement that the Supreme Court reached a decision that ultimately allowed the movement to expand to the point it has reached today.

In 1954, in the case of *Brown v. Board of Education of Topeka, et al.*, the Court ruled that the separate but equal system in public schools was in violation of the Fourteenth Amendment. The years of work by the Inc. Fund and a brave group of Black attorneys had paid off for them and their clients and was in a few years to have a profound and unexpected effect on all other people's lawyers. Following this decision, "separate but equal" was quickly shattered in the areas of public transportation and recreational facilities.

For the most part, the witch hunt ended with the silent fifties. In the spring of 1960, the House Un-American Activities Committee, apparently not aware that its time had largely passed, decided to hold hearings in San Francisco. Thousands of people, many of them students, turned out to protest the hearings. The police responded by dragging the protesters down steps, flushing them with fire hoses, and herding them into patrol wagons. The nation witnessed this brutality via television, and many people responded with horror and indignation.

This one event actually set the tone for the sixties, a decade of protest. From California, the action turned to the South. Increasingly, Black students sat in to protest segregation in public places. Beginning in 1963, a large number of northern activists began to go to the South in the summer to help in the quest for justice and equality.

They were greeted with clubs, hoses, dogs, arrest, and worse. Sensing that they were once again needed, most of the organizations and individuals in the people's law movement began to go south. This southern activity gave the people's law movement the boost that it needed to begin to move strongly after twenty years of limited, quiet actions.

Lawyers and law students poured into the South during that, and the following, summer. Those who went never returned with quite the same views that they had before. A new organization, the Law Students Civil Rights Research Council (LSCRRC), was formed to channel law students' energies both when they were in the South and when they returned to school. Four labor and civil liberty attorneys who had been radicalized by their southern experiences formed the Center for Constitutional Rights to allow them to continue with the work they had begun there. Several of the then existing legal organizations formed under the umbrella of the Lawyers' Constitutional Defense Committee so that they could work together on the legal problems of the South. The ACLU, the NLG, and the Inc. Fund all sent representatives to the South.

In 1964, in response to the "discovery" of the poor and disadvantaged second nation in our midst, the government passed the Economic Opportunity Act, which included a section providing for free legal services for the poor. Out of this came a new rights input into the people's law movement as committed young attorneys across the country drew up proposals for legal services programs, and received government funding to carry these proposals through.

In 1965, another rights input came into the people's law movement when Ralph Nader, a young attorney, published *Unsafe at Any Speed* and set the stage for consumer rights, or public interest lawyers.

As these new alternatives for rights lawyers began to emerge, all of the older legal organizations continued to grow. The ACLU and NECLC were infiltrated by activists.

The NLG had a renaissance as more and more young attorneys and law students became radicals, and joined the Guild. In the midsixties the Guild actively began to organize law students. It became known as the legal arm of the movement. Soon, it started to handle directly each year thousands of cases connected with demonstrations against the war, racism, and poverty. And there were thousands of cases to handle as protest spread across the nation. In 1967, the first Guild mass defense office was set up to handle protest cases in New York City. This office was so successful that at its 1968 convention, the Guild adopted this regional office concept and urged members to help it spread to facilitate the handling of those cases where mass defense was necessary, to obtain lawyers for political defendants, and to serve as the focal points for the Guild's efforts to organize law students and lawyers.

By the late sixties, second nation lawyers had begun to form their own, often militant, organizations. The Black American Law Students Association (BALSA) began in 1967. Shortly afterward, it merged with a group of Black attorneys to form the National Conference of Black Lawyers. Chicano law students formed the National La Raza Law Students Association. Indian law students formed the American Indian Law Students Association.

Until this time, many militant second nation organizations had utilized the services of white radical attorneys because most second nation lawyers had not been able—largely due to finances— to give free or inexpensive legal help on time-consuming political cases. With the organization of militant second nation attorneys came a challenge to these white radicals to surrender their legal control of the groups they had aided. In several cases, this challenge has been ignored both by the organizations and their attorneys, and white radical lawyers still act as primary defense counsels.

All of this organizational activity was matched by individual activity on the part of law students and attorneys. By the late 1960s, law schools began to report a large drop in the number of their graduates entering business firms; legal organizations outside of the traditional bar associations reported substantial rises in their membership figures; law students began to demand clinical programs that would allow them to help indigents while they were still in school; legal service organizations, ranging from Ralph Nader's Public Interest Research Group to OEO legal services programs, began to attract an ever-increasing number of

the best young lawyers; and large corporate firms were forced to
set aside pro bono publico (for the public good) time to help
boost their sagging recruitments.

Because there were so many young people's-lawyers coming
out of law school, new forms of organizations had to be found to
accommodate them—to let them do the work that they wanted to
do and still subsist. All of the legal organizations discussed thus
far took on as many people's lawyers as they could, either as staff
attorneys, interns, trainees, or cooperating attorneys. The NLG's
regional offices tried to steer paying cases toward attorneys who
were attempting to do a lot of free political work.

However, this was not enough. To meet this new need, a new
form of law firm came into existence, the legal collective. These
collectives, incorporating the ideas of the movement, allowed
young attorneys, by dividing all expenses and fees, to subsist
while still having the time to do free political work. They also attempted to change the conception of lawyers and law firms by
doing away with secretaries and replacing them with legal workers who had equal voice in the decision making, and who were
free to do whatever work interested them. In their daily work,
collectivists also tried to struggle against their own professionalism, elitism, and male chauvinism. This idea has caught on, especially with white radical attorneys, and there are now about a
dozen such collectives spread across the country. Their influence
in the NLG became strong enough that they were able, against
the protests of traditionalists, to convince the organization to
allow legal workers to join as full members.

To serve this need, the field of public interest law also began to
grow, and different financial schemes that will allow people to do
legal work in the public interest and still subsist are now being
tried in different parts of the country. These schemes include the
funding of public interest firms by students, lawyers, and "public
citizens."

All of these concrete changes in the legal profession have, of
course, begotten conceptual and philosophical changes. Many

radical and civil libertarian lawyers who had put their hearts into the legal work they had done in the South joined some of their second nation brethren in a general disillusionment with the legal system when they saw that changes within the law did not necessarily trigger changes within the society. Their disappointment was so deep that they refused to act any longer as lawyers were expected to act.

His honor, the captain of the courtroom, could no longer depend on all lawyers to act as dutiful first lieutenants. Lawyers began to raise their voices, and their fists, in court to show their solidarity with their clients. The expected conservative attire was often exchanged for mod, hip, or even funky dress. Hair grew longer and beards appeared on male attorneys. The language of the courtroom sometimes sounded like the language of the streets. In other words, lawyers stopped identifying with the exclusive courtroom clubhouse atmosphere and started relating to their clients, and the causes these clients served.

Attorneys began to hold numerous press conferences in which they would express their view that justice was not being served in the courtroom. Always implicit in these statements was the attitude, "If we can't get justice in the court, we'll get it in the streets; if we can't get a jury of peers inside the courtroom, we'll have one waiting outside."

These new attitudes were noticed by everyone. Traditionalists within legal organizations began to fight the activists, the people who espoused these views. Judges began to hand down sometimes heavy contempt sentences to so-called disruptive lawyers. Bar associations began to look into the "morals and fitness" of practicing attorneys. The character committees of these associations began more carefully to peruse the applications for admittance to the bar of law students with an activist history. Conservative attorneys suggested that lawyers who disrupt the courtroom be charged with a felony. Nixon's attorney general and the chief justice of the Supreme Court began to speak strongly against this new style of lawyering.

By the beginning of the 1970s, as the general movement began to splinter and fragment, the people's law movement *apparently* passed its peak. Corporate law recruiters noticed an upward trend in recruitment. General public interest in radical law and radical lawyers began to taper off. Disruptions in the courtroom became rarer. Legal organizations tended to cooperate less than they had during the decade of protest.

Yet, even without the unity and the excitement of the 1960s, there still is a larger number of people's lawyers and legal workers than ever before working for the rights of people all across the country. In the 1970s it appears that these people's lawyers and legal workers are being less flamboyant, and even more serious, about their work than they were in the 1960s.

The preceding is meant to serve as a chronological, interpretative outline of the people's law movement. What follows is a comprehensive history of the individuals and organizations who have come together to form it. The story is told, in large part, in the words of the people who are so central a part of this history.

1
RIGHTS LAWYERS

Roger Baldwin and the Early Years of the American Civil Liberties Union

Roger Baldwin, now in his late eighties, is the prototypical civil libertarian, just as the American Civil Liberties Union (ACLU), the organization which he headed for many of his adult years, is the prototypical civil liberties organization. Although Baldwin is not a lawyer himself, he has been the friend, supporter, and mentor of countless civil liberties lawyers for more than fifty years. In recent years, because of his knowledge of civil liberties law, he has served as a visiting professor of law at the University of Puerto Rico.

Baldwin was born in 1884 to a liberal Unitarian family in Boston. His father was a socially concerned businessman, his mother was an agnostic and something of a feminist, his paternal grandfather was a lay preacher and president of the Boston Young Men's Christian Union, and his Uncle William was a trustee of Tuskeegee University and a sponsor of Booker T. Washington. Given that background, it is not surprising that Baldwin eventually found himself doing social work.

"I started my infantile social work at about ten, went to church with unquestioning belief in man, if not God, and read history outside of school with a reformer's eye, always with the underdog and rebels. It was not that I did not like our society. I did. I liked it so much that I just knew it would perfect itself, that good people like us would triumph."

After attending Wellesley High School, "the inescapable Harvard," and spending a year in Europe with his family, he accepted, on the advice of his father's lawyer, Louis Brandeis, an offer to teach sociology at Washington University and work with a slum settlement house run by the Ethical Culture Society in St. Louis. He remained there for eleven years, also becoming chief probation officer of the Juvenile Court and, later, secretary of the Civic League, a reform organization for better city government.

When World War I started, he realized that he could have no part of it and was opposed to the United States' entry into it. He became the St. Louis representative of the American Union Against Militarism (AUAM), which was largely composed of social workers. When the director of the AUAM was taken ill, shortly before America's entry into the war, Baldwin agreed to leave St. Louis and take on the directorship of the organization.

"By that time I knew I was a complete pacifist, unwilling to take part in organized violence for any end. I have never faltered since. But the war issues that really gripped me were the civil liberties ones concerning freedom of speech, press, and association. And they were immediate. Repression became very bad with mob violence and governmental and political action against all people who were against the war. It didn't take long to get people hysterical because the experience was so new, almost unexpected. We went into the war so fast, after an election in which Wilson promised to keep us out of war.

"At once when the U.S. entered the war the AUAM was flooded with appeals for help from war opponents and conscientious objectors, many requiring legal help. Since the AUAM was not equipped to handle legal aid, a committee to render free legal services was set up. I concentrated my energies on running this committee—known as the Civil Liberties Bureau. In the fall of 1917, the Bureau split from the AUAM in Washington to become an independent agency in New York City, where the directing committee had always been located.

"Volunteer lawyers were quickly enlisted from all over the country to counsel conscientious objectors and to defend or advise persons charged with making antiwar speeches, or writing antiwar publications, or belonging to antiwar associations. At that time the government was attacking by indictments under war laws hundreds of people who opposed the war or the draft. The lawyers who volunteered their services were often themselves against the war, many because of their membership in the Socialist party or the Farmers Non-Partisan League, others as Quakers and religious pacifists. The Bureau enlisted in its New York office two able lawyers, Albert De Silver and Walter Nelles, who were able to give their whole time to legal aid; De Silver because he was wealthy and Nelles because he needed only bare expenses.

"The office kept cooperating attorneys all over the country advised of cases, decisions, and regulations by sending out bulletins. We were the first organization to do that. We also responded to thousands of inquiries, especially from conscientious objectors, whose problems under the first general draft law in the U.S. required major attention from the Bureau both in Washington with the War Department and in local draft boards. We also handled courts martial of people trying to get out of the army—unhappily, not often successfully.

"After the war, we thought that the services of the Bureau could be discontinued, but then the Russian revolution shook the world, causing terrific repercussions in the United States. It excited deep controversy, and the left and labor unions came under fresh attacks. It was evident that the Bureau would have plenty to do. We formally expanded the Bureau into the American Civil Liberties Union at a meeting in New York in January 1920. Instead of Washington and New York based groups we created a national organization with representatives all over the country. Before the ACLU actually formed I was doubtful that anyone who had served time in jail for being a war resister, such as I had, would be acceptable as director of an organization that now would include a wide range of civil libertarians. So we took a poll and not one objection was voiced. I accepted the position of director and, in one way or another, I've been with the ACLU ever since.

"As a legal defense organization the Union then as now relied largely on volunteer counsel. After the war the number of such volunteers increased to over a thousand from all over the country, including many defenders of trade union rights, which were then under sharp attack in the open shop movement. These lawyers worked for us without fee, and usually without expenses. We selected cases because of their usefulness to constitutional principles, and we usually took them at the appellate level. When protracted court trials were involved, the defendants would engage other than Union lawyers for fees, but we would often assist them in raising funds or with legal advice.

"We enlisted some of the most distinguished lawyers in the country for important cases—Clarence Darrow of Chicago; Wendell Willkie of New York; Henry P. Hunt, one-time mayor of Cincinnati; Frank P. Walsh of Kansas City and New York, a former chairman of the War Labor Board; Professor Felix Frankfurter of Harvard, who later became a Supreme Court justice; former U.S. Senator Thomas W. Hardwick of Georgia. These lawyers, among many others, represented the defense of the Bill of Rights for the ACLU, and did it regardless of the politics of the client. Many more well-known lawyers signed friend-of-the-court briefs in Supreme Court cases taken on by the Union to establish constitutional principles, always acting on behalf of the public interest.

"Throughout the years the Union has been advised closely by its general counsels, all volunteers who have given substantial time. In our early years Wolcott H. Pitkin served in this capacity; later Arthur Garfield Hays and Morris L. Ernst did so; and, more recently, Osmond K. Fraenkel, Norman Dorsen, and Marvin Karpatkin.

"For its first few years the ACLU was kept busy fighting for the free speech rights of the Industrial Workers of the World [IWW] and other radical unions, fighting against deportation of alien radicals, and striving for amnesty for the hundreds of wartime prisoners and conscientious objectors. Although the Union often used publicity tactics such as sending people into trouble spots to test the right to hold meetings, it did not come to front-page attention until the Tennessee 'Monkey Trial' of 1925."

In March of 1925, Governor Peay of Tennessee had signed into law a bill that made it illegal to teach evolutionary theory contrary to the story of creation in the Bible. In April the ACLU sent press releases to Tennessee newspapers guaranteeing legal and financial assistance to any teacher who would challenge this law. A young science teacher, John T. Scopes, volunteered and was indicted by a grand jury in May.

For eleven days in July the trial attracted world attention, with Clarence Darrow, an agnostic and a member of the Union's National Committee, leading the defense team and William Jennings Bryan, a Fundamentalist and three-time Democratic loser for the Presidency, heading the prosecution. Scopes was convicted, and fined $100. On appeal, the Tennessee Supreme Court upheld the law but reversed the conviction, making it impossible to appeal to the Supreme Court.

"No case was ever again brought in Tennessee, but it was not until thirty years later that the Supreme Court had the chance in an Arkansas case to strike down such laws. No other striking court case of national note marked the Union's always full docket until the New Deal years began in 1932. But our lawyers were busy with labor and left defense and our committees were expanding their interests into the rights of racial minorities—Indians, Negroes, Orientals, and Spanish-speaking people in the Southwest. We also had an influential Council on Censorship which enlisted expert legal advice to tackle the problems of the mass media with state and local censors, and to tackle the post office bans on 'obscene' and 'subversive' matter as well as the barriers to importing from abroad all sorts of 'objectionable' material, including some world classics.

"Almost at once when the New Deal administration took office in 1932 the efforts of the ACLU found a favorable response in Washington. Many ACLU members held office in the administration. The expansion of federal agencies to protect rights, notably, the Labor Relations Act, and the novel services of a welfare state opened new avenues for ACLU activity. Resistance to New Deal measures by conservatives and anti-trade union employers brought on renewed industrial warfare, and the Union's lawyers were enlisted time and again all over the country to help protect the rights to organize, strike, and picket and to defend union people against injunctions and police and employers' gunmen. It was not until the Supreme Court upheld the Labor Relations Act in 1937 that the resistance stopped.

"The 1930s were years of momentous concern to champions of democracy and civil liberties with the rise of the Nazis in Germany, fascism in Italy, and the civil war in Spain. United fronts organized by Communists in Europe and the U.S., with a wide range of liberal and labor support, fought fascism and backed the Spanish 'Loyalist' government. Many of the leaders in the ACLU joined in these efforts, Dr. Harry Ward, the board chairman, and myself included. This cooperation with Communists gave the Union, in many circles, a reputation which should have been confined to the personal connections of its officers. But, it was inescapable that confusion resulted."

It was in this atmosphere of confusion and shock following the Nazi-Soviet pact of 1939 that the ACLU, in 1940, took an action that caused its first large internal split. It passed a resolution barring from its governing committees or staff any person who "is a member of any political organization which supports totalitarian dictatorship in any country or who, by his public declarations, indicates his support of such a principle."

While the ACLU specified that the resolution was aimed at excluding anyone who failed to meet "the test of consistency in the defense of civil liberties in all aspects and all places," it was most clearly aimed at Communists and, more specifically, at Elizabeth Gurley Flynn, one of the Union's founders and a longtime board member, who had publicly declared that she had joined the Communist party in 1937. In March the board asked Miss Flynn for her resignation which she refused to give. In May she was "tried" by the board and ousted by a ten to nine vote. Subsequently the National Committee, composed of fifty people, ratified the board's actions by a twenty-seven to twenty-three vote, and Miss Flynn's membership on the board was terminated.

"I had two feelings about the matter. In the first place I admired Miss Flynn. She was a friend of mine. Yet, I felt that her presence on the board was inconsistent with our principles. Anybody who believed in the principles of the Communist party and in dictatorship in a foreign country was not the type of person who would be convincing to our constituency, however sincere they were in supporting civil liberties in the United States. It was for that reason that we excluded Communists. But then other civil libertarians and liberals accused the ACLU of practicing the guilt by association that it had fought against for so long. We answered that by saying that guilt by association in a private organization was different from guilt by association in a public position where there should be no tests of people's opinions. A private organization has to test your opinions and your loyalty to its own principles. A church does it; any organization does."

Another accusation aimed at the Union was that this resolution provided a model loyalty oath for other organizations, as well as for government agencies.

"I think that other organizations that followed our example just felt the same way that we did. They were faced with the same dilemma. Remember that this was a period when Communist infiltration of liberal organizations was a problem that often resulted in Communist domination. It didn't get anywhere near that in the ACLU although it did in some of our local committees, and we had to dissociate ourselves from them. The Communists were using the ACLU for political purposes, and we have tried always to keep clear of any political influence.

"The policy laid down by the resolution was followed for years as a useful answer to those who charged the Union with Communist sympathies, and as a declaration of principle consistent with the Union's purposes. Rather than modify or repeal the resolution, as some critics from time to time urged, on the ground that it was outdated, in 1970 the Union's board strengthened it in a constitutional provision requiring of all ACLU personnel 'uncompromising support of civil liberties for all peoples.' This action also excluded the advocates of racial or religious discrimination from working for the ACLU, and it has ended the debate by making it clear to all that the Union is directed only by persons faithful to its principles.

"It cannot be said that the Union has always lived up to its principles without compromise. It has avoided some issues it should have met, like the wholesale violation of civil rights in the enforcement of prohibition."

Critics also cite the World War II period as one in which the ACLU did not perform with its previous zeal. They especially note that the Union responded weakly when Japanese-Americans on the West Coast were interned in concentration camps on the presumption that they would cooperate with a Japanese submarine attack.

"The character of World War II, unlike World War I, brought comparatively few prosecutions for opposition to it, for opponents were few. The Union defended the cases brought to it and ran a legal aid bureau for conscientious objectors. The main controversy over policy was in cases of the rights of enemy agents or persons charged with enemy association. The board finally compromised by not extending to such persons the usual defense of rights that it would have defended in peace time. I didn't like it, but I accepted its necessity."

The period following the war was undoubtedly one of the most trying for liberals and civil libertarians. Following a short period of being allied with the Soviet Union, the cold war began. The government resurrected the Smith Act, also known as the Alien Registration Act of 1940, which, in part, forbade the advocacy of the overthrow of the government by force or violence and conspiracies to bring about such an overthrow. Beginning with Churchill's Fulton, Missouri, speech which implied that enemies within caused the cold war and continuing with Senator Joseph McCarthy specifying just who these enemies were, civil liberties were forgotten. The witch hunt was on!

By the time the witch hunt was in full swing, however, Roger Baldwin was no longer the director of the ACLU. His close relationship with the organization took on a new character after the war. In 1947 he was invited by the War Department to go to Japan and Korea to assist the occupation in developing civil rights agencies. With the ACLU's blessing he went as a private citizen, spent several months, and set up civil liberties organizations that are still functioning.

"General MacArthur's understanding of what I represented was a surprise; we never in our many conferences had occasion to differ. His reputation does not reflect his depth of commitment to peace, to democracy, and to international order. I found him the philosopher with the long view, which many of his speeches reflect, but which is obscured by his military career. He gave me every encouragement and aid in the mission he had invited me to undertake. To know him was an inspiration."

The following year Baldwin, Norman Cousins, editor of the *Saturday Review*, and Arthur Hays were invited to Germany as ACLU representatives to do a similar job. Baldwin, who remained longer than the others, set up several civil liberties organizations but with poorer results than in Japan and Korea, because of the division of Germany. Baldwin returned to follow up his efforts in 1950 and 1952 under State Department auspices.

"Starting with the oriental trip I had entered a new field of civil liberties work under United States auspices. The whole experience threw me into a new world of activity and interests which I have continued ever since."

In 1950, having reached the age of sixty-five, Baldwin resigned as director of the ACLU, but he has remained active in the organization in different capacities. He was chairman of the National Committee for the next five years, and he also has an arrangement, still in effect, by which he remains on the payroll at a modest retirement salary. Baldwin watched the McCarthy years with horror, but with a sense that the ACLU did the best job that it could.

"Despite the ACLU's close association with the defense of victims and its opposition to all witch-hunting agencies, it was never called before an investigating committee or blacklisted by any federal agency, although it was extensively investigated. It was charged by some state agencies and many right-wing organizations with subversion of our institutions in favor of communism. But the ACLU weathered all of these attacks, as it had weathered previous ones, with a growing membership. Indeed, the attacks attracted a lot of supporters fearful for American liberties. McCarthy was among our best membership recruiters.

"Then, as always, if the Union did not consciously play favorites, its clients came mainly from the 'underdogs' of the left, the minorities and activists of all sorts demanding one right or another. But the Union has, on occasion, come to the aid of conservatives and extreme rightists, whether or not they asked for it. It defended the right of employers to free speech against unions, of the Ku Klux Klan to meet on private property, of the anti-Semite Gerald K. Smith to hire a hall, of a white supremacy party in the South to run candidates for office. I do not recollect a single case where aid was refused because of the views, race, religion, or associations of an individual or group. This has been our enduring policy which is the test of good faith in the principles upon which we were founded."

Most of Baldwin's work since his nominal retirement has centered around international affairs, particularly human rights work for the United Nations and the International League for the Rights of Man.

"Much of this work has dealt with the pioneering effort to write international law for human rights of individuals, and to attempt remedies for their violations, so far frustrated by the jealous defense of national sovereignty."

Although spending most of his time in New York City, Baldwin has, in the years since his ACLU retirement, traveled all over the world in the interest of human rights. He has concentrated in recent years on civil rights problems in Puerto Rico. He was invited to do so by a former governor, who asked him to come and help set up a civil rights commission, in line with a policy encouraged by the United Nations. This work resulted in his appointment as a visiting professor of law at the University of Puerto Rico Law School, where he has helped to conduct a seminar on civil rights for more than a half-dozen years.

"I go there every winter because I like to keep busy at what interests me, and because Puerto Rico in winter is a refuge from the deep freeze in New York."

When the ACLU celebrated its fiftieth anniversary in 1970, Baldwin, along with former Chief Justice Earl Warren of the Supreme Court, and other distinguished names in the legal field, spoke at the celebratory dinner. Other honors have also come to him in his later years—the Order of the Rising Sun from the Emperor of Japan, and honorary degrees from Yale, Brandeis, and Washington University in St. Louis where he began teaching. When he is in New York, Baldwin still goes in to the ACLU office at least once a week.

"I'm still as intrigued as ever with this ceaseless conflict over rights and liberties in our democracy and throughout the world. Certainly we can chart progress toward a rule of law at home and abroad, despite the disorder and division of the world. My greatest satisfaction in a long life is to have had the chance to play a part in so hopeful a struggle."

2

Leonard Boudin and the National Emergency Civil Liberties Committee

Leonard Boudin is a man with a mission: using the law as set up in the United States Constitution, particularly the Bill of Rights, to protect U.S. citizens from encroachment of rights or excesses of the U.S. government. Boudin is a civil libertarian lawyer par excellence, an intellectual who, while leaning slightly in the direction of the left, is not really political. Aside from the law his favorite subject is chess, and he sees a connection between the two.

In his own practice and, later, as general counsel for the National Emergency Civil Liberties Committee (NECLC), the civil liberties group that came into being when the ACLU was more concerned with protecting its own reputation than people's rights, he has handled many of the noteworthy libertarian cases of the past three decades, most on the appellate or Supreme Court level. Included in these are security risk cases; censorship cases, including the one that lifted the ban on Henry Miller's *Tropic of Cancer*; cases of union officials, members, teachers, and others who were accused of being Communists during the witch hunt years; espionage cases, including that of Judith Coplon; and many freedom of travel cases, including the case of the late Rockwell Kent.

In the late 1960s and early 1970s Boudin took on some important cases at the trial level: the draft conspiracy case of Dr. Benjamin Spock, the Pentagon Papers case of Daniel Ellsberg and Anthony J. Russo, and the conspiracy case of the Rev. Philip Berrigan and seven others.

At fifty-nine Boudin's unruly gray hair doesn't quite set with his middle-aging, pleasant face. When he speaks he is restless, toying ceaselessly with three sets of glasses. His clothes, while vaguely coordinated, give him the look of a rumpled, absent-minded professor. He speaks slowly, yet his movements are quick, almost jerky at times.

"I was born in Brooklyn, into a family of lawyers. My father, Joseph, specialized in real estate law. My Uncle Louis was a well-known constitutional and labor lawyer, an international Socialist, a friend of Lenin and Trotsky. Louis was a lovely man with strong views. He left the Socialist party in 1917 to join the left wing of the Socialist party. He quit that within one day saying that he had not gone from a party of knaves to join one of fools. He not only exercised a very great influence on members of the family who were lawyers such as his daughter, my father, myself, and my son, but also upon anybody associated with the firm which he headed, Boudin, Cohn & Glickstein.

"I went to public school, then to Richmond High School, where I was number four on the chess team. From there I went to the City College of New York where I was number eight on a chess team of eight. I spent most of my time there in introspective revelations. I also worked along with Paul Goodman, Abe Polensky, and several others on *Lavendar*, the literary magazine. I was a terrible athlete. A sociology major, I vaguely planned to teach English.

"However, I ended up at St. John's Law School. Of course that idea had always been floating in the family air. While I was in law school it was the era of the Depression, and my father and his clients were in trouble with foreclosures. I became sort of traveling manager for my father, collecting rents from policemen and firemen who lived in Queens, and going to law school in the evening. For a short time after passing my bar examination I continued to work for my father. Then, in 1936, I became part of my uncle's staff. At that time his firm specialized in trade union law, representing many of the CIO unions, and the more radical of the AFL unions. I worked there for eleven years representing white collar unions, and occasionally doing some constitutional work. The night courts and picket line arrests kept us lively and busy during that time. For a few months I also worked for the War Labor Board in New York City. While I was doing that I was also doing some writing. Very early in the game I started writing scholarly articles, mainly on legal subjects. My first one was in the *American Spectator* on protective custody. By now I've written several scores of articles and book reviews, had some chapters in books, and I may soon be doing a book if litigation permits, which it probably won't.

"Although I was probably a nominal member of the ACLU then, I never had much to do with it. I did become active in the National Lawyers Guild [NLG] in the late thirties or early forties. I was chairman of the Committee on Labor Law and possibly also the Constitutional Law Committee, and we ran several large conferences.

"During the war it just went on around me. I played no active part. I was concerned with cases and family. In 1939 my wife Jean and I had our son, Michael, and, in 1943, our daughter Kathy was born.

"After my uncle's death and because of attachments to my peers who were younger and synonymously more radical, I left my uncle's firm to become a member of the firm of Neuberger, Shapiro, Rabinowitz, and Boudin. We concentrated on labor law, representing the more aggressive of the left-wing unions, the ones that were the objects of all the government investigation. The Taft-Hartley Act [which severely curtailed the power given to unions by the National Labor Relations Act of the New Deal years] had been passed in the spring of 1947, shortly before I joined the firm. If I hadn't been looking for trouble I probably wouldn't have joined the firm because that act meant trouble. We began representing people in front of congressional committees in the late forties, and we were engaged in very bitter inter- and intra-union disputes with the parent bodies of the unions. However, we successfully protected the assets of the unions we represented, which was the important thing at the time.

"In 1950 Judge Sylvester J. Ryan of the U.S. District Court 5th Circuit appointed me as counsel for Judith Coplon, who had been charged with conspiracy to commit espionage. I eventually won that case, and then we won a similar case for her in the Court of Appeals of the District of Columbia. Because of my taking that case, guilt by association started its operations. Our trade union clients became afraid that they would lose union elections because of their association with us and our association with the Coplon case. Our relations with these unions deteriorated and were finally terminated. From a financial point of view we were badly off.

"However, the congressional investigations [regarding alleged Communist infiltration of just about everything]—House Un-American Activities Committee, Senate International Securities Subcommittee, McCarthy—continued with Victor Rabinowitz and I, as specialists in constitutional law, doing most of this work for our firm. Over the years we represented hundreds of people—not just labor people—in front of those three committees."

A good deal of Boudin's work in front of these committees was done for the NECLC, which came into being in the fall of 1951, founded by Dr. Paul Lehmann, a professor of religion at Princeton; I. F. Stone, the journalist; E. Franklin Frazier, a professor at Howard University; Henry Pratt Fairchild, a professor at New York University; James Imbrie, a retired Wall Street banker; H. H. Wilson, a politics professor at Princeton and a member of the ACLU's Academic Freedom Committee; and Dr. Corliss Lamont, a writer, teacher and one-time member of the ACLU's board of directors who became a sharp critic of that organization

after it purged Elizabeth Gurley Flynn from the board on the
basis of its 1940 resolution. The people involved with the
NECLC were, for the most part, non-Communist liberals who
were not afraid of being labeled pro-Communist, as were their
civil libertarian brethren in the ACLU at that point.

"In 1952 I became the general counsel for the NECLC, and
have remained such to date. In a general way the NECLC represented people who either had been connected with the ACLU in
some way, or who were generally sympathetic to the ACLU but
who decided that it wasn't sufficiently protecting the rights of
American citizens. For example, in the years that followed the
NECLC's founding, the ACLU said that Communists should not
have the right to travel, and that was characteristic of the ACLU
then. Today it's a very changed organization, in part because of
the NECLC, in part because of younger people, in part because
we all learn. Now I feel it is a splendid organization whose attorneys are my friends.

"In the NECLC we formulated some philosophy because of
the cases we took, and took cases because of the basic philosophy
we had. Civil liberties is the key to our philosophy: the politics of
the client, the nature of the charges, the context of the litigation
—in court or in front of a committee—didn't make much difference. We weren't afraid of being called 'Communist,' and we
were placed on a subversive list of HUAC and SISS but were
never named by the attorney general because that would have
meant litigation which we would have won."

Because of his work for the NECLC, because he remained active in the National Lawyer's Guild after it was accused of being
Communist-oriented, and because he wrote for *The New Masses,*
a Communist publication, and lectured at the Jefferson School for
Social Science, which was considered a Communist hotbed,
Boudin was thought of by many as a Communist or fellow traveler. The passport office wrote him at one time that they had evidence that he was a member of the Communist party and under
its discipline. Eventually he was called in front of a congressional

committee and questioned about his affiliations. At a time when the Fifth Amendment was the common answer to all such questions he shocked many people by flatly answering that he was not, nor ever had been a Communist. He decided to answer because he was not a Communist, felt that answering would enable him to better defend his clients, and wanted to show that the government was lying. While Boudin was impressed with some of the social possibilities of reform that socialists and Communists discussed he would never commit himself. He felt that his work was as a lawyer.

"During that whole period the passport litigation always interested me most. It seemed, in its own way, as bizarre as McCarthy. That ended, for the most part, in 1958 when we won the Kent case. [In *Kent v. Dulles,* the Supreme Court held that the secretary of state could not deny a passport to an individual for political reasons.] We then moved into problems of area restrictions on travel, for instance, to Cuba. We did not succeed in compelling the secretary of state to validate passports to Cuba, but we did succeed in preventing visitors to Cuba from being convicted for their journeys and/or having their passports seized.

"While all of this was happening, our firm was still experiencing financial difficulties. Some partners left, and then Michael B. Standard joined us and the firm became Rabinowitz, Boudin, and Standard. Now we also have four very able associates with us.

"In the sixties, the firm has had a number of different lives: the NECLC life, the general civil liberties life, some trade union life, some commercial and general work life, and some criminal work life, usually with political or at least constitutional overtones. People think of us as appellate lawyers, but we do work in the lower courts, although not often in criminal cases.

"We have also represented the Algerian and Kenyan governments, and we do represent the Cuban and Chilean governments in their American legal problems, mainly in commercial litigation.

"About half of our work now is NECLC work, and half is private. We run an informal household and only differentiate by which door it comes in. Almost any case today is tailored to be a civil liberties case."

A good deal of the firm's fee-generating work is involved with defending draft resisters. It also receives a retainer each year from the NECLC. Yet the firm is by no means a rich one, a fact which doesn't seem to concern the people who work there.

"Aside from civil liberties, I have never formulated an ideological or theological goal for myself in my work. Being somewhat limited in my range of interests, I've found that the defense of civil liberties is sufficient in itself, as long as chess is around. It's a fulltime job to concentrate on a few constitutional amendments. Three of my four favorite subjects are pretty related to that: law, lawyers, and judges. The fourth, of course, is chess."

Leonard Boudin left his firm in New York in the winter of 1971 to teach for a year at Harvard Law School. With him was his wife, Jean, a poet and women's libber who took two courses at Harvard while he was teaching. Absent was his son, Michael, a lawyer with the firm of Covington & Burling in Washington, who has also been invited to teach at Harvard Law, and his daughter, Kathy, who has been active in the underground since the spring of 1970.

"Our son is an unusually fine lawyer. I remember with dismay and pride, after having worked myself to the bone on a Supreme Court argument, I gave it to him to read the night before argument, only to hear him casually give me two new important legal approaches. I would probably have won anyway, but it was his unusually well-organized thinking that won me, I believe, a unanimous decision.

"Our daughter is remarkable, wonderful, and beautiful. She always has been idealistic and concerned for the welfare of her fellow human beings. Now that she is in the so-called underground I am as ill-informed as the press on what she is alleged to have done, and I will not express an opinion until the appropriate time. I do know of her indictment under the antiriot act, which is both constitutionally and morally wrong.

"As to my own future, I'd like to practice law every fall with my firm, and teach in a different law school every spring."

Boudin's quiet plans changed, at least for a while, because of his involvement in the case of Daniel Ellsberg and Anthony Russo, Jr., the men accused of espionage, conspiracy, and unauthorized use of government papers for allegedly releasing the Pentagon Papers, a once-secret seven-thousand-page history of U.S. involvement in Vietnam.

The trial is considered by many people to be one of the most important ones of the century since it could produce either an "official secrets" act, which officially doesn't exist now, or a more open government.

Pretrial motions began in May 1972 and a jury had been picked and sworn in by the end of July when the trial was stayed by Supreme Court Justice William Douglas. At issue was the trial judge's refusal to let the defense see a transcript of a conversation between one of the defense attorneys and a "foreign national" whose phone was illegally tapped by the government.

In issuing the stay Douglas said, "The present case is one of several that have come across my desk this year involving not surveillance of a defendant in a criminal case but surveillance of his lawyer. It is time, I think, that we hold that the confidences of a lawyer-client relationship remain inviolate." However, in November, the full court refused seven to two to hear the appeal at that time, and the trial was scheduled to begin again, which it did, with a new jury, in early 1973.

Consistently the prosecution has made it clear that it wants only the narrowest "criminal" definition of the trial, while the defense wants to attack the whole government classification system, and, if possible, test the legality of the war.

This is Boudin's third recent case in which the legality of the

Vietnam war could be an issue. In the Spock and Berrigan cases the government managed to skirt that issue in court. If they manage to do it again in a case of this magnitude, Boudin isn't sure that he'll feel that the law is the answer he once thought it was.

3

Mel Wulf and the New ACLU

Mel Wulf has been with the American Civil Liberties Union (ACLU) since 1958 and has been its legal director since 1962. He is an activist, and the views he holds are becoming more prevalent throughout the Union.

Wulf's physical presence gives the first hint of the difference beween the ACLU of Roger Baldwin's time and the ACLU of today. Where Baldwin is a gentleman of the old school— properly attired, exacting in speech, courteous to the point of being chivalrous—Wulf is a gentleman of the new school. His tall, husky frame is casually attired in mod, ivy league clothes. His brown hair, speckled with gray, cascades over his ears, forehead, and collar. When he speaks, his voice is soft and modulated, and now and again it drops almost into a mumble.

Born in Brooklyn in 1927 to a successful businessman who had immigrated here from Latvia in 1905 and to his wife, a lower East Side native of Polish extraction, Wulf lived in Brooklyn until he was nine. In 1936 his family moved to Troy, New York, where his father's clothing factory was located. He attended public school there.

"I enjoy the fact that I grew up in Troy instead of Brooklyn. It speeded up my assimilation into American society. I was totally unpolitical in public school. I was social; I played football. In '45 with the war going on and the draft on my neck, I joined the Merchant Marine Academy as a way to avoid getting shot at, and I stayed there for two years here in New York. I still was totally unpolitical, and social, and I also drank a lot.

"In 1947, fully expecting to go into the family business, I went to Lowell Textile Institute in Massachusetts. It was there I began to catch on to what was going on. I joined a fraternity, half of which was political novitiates like me and half of which belonged to the Communist party. I began to get political in '48, around the Wallace campaign, but the effect of all of the left-wing politics around me at Lowell, a predominately working-class school, was that I became right-wing. I voted for Eisenhower, had a picture of John Foster Dulles over my bed, and I used to go around screaming at the dirty commies. Finally the left-wing politics got to me the last year I was there, and I moved from Republicanism to Democratism.

"Then I came down to Columbia where I got my degree in economics after two years. I spent most of that time not going to class and reading about politics, Fabian socialism. This was in 1950 when the cold war was heating up. There was no political activity on campus so I kept on reading and became a socialist of no particular variety.

"I got my bachelors in '52, and the draft board was still after me—the Merchant Marine Academy hadn't counted. The war was going on in Korea, and I certainly didn't want to fight North Koreans—I had nothing against them—so to avoid that, I arbitrarily decided to go to law school. I applied to Columbia only and got accepted, and I went there with no distinct idea of what a lawyer was all about.

"I went to law school, found it a terrible bore, continued my outside reading, didn't study much, and didn't do very well. There weren't many interesting people there. Most of them just wanted to go into law to make lots of money. I didn't know what

I wanted to do. I thought about going into labor law cause I still thought the Labor Board was a left-wing institution.

"I got out of law school in '55 and the draft board was *still* after me so I went into the Navy. I was assigned to a Seabee base in California as a legal officer. All the other guys there were recently graduated engineers so I came out like a left-wing radical. I tried to get into trouble but couldn't. I got secret clearance. I went around talking socialism a lot but nobody took me seriously.

"I got out of the Navy in '57, had no idea what I wanted to do. I played tennis, went to the movies, went camping, took out a lot of girls. I went to Europe, came back and lived in Berkeley for a while, then came back to Troy. Eventually I took a job in a law firm in Albany. I stayed there for four weeks, woke up one morning, and decided to come to New York City. I did but still had no idea of what I was going to do. I went to work at the Columbia bookstore where I'd worked while I was in law school.

"I dropped a note to the then legal director of the ACLU, Rowland Watts, and asked if they had anything they wanted me to do. I wrote cause I had joined the ACLU while I was in the Navy. I used to leave the literature lying around thinking it was really provocative stuff. Little did I know the ACLU was a useless organization in the early fifties. I also belonged to the NAACP at that time. Used to go around showing my credentials and saying 'Look how radical I am.' And all that time I was living off the fat of the land. Right? Right! I sound like Mort Sahl.

"Finally I heard from Watts and he said, 'Come on down,' so I kept coming in for about ten days a couple of hours each day doing volunteer work. One day Watts asked how I'd like to work here. I said, 'Holy Christ, terrific.' He had just gotten permission to hire a second man. The next week he offered me a hundred dollars a week which I thought was really terrific since I never expected to make a hundred a week doing anything, let alone something I thought was important. I took the job as assistant legal director, practiced under Watts, learned some law.

"About that time I met some Young People's Socialist League [YPSL] people. That was about the most radical thing around in '58. Met a terrific girl who turned me on to grass. I remember that Thanksgiving we got together and had a traditional dinner then all turned on, which I thought was a parody of American society. I did some writing then, and running around. I remember I was at one of the first anti-civil defense demonstrations down at city hall. But I still never joined anything. I was just a seat-of-the-pants instinctive socialist. I was working and living the life of the Village, left-wing bachelor. Terrific, just terrific.

"In '62 I became the ACLU's legal director, my predecessor having left. At that time the ACLU was small, I don't think it had more than 10,000 members in the early sixties and few affiliates. There were two lawyers on the national staff before Watts left, and it was the biggest collection of ACLU lawyers anywhere. My predecessor was a good guy and had done some stuff but his predecessor, Herb Levy, who was here from 1949 to 1956, mostly had a reputation for saying no to anybody who came in here with a case. In 1962 the whole legal budget for the ACLU was $8000; last year we spent over $100,000.

"When I began as legal director I was mostly doing office work. I went to court a couple of times, but we were mainly using volunteer lawyers. I didn't have an assistant, but I decided that the ACLU could be most useful by helping the victims of the government. I took fifty or sixty cases that year. Then the ACLU started to grow with the civil rights movement; I don't know who was the tail and who was the dog. In '62 I started going down South cause there were no lawyers down there. I tried a couple of capital cases and worked on the jury exclusion thing. It was terribly exciting, I felt like a goddamned pioneer. There were some local lawyers down there who got their ass handed to them every time they surfaced. They literally whispered to you, 'I'm on your side but I can't do anything.' I was working with Jess Brown, a local black lawyer in Jackson, Mississippi, and I must say we singlehandedly abolished capital punishment in Mississippi. There were three black guys on death row all convicted of raping white women. Jess and I got their death sentences set aside. Between '62 and '64 I was going down their every month or every other month.

"Then in '64 the Lawyer's Constitutional Defense Committee [LCDC] started, for which I'll take some credit, and later Chuck Morgan set up our regional office in Atlanta. LCDC was set up in a month by us, the Jewish Congress, CORE, and, reluctantly, the Inc. Fund [NAACP Legal Defense Fund, Inc.]. After SNCC announced Mississippi summer, we held a press conference and said we'd take applications for lawyers to go down South, and we got something like five hundred applications in a week. You know that was the old northern liberal 'we want to do good in the South because we don't want to have too many problems up here' thing. It was a very romantic period where we thought we were going to smash the racist barriers down in one summer.

"In '65 I had Eleanor Holmes Norton [now Human Rights Commissioner in New York City] working here with me, and about that time the Vietnam war thing began, and the Selective Service thing and the ACLU was getting very big. I've been here since."

As the ACLU began to grow again in both numbers and power, an internal struggle began to surface between the traditionalists, those who thought the ACLU should stick to its old amicus curiae mode, and the expansionists, who believed that the organization should directly aid victims of repression.

"This battle both came to the surface and exploded at the same time, in 1968 around the Spock indictment. There were people on the board who thought we were getting into cases they didn't like very much; they thought it was civil disobedience that we were defending. That had begun before, but it came to a head then.

"The indictments came down on a Friday and I got together with our then public relations woman and announced the indictments and announced that the ACLU would defend any of the defendants who wanted our help. A week later we had a board meeting in which I was denounced and my stand repudiated. Some of the big affiliates denounced the action of the National Board, defended what I had done, and demanded a recount. Six weeks later there was the biggest board meeting ever held in the history of the ACLU and I was vindicated."

Around the same period as the battle between civil liberties traditionalists and expansionists, another battle was brewing. A movement for repeal of the Union's 1940 resolution, which resulted in the expulsion of Elizabeth Gurley Flynn from the organization's board of directors, was gaining momentum among the more militant civil libertarians in the ACLU. In 1966, the board of directors appointed a special committee to study that resolution. In the late sixties, after much political maneuvering, two new provisions already mentioned by Baldwin were voted into effect to supersede the 1940 resolution.

The vague language of the new provisions is seen by some civil libertarians as being dangerous whenever pressures for conformity mount. Others in the Union, Wulf for one, don't take the provisions so seriously.

"The matter was important symbolically. I could never understand why the ACLU, which was in court all the time attacking loyalty oaths and guilt by association, was guilty of the same things in the 1940s. When the issue was raised in the sixties, I never got the sense it was the same kind of acerbic issue as the one that came out around the Spock indictment. I kept pretty much out of it. I denounced the forties resolution whenever I could, and I never followed the ACLU policy of denouncing the Communist party in all cases involving it. I'm not a fan of the CP, although I happen to be a Socialist, but I felt that denouncing the CP was hardly the role of a civil liberties organization.

"After we got the Spock thing back on the track, the battle with the traditionalists continued over other cases for about a year and a half. I persisted in my views because I thought I was right. Finally, the conservative faction that was making all of the trouble for me got voted out.

"By this time the ACLU had changed from an organization with ten thousand members and half a dozen affiliates to an organization with over a hundred thousand members with affiliates in practically every state. Since I came in I've been trying to set an example of what I thought was the utility of a very active, visible, aggressive litigation policy. Around 1962, 85 percent of our cases were amicus briefs, and we only took part directly in the remaining cases. By 1965 we hit a parity between direct and amicus cases, and now we file amicus briefs only if we can't get our hands on the cases; that's about 10 percent of the time.

"We're getting back to the roots of the ACLU. The organization was doing more in the twenties than in the forties or fifties. It was very radical in the twenties. Baldwin was a mad bomb thrower, for Christ's sake. He did the Scopes case; he got arrested in Patterson; he was involved with the silk strikes . . . all of that. But the cold war and all of the anti-Communist rhetoric finally got to the organization. It's the natural history of the conservatizing influence of time on an organization. In the forties the ACLU was still okay. Roger Baldwin became very anti-Communist, but he was still a damn good civil libertarian. In the fifties, after Roger retired, the new executive director was weak, and the staff was fearful and timid. One of them is still here, out of habit if not conviction. He personally bears a lot of responsibility for the pitiful condition of the Union in the fifties.

"I think now the ACLU has regained its reputation with the left. We get along fine with the pacifist movement and the antiwar movement."

The ACLU is now active in cases concerning drugs, military law, antiwar activities, Selective Service, privacy, women's rights, the rights of the gay community, abortion, academic freedom, the rights of children, and high school rights. It also has a prison project it's trying to expand.

The national staff of lawyers does litigation, some consulting, and some coordinating of the legal work done by the affiliates. They also have prerogatives in Supreme Court cases. While some affiliates have staff lawyers, much of the day-to-day legal work of the Union is handled now, as it has always been, by volunteer lawyers willing to devote some of their time to ACLU cases. Wulf says that his preference in volunteers is law professors who like to litigate, and lawyers in whom he has special trust. He feels that the use of young lawyers, especially those getting pro bono time from large firms, requires too much supervision.

Concerning his own future, Wulf says, "I still think the ACLU is doing vital work. I still think civil liberties are important. I think my politics are more radical than the ACLU's, but I've chosen to work within this framework. I've been here twelve years, with the exception of one six-month leave of absence when I got a grant from the Ford Foundation to investigate police work in England, and sometimes I think about doing something else, but I can't think of anything else I'd really like to do nearly as much."

Anthony Amsterdam: A Practicing Civil Libertarian Law Professor

Professor Anthony G. Amsterdam of the Stanford University School of Law wears his genius with a worried look. According to many lawyers of all radical hues, Tony Amsterdam has one of the most brilliant minds in law today. He definitely carries one of the heaviest caseloads.

Amsterdam is tall and thin and all of his features seem to follow the general contour of his frame: his face, his nose, even his lips are thin and almost pointed. His hair is brown and wavy and his eyebrows are bushy, framing a forehead that is wrinkled before its time. His hands, constantly clasping and unclasping, give a hint of the intensity behind his low, unhurried speech.

"I was born in Philadelphia, Pennsylvania, in 1935. I had essentially no interest in law until my senior year in Haverford College, and I had very little then. In fact, I had very little interest in law when I went to the University of Pennsylvania Law School. Throughout the earlier parts of my education I was more interested in the humanities and art. I got into law eventually as a backsliding operation— I think many people do. In the humanities it seemed to me there was no opportunity for one to make a living and still have the freedom to do individual work that one might find in the professions. Among the professions it seemed to me that law was the one most relevant to working with society as a whole and its problems. But it was a very amorphous sense of that that caused me to go to law school.

"I got all the way through law school without having terribly great inspiration or fire for the law built up. When I got through I was thinking of going to work in the antitrust division of the Department of Justice because at that time the intellectual problems in antitrust law seemed to me most intriguing. One of the things about law school is that the focus is on intellectual problems, not human problems. To the degree that I was interested in law, I was interested in the intellectual problems.

"Then one of my professors prevailed on me to clerk for Supreme Court Justice Felix Frankfurter. I was very reluctant to do so because people all over the U.S. have a very great reverence for the Supreme Court, great anxiety to clerk there, and I really did not, and I thought it was unfair to deprive students who really believed in the whole thing from doing it when I had very great doubts about the Court and the importance of the Court. But I finally went to see Frankfurter, and I was persuaded to clerk for him for a year. I was the only Frankfurter clerk not to come out of the Harvard Law School but because of his close relationship with my professor, Louis Henkin, he was persuaded to take me on. I clerked for him for a year and it was at that time that my interest in law developed.

"One would think that clerking for Frankfurter would send one off in a very different direction from the direction I've gone, since Frankfurter is generally regarded as a conservative. He was not, in fact, a conservative. He felt very deeply about the human problems in the law and he very often felt helpless and hopeless because of the limitations of a Supreme Court justice to deal with those problems. He felt that the Constitution didn't give the Supreme Court enough power to deal with all of those problems.

"So I was confronted daily with a sensitive human being, deeply concerned and troubled by problems he felt that the law couldn't get a handle on. That's been important in what I've done since. I've been trying to make the law get a handle on those problems, and trying to have judges break the shackles that Felix Frankfurter felt bound in, trying to tackle some of the major problems in our society using the Constitution as a tool.

"When I left Frankfurter, I was a prosecutor for a year in the office of the U.S. Attorney for D.C. who was then Dave Acheson, Dean Acheson's son. Dave was an enlightened prosecutor, a fairly liberal guy, and I thought that would be a good office to learn the ropes in. If you're going to eventually be on the defense side, as I had a feeling even then that I would probably be, it pays to know what the other side is all about. Following that, in 1962, I began teaching in the University of Pennsylvania Law School. I stayed there till 1969 when I became a teacher at the Stanford University Law School where I now am.

"Right after I left the U.S. Attorney's office I began to set up lines of communication with various groups involved with defense work and with which I've been involved since. Beginning in 1962, I began to do consulting and was a litigating attorney for the NAACP Legal Defense Fund, Inc. [Inc. Fund] in New York. I began to do consultative work and some litigation for the national ACLU operating out of New York, and I began to do work for the Philadelphia chapter of the ACLU. That increased very considerably over a period of years. When the Lawyers' Constitutional Defense Committee [LCDC] was formed in the summer of 1964, I began to work for them. I've also worked for the Southern Christian Leadership Conference [SCLC], and, eventually, as things grew, I've worked with virtually every civil rights litigating organization in the country.

"I was in the South for two months of the summer of 1963, all of the summer of '64, and most of the summer of '65 and I have been there since periodically from periods ranging from a few days to a month. Now that I have a national litigation practice, I move around all over.

"One of the fortunate things about my position, which is one of complete independence, is that I can work comfortably with all of the groups. They may be fighting with each other some-times since they have very real ideological and financial problems in relating to each other often, but I have had no problems in relating to all of them. That is one of the reasons why I tend to crop up in everything from representing *New York Times* re-porter Earl Caldwell to representing Bobby Seale along with Charlie Garry on the one hand, and representing the Chicago Seven with Bill Kunstler and the Law Center, and, indeed, representing Kunstler and Kinoy privately in their own tussles with the law, to the school desegregation cases and that sort of classic litigation with the Inc. Fund and the very classic ACLU stuff. I was also in charge of the national campaign to knock out the death penalty by litigation. I had primary responsibility for representing more than four hundred of the six hundred men on death row. I managed that overall court campaign for the Inc. Fund—in cooperation with the ACLU in some places.

"I've been involved in all of it simply because of great luck on my part. Being in a position of independence where I don't have to worry about making a living with any of this—my law teach-ing is enough to keep me going—I have been able to offer assist-ance to all of these various groups and I have made good friends with all of the people involved.

"In a sense I have a responsibility and a role in formulating new policy for the organizations I work with, and not just in han-dling cases that come in to them. But the only organization where I was on the board of directors was LCDC, and that was because it never had a staff of any size so the board was in a close rela-tionship with the staff, handling litigation and everything. With the other organizations I've had such a good relationship with the staff that it has never seemed appropriate to me to be on the board. I really see myself as one of the workers in all of these or-ganizations, and I really don't like the role of boss. I think I can accomplish the kind of things I want to do much better by being in rapport with the staffs. I'm on the boards of several other or-

ganizations, but not the kind I work with on a day-to-day operation, for example, California Indian Legal Services, the Northern
California ACLU, and the Center for Law and Social Policy, a
new pro bono publico organization."

Working with all of these groups, Amsterdam has such a heavy
caseload that he has difficulty giving an exact estimate of its
breadth.

"In the course of a year now I handle a countless number of
cases. I simply can't estimate the amount particularly since a
large part of the time they may be a one-shot, fly-by-night operation.

"For instance, a friend of mine in Boston called up when they
had the so-called police riot there and asked me to give them information on filing a civil action against the police. I spent a couple of days talking about that, looked over the papers in the case,
and didn't do anything else with it, since it seemed to be going
along fairly well. How do you count these? Things like that may
be one phone call. Guys all over the country that I've worked
with for years will call up with a problem and we'll talk it out."

Amsterdam, like most other Bill of Rights lawyers, concen-
trates on cases that have reached the appellate level.

"I'll handle cases at the trial level when I get in at that stage
and it looks to me that it is vitally important how the record
looks at that level. Nine-tenths of the issues I'm involved in are
issues where we are trying to make new law. The likelihood of
winning at the trial level is zero. So I'll only get in if the
contentions we're making at the appeal level have to be firmly established in the trial record. But for the larger percentage of cases
that I handle, you can talk about my involvement in terms of litigation, strategy, and planning, choice of court, choice of a form
of action, drafting of pleadings, and then working on appellate
stuff.

"Besides this, in a normal year here I'll teach a normal load of
courses—three or four. I find time to do all of this because it's
what I like to do. Also my wife, Lois Scheinfeld, is a lawyer, and

it's also her bag. She's been much more involved on the civil side than I have—poverty law, welfare, and that sort of thing—so all my work is not too much interference with our family life because she and I work together on these things. She understands my commitment to them. Some of the cases we handle, we handle together.

"Another thing that is helpful is that the idea of what a law professor should be like has changed. When I started at Penn in 1962 the idea was that a law professor taught and wrote law review articles and books. The one thing I hope to have done by the time I get finished is to change that model, and I think I already have. The one thing I feel like claiming any credit for is that I think I've sold the notion in the law school teaching profession that that is not the only viable model for a law school professor. I wouldn't play that game. What I wrote was manuals for lawyers who shared my point of view. But what I've spent most of my time at has been litigation, and I have, in a sense, made respectable the idea that that's what a law professor can do. Now almost every good law faculty has at least one guy who is doing this sort of thing, and some have more than one. The faculties that don't have them are looking for them. If I had told Penn at the beginning what I was going to do I don't think they would have taken me on. What I've tried to do is integrate litigation and teaching by using students on my cases, posing problems that come out of these cases. So I've been able to blend the two and prove that it can be done. There's a real benefit to posing problems from the real world and to using student manpower on these cases because about the only good thing one can say about legal education as it is now is that it's about the cheapest kind of professional education. You can't train doctors, engineers, dentists for what we train law students. I don't think it's a good education for business-oriented banking lawyers any more than for movement lawyers. But with the 'real world' approach I think there is some but not great prospects for significant change.

"The major problem is a political one—the politics of law

schools. They aren't terribly interested in educating lawyers. Unless we face up to this, all of the business about curriculum change is nonsense. What I mean by that is that we have attracted people into law teaching for the most part on the promise of a style of life, in which research is primary and teaching secondary. Most law faculty people have joined law faculties for the same reason that novelists join English faculties. It lets them bring home the bread and do their own writing on the side. Ideas for reform of legal education have been floating around since 1930. I have some ideas but the real question is how you pull it off. You're confronted with the basic fact that legal education is incredibly cheap. This idea of herding sixty or a hundred and twenty students into a room and letting them hear a professor talk for an hour with little individual instruction is something we don't do in medicine or even in graduate work in the humanities or art anymore. That is very cheap legal education, and if we try to change that very much we're going to require the investment of vast amounts of resources. God only knows where they're going to come from. So the problem of changing legal education is a very significant one, and its problems at the moment are great. I have somewhat more hope of changing them than of changing the problems of society, but that is only because the problems of society are so unlikely of being solved at all that you have to be supremely pessimistic about them.

"I'd like to see a good deal more clinical stuff in the law schools, but I'd like to see far more than that. I would like to see law schools become true graduate schools. I would like to see law students working with their professors on the frontiers of the law as a matter of research and thinking, quite apart from litigation and clinical stuff. Most law schools today are more like undergraduate than graduate schools. I defy you to find in the history of the legal profession really frontiersmanlike work being done by law students. The only place it could happen now is on the law reviews, but even the people who get on these only get to a pretty pedestrian frontier at best.

"The nine-tenths of the students who don't get on the law review never do any imaginative or individual thinking. One of the changes called for is to make law students move out from just learning the accumulated wisdom of the professors, to make them think about problems.

"The second thing we don't do in law school is almost not to be believed. We don't make decisions. We don't force students to make decisions, and we don't teach them the problems they'll have when they have the responsibility for making decisions. Now, the theory behind this is that we don't know enough about the facts here in law school to make those decisions. We're training them in the process of identifying the issues and considerations. Then when they go out into the world and get a particular concrete problem they'll figure out what the poles are and work them through. The fact of the matter though is that I suspect we set them up in a frame of mind so that we discourage them from ever making the ultimate decision and making it right.

"Simply as an academic and research matter—again, this is almost not to be believed—we are one of the very few disciplines that has an organized, systematic mode of thought but has no philosophy as to what that thought is. You can't find anybody in law school who is concerned with answering the question 'What is the proper mode of proof of a legal proposition?' I'm not talking about proof of a factual matter, I'm talking about proof of a legal proposition. A judge or a governor or a lawyer or somebody asserts the following legal proposition: that the death penalty does or does not violate the Eighth Amendment and then he goes through a reasoning process. It is not to be believed, but we are not able to talk about the rightness or wrongness of that reasoning process. The process goes on, we teach it, but we don't have any science of it. This would be the analog of an empirical scientist—be it in the natural sciences or the social sciences—who was trying to prove propositions without probability theory. If you don't know why you pick .05 as the basis for going out and making statements with or without confidence, then you have no business going out and making statements. In the law for hundreds of years we've been making statements and we have no intelligent science.

"So there is everything wrong with law schools as they are now. Socially oriented or not they don't light a fire to the tails of young people and make them go out and want to grapple with the problems of the world. We don't equip them with the kind of knowledge and information they need about people, about institutions, about the other sciences. But even in the most strict, stodgy academic senses, legal education is lousy. We do not as a respectable science concern ourselves with the fundamentals of our own discipline. We don't have a logic or a philosophy of law or of legal reasoning. We don't assume the responsibility or place the responsibility on students for what is ultimately the lawyer's job: making decisions and evaluating them. All of this needs radical change and whether we're going to get it or not I don't know. I think the litigating/teaching approach, which is really the idea I'd like to sell, is at least one step in the right direction.

"As far as the outside world, basically what I would like to see is a completely open society. What I mean by that is that every individual born into a society should have the greatest opportunity the society can give him to fulfill his own potential, his aspirations, his own instincts: to make of himself a complete and full human being. Our society is very far from that. It would be ridiculous to assert that our society is farther from that than other societies. It is not. In many ways our society is closer to that than it has ever been historically, and it is certainly closer to that than many other societies in the world are. But it is still so far from that that my major thrust is trying to get change so that we can eventually get closer to that goal of an open society where every individual has a fair shake and a fair opportunity, not handicapped by poverty or race or all of the other discriminations that beset our people.

"Of course, at this point in time that raises a serious question. Do you stay within the law or do you, as the 'revolutionary lawyer' would say, see the prognosis in the legal system as being so bleak that you can't, working within the law, hope to do very much. The answer for me now is that I haven't given up all hope that it can be done within the law. It is clear to me that it can't only be done within the law, that we do need something that is in the nature of a revolution. Now whether I mean a political revolution or whether I mean Charlie Reich's bloodless revolution or whether I mean a very profound shakeup of power that would let us start out in new directions, I'm not sure. I do know this though, until I completely and totally despair of the legal system as reformable, until I come to the conclusion that you can't work within the system, it makes sense for me to keep working at it simply as a matter of Adam Smithian economics. There are a lot of people who can get out on the barricades and fire guns. I probably shoot worse than most other people. But the people who have had the kind of training and experience I've had are relatively few, and so I can make a greater contribution now by being a lawyer than by being on the barricades. That's true until such time as I come to the conclusion that there is no contribution lawyers can make. Then, I'll have to rethink that question. But, for the moment, my point of view is to work within the system to achieve the change I'd like to see.

"I'm close to revolutionaries in that I agree that major change is necessary in our society and I have at least a doubt that that's possible within our present legal system. I agree with them completely that if it is not possible within the legal system, the legal system is going to have to be changed by any means necessary to change it. I disagree with them at the moment in that (1) I am not yet convinced that the present legal system is so unreformable that one ought to abandon it without the prospect of anything better, and (2) I don't see in any revolutionary scheme the prospect for anything better. That doesn't mean you don't have a revolution. If a society is bad enough, you tear it down without anything to replace it. But I'm not yet there at that level. I may change my mind any day though.

"The only point where I seriously disagree with the revolutionaries is that after the revolution I'm probably going to be representing the bourgeoisie. That's just a cute phrase because there isn't going to be a revolution in that sense and if there is I don't know if either the bourgeoisie or I will survive it. What I mean is that my motivation or ideology is not essentially political. I do not believe that communism or anything else is going to bring our society to an an open society. An open society is possible with any form and highly unlikely within any of them because there's going to be an oppressed class under any system. And what I'm interested in is being the spokesman for, the representative of, the guy who tries to protect the interests of the out groups, in whatever society we happen to have at that moment.

"I'm pragmatic enough to know that no society is going to function without a government so I wouldn't describe my view as anarchistic. I would describe it as extraordinarily pessimistic with regard to the hope of any government being run in a way so that people don't get screwed. Under any government that we now have, or are likely to have, large classes of people are likely to get screwed. I define my role as standing up for the guy who is getting screwed. I want to be the balance wheel against government in whatever government there is. I see the highest calling of a lawyer in any system as trying to keep whatever system you have alive enough and awake enough so that you can pepper it, keep vulnerable points, so that a spokesman for the outsider can come in and hit hard enough to hurt when he makes his points. I just have no optimism about any human form of government doing the greatest good for the greatest number. I'm antirhetoric but not anarchistic. It's kind of the American equivalent of French anticlericalism.

"I confess to being a humanist. I think, although there are many people, both in power and out of power, who are ugly and corrupt and misguided, basically human beings are good, and I think the job of society is to let them realize that good and not to pervert them or distort them."

5

Poverty Rights Lawyers

The Supreme Court's decision in *Brown v. Topeka Board of Education* in 1954 began to have a far-reaching influence in the people's law movement by the early 1960s when lawyers were needed in the South to help gain basic civil rights for the country's disenfranchised citizens. Many civil liberties lawyers responded to this call and some of them never again were Bill of Rights lawyers in the old sense.

During this period many rights lawyers became radicals, as did many young lawyers and law students who previously would have been rights lawyers. While the southern civil rights movement radicalized all people's lawyers, it did not make them all into radical lawyers.

Some returned to civil liberties work, and, with their new perspective, changed the emphasis of this work, made it more concerned with defending real people along with abstract rights. Others began to re-evaluate their priorities, to wonder whether lawyers were needed to obtain more basic rights for America's disenfranchised. How important is the right of freedom of speech to people who do not know where their next meal is coming from, who do not have the right to vote? As it became clear that many of the problems of the South also existed in all other parts of the nation, a larger number of lawyers than ever before began to wonder how they could help the country's seemingly newly discovered poor, disenfranchised minority.

Theoretically, there have been Legal Aid societies, usually in large cities, to help indigents since 1876. In 1920 there were enough of them to call for the founding of the National Legal Aid and Defender Association (NLADA). However, the performances of these associations were most often inadequate. After the *Gideon v. Wainwright* decision in 1965 which gave all defendants the right to counsel in state as well as federal courts, the performances of legal aid programs deteriorated. While all states had to set up some kind of public defender system for criminal cases, the number of cases far exceeded the number of lawyers. Talking to any former Legal Aid attorney one gets the impression that members of the Legal Aid boards of directors still consider this service somewhat akin to their wives' charity work. Whether indigents received aid in civil cases varied from state to state. In part because the southern civil rights movement made concern with the second nation in the midst of the U.S. so popular, the American Bar Association (ABA), the same ABA that was formed in 1877 to protect lawyers' big business clients from populist-oriented legislatures, was instrumental in pressuring Congress to add a Legal Services section to the Economic Opportunity Act of 1964. Before the passage of this bill there had been in some poverty areas pilot legal services programs funded by private foundations, most notably the legal services division of Mobilization for Youth (MFY) in the lower East Side of New York City, and a similar program in Oakland, California. Because of the success of these programs, and the atmosphere in the country, a National Conference on Law and Poverty was sponsored in 1964 by the Department of Health, Education, and Welfare (HEW). Out of this came ABA backing for the legal services idea, and out of that backing came the Legal Services Program of the Office of Economic Opportunity (OEO).

Because the ABA pushed for the program, it still has a great deal of influence over it. Local bar association bigwigs sit on all local boards of directors, while the national bigwigs sit on the national program advisory committee. Sometimes this is helpful, but on a day-to-day basis, it often is not. Bar Association officials, for the most part, in no way qualify as people's lawyers, nor do they really sympathize with attorneys who are.

Nevertheless, the beginning of the OEO Legal Services programs provided a new golden age for rights lawyers.

When the bill became law and money was appropriated for such offices, they opened all over the country. And, as they proliferated, they received more favorable attention than the other projects of OEO. Not only were the poverty projects attracting some of the brightest former civil liberties lawyers and some brilliant young law students, they were also seducing some fine corporate lawyers away from their corporations. Sargent Shriver, then head of OEO, was happy; President Johnson was happy; even some poor people were happy with the programs.

That was in the beginning, before some sour notes started to spoil the happy tune. What happened was that a lot of these rights lawyers took their work seriously. Instead of just taking care of the personal civil problems of poor people—things like divorces, adoptions, name changes, consumer frauds—as the government had intended, they began to defend poor people in criminal prosecutions, and they even had the effrontery to bring class actions (suits that affect a large group of people) against government agencies on issues that would affect the poor communities, that would give them power.

The government took care of the first sour note easily enough. It amended the bill so that legal services lawyers could rarely take criminal cases without the explicit permission of OEO. This happened in January of 1968, shortly after the summer that saw the battles in Detroit and Newark, at a time when many Legal Services lawyers were helping the people who were being tried for their part in those battles.

But the second sour note was not so easily silenced and has remained as a consistent disharmony in the ear of the federal government. One Legal Services program that has proved particularly jarring is the California Rural Legal Assistance Program (CRLA), a statewide program to help with the legal problems of California's rural poor.

Jim Lorenz, a founder and former executive director of CRLA, who is now a deputy director, is a good illustration of a former corporate attorney who left those ranks to become a lawyer for the poor. Born in Dayton, Ohio, he attended public school, Phillips Academy in Andover, Massachusetts, then Harvard College and Law School, "with the usual academic and extracurricular activities and honors along the way that you're supposed to get to continue to be a high achiever."

After his second year of law school he worked in a corporate law firm in L.A. and says he remembers nothing about the summer except an immense cloud of boredom that hung about his head. He returned to his last year of Harvard confused about what to do after he finished. He interviewed with a large corporate firm in Cleveland and tried to get a special arrangement whereby he would spend less time in the firm and take less pay, but the firm wouldn't buy the idea. Finally he decided to play for the short run, to take a job with a large corporate firm in L.A. for the experience.

"At the end of this educational assembly line you had this bunch of bright, extremely trained, highly motivated people with no outlets for these attributes. The firm I was with was better than some I'd seen, but people were anything but fulfilled. I began having some doubts about what this American success story was that I'd been primed to run for for fifteen or eighteen years."

In 1966 during his second summer at the firm Lorenz met some people who had been working with a citizens' group called the Emergency Committee to Aid Farmworkers which was trying to get support for Cesar Chavez, a Chicano leader and organizer, in his efforts to organize farm workers.

"I took some field trips, talked with some farm workers about their problems, and became convinced that there was little I could do for them as an individual lawyer. I'd read about the legal services program, so I went around and asked Cesar and some organizers for rival unions if they'd be interested in such a program. They all joined the board. I was still working for the corporate firm, but I was driving all around the state trying to get this started. We got some liberal lawyers on the board; I wrote a proposal that winter; and we had the first meeting of the board of directors.

"Some of the members of the board wanted the proposal sent to the state bar association first for approval. Although we thought that would be leading with the chin since the state bar was solidly stacked on the side of management, not workers, we ended up sending it to them anyway. After a month they sent a telegram to OEO saying they unanimously opposed the OEO grant since it was 'an effort to take part in an economic struggle still pending.' [This meant they were afraid that the farm workers trying to unionize would get some leverage against California's giant agribusiness industry.]

"At that point any group could get together, form a nonprofit corporation, and put in an application for an OEO grant, and we hit OEO at a good time because Clint Bamberger was then director of Legal Services, and he would stand behind any decision he made that he thought was important, and Shriver was enthusiastically supporting Legal Services because it was the only part of the war on poverty that was receiving favorable press notices. The funding was very touch and go, but Shriver was enthused enough about Legal Services and farm workers that he was willing to take a risk. However, most people drew the conclusion from the original proposal that we would be the legal arm of United Farm Workers Organizing Committee (UFWOC) so that they wrote into the funding that we could do no work for Chavez."

From talks with other people who helped to form CRLA but

who have since left, it appears that that conclusion concerning UFWOC was quite correct. These people, men like Gary Bellow and Dan Lund, intended CRLA to play a part in making UFWOC a stronger organizing vehicle in the farm worker community by providing it, and its members, with needed legal services.

"We accepted that stipulation because we felt that if we couldn't represent the union directly we could represent individual farm workers or groups of farm workers on issues that would be essentially the same.

"Coming from corporate practice I had a good education on how law is actually practiced and on how power is exercised through the law so we started out with a big firm model. We wanted to do the same things for farm workers that corporate firms did for their corporate clients. I had this vision of the law as a mechanism to redress a power balance. Exactly how was not so clear.

"We started out with a couple of guys who came to us in all different ways. Some were just out of school, some were also bored with corporate work. By and large the people who came in had not had much experience, but we decided to go with young, inexperienced, very bright, highly motivated people who had the kind of motivation that would fit in with this organization. And we were right because all of the older lawyers we hired didn't work out. They had a different concept of what the law and a lawyer is.

"The funding had come through in May of 1966, and our central office was located in Los Angeles then. From the beginning we did have a problem with turnover in the rural offices. Because of it we decided to pull some of the attorneys together in a place where they would be likely to stay because we needed some continuity, and we wanted to get Cruz Reynoso out here to work. He was an original member of the board and had been a rural lawyer, but then became assistant to Governor Pat Brown and was then with the Fair Employment Practices Commission in Washington, D.C. We needed a good Chicano lawyer, and we wanted him to succeed me as director.

"We moved the office to San Francisco, and Cruz came out as deputy director for seven months during which time we decentralized the decision-making in the office a lot. Then I stepped down, and Cruz stepped up. Now we have five lawyers in the main office, three who work in a back-up center as well as in the field, and thirty-two others scattered in nine regional offices throughout the state."

In 1972 Reynoso left CRLA so that he could teach fulltime at the University of New Mexico Law School, a school which has been a pioneer in enrolling and instructing Chicano and Indian law students. Martin Glick, who had directed litigation for CRLA, succeeded him.

By the time Reynoso became director, those lawyers who had wanted CRLA to play a house counsel role to UFWOC had, for the most part, become disillusioned with the way the program had worked out and had left it. Although they felt it was playing a vital role, they did not feel it was helping to strengthen the farm worker community.

Despite these criticisms, in its first five years of existence, CRLA had a long list of accomplishments. Through lawsuits or threats of lawsuits it had stopped the importation of braceros (foreign laborers, usually Mexicans, imported by the farmers for the picking seasons to keep the wages of farm workers down); stopped cuts of the Medi-Cal program that would have effected the health care of many poor people in California, both urban and rural; got the minimum hourly wage for farm workers raised from varying low figures to a standard $1.65; improved the health, sanitation, and safety facilities for farm workers; got legislation that improved the regulation of the use of pesticides, aiding both farm workers and consumers; had the federal food stamp and commodity programs instituted in all California counties; tried to ensure that farm workers could not be fired for union membership (although this can only be truly achieved when the union is firmly established throughout the agricultural industry); forced the state to provide free milk to three hundred thousand hungry school children, and to provide free lunches to those that qualified for the school lunch program; had an appeal before the Supreme Court that would ensure that farm workers would be covered by unemployment benefits; forced the retesting in Spanish of twenty-two thousand Chicano school children who had been placed in mentally retarded classes as a result of an English only IQ test; successfully completed a suit that allowed people who were literate in Spanish, but not in English, to vote; and had done much work on food and consumer fraud cases and on minority employment practices.

From their beginnings through 1970 they had handled 72,000 individual cases. In 1969-70 alone they handled 18,823 legal problems. Of the problems that went to court they won 80 percent of the cases. Seven percent of the cases in that fiscal year were class actions which affected approximately 2.5 million people.

All of these successes did not go unnoticed, either by CRLA's friends or enemies. In 1968 it was named the outstanding Legal Services program by OEO's National Advisory Committee, by the National Legal Aid and Defender Association, by the American Bar Association and the National Bar Association.

The person in California most consistently opposed to CRLA is Governor Ronald Reagan, a man not noted for his liberal views on anything. As far as his friendliness toward the nation's poor, in his second inaugural address in 1971 he announced that the principal goal of his second term would be slashing state welfare expenditures by eliminating those welfare recipients whose "greed is greater than their need." Another consistent opponent was California's booming agriculture business. While California contains only 2 percent of the nation's farms, it accounts for 10 percent of the national gross for farming. Its agribusiness, as it is called, leads the nation in the production of forty crops that

range from grapes to honey. The agribusiness people, farm own-
ers and people in related areas, exert a good deal of influence on
California's politicians, and are not fond of organizations that
help farm workers.

"CRLA started getting in trouble even before we were
funded," Lorenz said. "I had written the proposal for funding in
colorful language and had submitted it at the time when Cesar
was marching to Sacramento, and unionization of farm workers
was a hot issue. That got us in trouble with the state bar since
many of the lawyers in it work for the growers. We were funded
anyway, and by the summer of 1967 we had concluded a peace
treaty—and it was literally that—with the state bar, so things
cooled off in that area.

"Then that summer the Department of Labor announced that
it was going to try to import nine thousand braceros, and simulta-
neously Reagan announced cuts in the Medi-Cal program. The
result was that we filed major lawsuits to stop both actions, and
we succeeded in both of the suits. The upshot was the first major
political controversy with a Legal Services program anywhere in
the country. CRLA was always the center of that controversy because of Reagan and the agribusiness community. It was a tinder-
box situation. Chavez was moving, the valley was hot, the agribusiness community was upset, and we come in and file a lawsuit.
It had all the makings of a controversy and produced exactly
that.

"As a result the first amendment of the Legal Services program
was introduced into Congress in 1967. It was pretty unsophisticated. It talked about barring Legal Services from suing any governmental agency, and it was defeated. But it did kick off the
original controversy and got a lot of people after us.

"Then the amendment that barred Legal Services from doing
criminal work was passed in 1968, but that did not affect us that
much since we didn't take many criminal cases because the public
defender program was there in many communities. As I remember, the rest of '68 was an off year as far as getting into trouble.

"Then came 1969 and Senator Murphy of California introduced an amendment that would have given the governor absolute veto over any Legal Services program. That was the second big wave because Murphy introduced it on the floor and sneaked it through the Senate.

"Finally a group of us from Legal Services programs from all over the country went to Washington and, with the help of Rumsfeld's [Donald Rumsfeld, then director of OEO] office, set up a task force which finally got the Murphy Amendment beaten in the House. Then came a subsequent threat, the Green Amendment which would have given the state's programs grant power over the Legal Services programs. That was beaten in early 1970. Then later in '70 came the decentralization proposal, followed by Lenzner's firing. [Terry F. Lenzner and his deputy, Frank N. Jones, were dismissed as the heads of the Legal Services program in November of 1970 following weeks of argument over the decentralization proposal which would have shifted control over legal services from Lenzner to regional antipoverty officials who were not lawyers. Rumsfeld said the dismissals took place because Lenzner and Jones were unwilling or unable to carry out his policies. Lenzner and Jones contend that they were dismissed because they weren't willing to buckle under to the political pressure and buffeting that was aimed at emasculating the Legal Services programs. Following the dismissals, the reorganization proposal was dropped.]

"Then in December Reagan announced that he was vetoing the CRLA grant that OEO had given for the next year under a provision of the law that allows a state to veto federal poverty funds. He had just received the Uhler report and said that that was his reason for the veto."

Bob Gnaizda, another attorney in the main office of CRLA said that before the Uhler report Reagan had stayed away from attacking them.

"But when he got that report he thought that he had us and

might as well take credit for it so the agribusiness would applaud him. But the report was sloppy and full of holes."

The Uhler report is a fascinating document, reminding many readers of similar treatises brought out during the 1940-60 witch hunt days. Lewis Uhler, appointed by Reagan as the director of the state's Economic Opportunity Office (a federally funded office whose principal task is to provide technical assistance to California's antipoverty programs), and a former member of the John Birch Society, sent out three thousand questionnaires to California lawyers and public officials, asking them for information for or against CRLA, and inviting them to reply anonymously if they desired. Using the adverse replies as leads, a team of investigators from Uhler's office then toured the state collecting anti-CRLA affidavits. The result was a 283-page report containing 127 complaints against CRLA. On the basis of these charges, Reagan vetoed CRLA saying it did not represent "the true legal needs of the poor." Only after his veto and announcement did he allow anyone, even CRLA officials, to see Uhler's report.

The actual unveiling took place on January 6, 1971. Among the more amusing charges were ones saying that CRLA attorneys go barefoot to court, carry pocketbooks, and have posters in their offices. Then there were treacherous charges, ones implying guilt by association with people who are guilty of nothing except having views quite a bit to the left of Reagan's and Uhler's. For instance, one charge said that CRLA attorneys had a close association with Fay Stender who was characterized as "a movement lawyer." Miss Stender, who will be discussed in section II, has, in fact, handled cases for movement people, but at this time that does not constitute a crime. Another charge was that CRLA attorneys had tried to arrange a visit at Soledad prison between Angela Davis, who had been accused of complicity in a Marin County courthouse shootout, and the late George Jackson, one of the Soledad Brothers. The wording of this charge made any denial of it by CRLA sound like it was implying that there was a reason that they shouldn't be identified with Miss Davis—that is, that she was guilty of some crime. While CRLA knew that the substance of the charge was incorrect, they were very uncomfortable with the implications of a denial.

In analyzing the complaints CRLA found that 119 of the 127 charges were groundless, 5 complaints that had merit had been remedied prior to the report, 1 concerned an attorney who had already left CRLA, and the remaining 2 were remedied after the report.

"The Uhler report was very interesting," Lorenz said. "It's the New McCarthyism, the guilt by association technique. When you deny everything and there are 283 pages there to deny, most people think that there must be something there. It's like when McCarthy held up a list of forty names, people thought there must be something wrong with some of the people."

With the veto, CRLA became a political football. Observers felt that Reagan was trying to push Nixon into appearing socialistic, by comparison, if he or Frank Carlucci, the federal head of OEO, overrode the veto and refunded.

After the report had come out, Uhler said, supposedly paralleling Reagan's thoughts, "What we've created in CRLA is an economic leverage equal to that of large corporations. Clearly, that should not be. When businesses sue to collect debts or protect patents or challenge government rulings, that's all in the spirit of free enterprise. When farm workers sue not to change laws but to obtain enforcement of existing laws, such suits constitute harassment."

With the possibility then of Reagan challenging Nixon for the Presidential nomination in 1972, Nixon did not want to override the veto, so he found a way around the issue. CRLA was given a six-month provisional grant that funded it through July 1971. In those six months a three-man panel, composed of state supreme court justices, looked into the charges in the Uhler report. In twenty days of public hearings at ten locations in California they took testimony from 165 persons. In time the Commission members gave CRLA a clean bill of health.

In its report the Commission said: "The Commission expressly finds that in many instances the California Evaluation has taken evidence out of context and misrepresented the facts to support the charges against CRLA. In so doing, the Uhler report has unfairly and irresponsibly subjected many able, energetic, idealistic, and dedicated CRLA attorneys to totally unjustified attacks upon their professional integrity and competence. From the testimony of the witnesses, the exhibits received in evidence, and the Commission's examination of the documents submitted in support of the charges in the California Evaluation, the Commission finds that these charges were totally irresponsible and without foundation. . . . [T]he Commission finds and concludes that the operations of CRLA as conducted presently and within the recent past are within applicable OEO standards and applicable standards of professional responsibility. The Commission finds that CRLA has been discharging its duty to provide legal assistance to the poor under the mandate and policies of the Economic Opportunity Act of 1964 in a highly competent, efficient, and exemplary manner. We, therefore, recommend that California Rural Legal Assistance, Inc., be continued and refunded."

Finally, Carlucci, the OEO director, announced CRLA's refunding. In a twenty-three-page report Carlucci added that more stringent controls would be exercised over CRLA. However, all of the conditions were ones that were contained in prior grants or internal policy.

"We gave up nothing," said Cruz Reynoso, noting that CRLA had been funded through 1972—not just to the end of 1971, as is usual.

"Even when we were on a provisional grant," Lorenz said, "none of our attorneys or staff left, which shows the solidarity of the group."

The solidarity that held CRLA together even through hard times stems, in part, from a common philosophy.

Lorenz, who at thirty-two looks like an Andover-Harvard graduate who has let his hair down, feels that his actions in CRLA both depart from the system and reinforce it.

"I'm a populist, an antistatist. I'm for working out a way whereby people themselves can have control of the economy and thereby have control of the political arena. I'm afraid of any large concentration of power no matter where the people in control are in the political spectrum. One of my jobs as a legal technician has been to facilitate the diffusion of power. The old liberal game of 'find another charismatic leader' is nonsense as far as I'm concerned. In that situation the leader does initiate new programs, but they still flow from the top down. It's harder to have five hundred people making a decision, but that is one change some of us are committed to. Another is stopping growth for growth's sake. That destroys community.

"Here we've used the court system for the people's ends, but the number of cases where we haven't been able to are just heartbreaking and maybe greater than the number where we've succeeded. In part we've been playing for time, in part we've been trying to neutralize the power of corporations, in part we've been trying to begin reversing the legal processes now at work, but for that to happen requires a change in consciousness and in the larger political processes."

Gnaizda added, "Here we've learned to play with the powers that are to get what we want. Militant people wouldn't do that, but then I feel the presence of more militant groups in our society has helped us get a good deal of the things we have. If you look for justice solely within the courtroom, you'd be denying poor people justice. I think adverse publicity has as much influence on the defendants as what happens in the court, and I make maximum use of that. I think the greatest protection for poor people and for civil liberties is with the press, but that isn't to say that the press is always fair.

"We don't sell out in the confines of what we do. I don't like to put labels on my views. I just do whatever is necessary to make changes within the confines of what is lawful. I have no respect for the institutions or the system per se, but I can't think of a viable alternative that isn't going to cause enormous bloodshed and not be acceptable to the majority of the people. As far as courts, I don't think the court system now is capable of remedying what's wrong with society, but I don't think there's ever been a court system that has been. Ours is one of the few court systems that allows challenges to those in authority.

"But I think the system in the abstract tries to destroy poor people, and since they or the people who would help them aren't going to be in power, we might as well in a limited sense try to change things by making the system work for us through combining creative, good legal skills with aggressive action. Overall though, I have little respect for Legal Services programs."

Lorenz agrees with that feeling.

"The war on poverty is ultimately part of the strategy by the people in power, who are the minority, to split the large majority of people in this country, who do not have real power. It assumes that the only people who have real problems of alienation, and lack of decision-making, the only people who are impoverished are those making less than $3000 a year. That is a fallacy. The vast majority of people in this country are in the same situation. Also, the war on poverty gives a large number of resources to lots of people who have very little and really need them, but then the guy who makes $5000 a year sees he gets nothing, gets resentful, and the class or racial split is increased. The war on poverty is used very skillfully by the ruling people to have this effect."

Because many CRLA attorneys hold similar philosophies and feel they work well as a team, they had considered forming their own private law firm if the program wasn't refunded.

"We would have had to go much more into middle-class practice," Lorenz said, "but we'd still be with the people who don't have much real power, and we'd still be doing public interest work and continuing the fight in that guise. I think ultimately we're only going to have an effect if we establish a private base.

This fight convinced me of that. You cannot talk about long-term change in this society with a political effect if you're on government money. They can cut you off too easily. We were running the cleanest program in the country, with no financial excesses, all the Uhler charges were ridiculous, and still we got hung up by what was a political decision in the White House.

"If you're operating as close to the line as we are in as difficult an area, realistically you can't go on over a long period. And the changes some of us are committed to are going to take twenty years if they're going to happen at all.

"For the next five years I want to go more into political organizing, trying to work with the people in the state who are split on the race and student issue. I have a feeling that the law is a good tool but to suggest it is the only way that reform comes about is absurd. We've gotten to the point where we can influence by responding to a situation, but the real power of government and private power is in who makes the initial decisions, and we don't have much access to that right now. That's the political gap the public interest movement has to face, and that interests me for this next period. Maybe what we have to talk about is middle-class organizing with the women's movement, the environmental movement, the consumer movement. It's hard for poor people to have sustained political effort when they don't know where their next meal is coming from."

"The guys who run CRLA have real political moxie like I've never seen," said Martin Spiegel, a former lawyer in CRLA's Santa Rosa office, who is in the minority of lawyers who don't feel that solidarity with the program. "It's a miracle that CRLA has stayed alive. But the people in it are really able, fantastic lawyers, and they know how to get their friends to back them and how to confuse their enemies. But CRLA never panned out for me."

Spiegel, who is the same age as Lorenz, came to CRLA with a somewhat different background. A Brooklynite and a graduate of Columbia Law School, he did have a job with a corporate firm in the corporate firm capital—Wall Street—for one and a half years after law school.

"It was really boring, and the clients were companies who did more to hurt the United States than the criminals I defended later. I specialized in income tax law, and the whole hierarchical scene got me. The people who worked there were only interested in golf, professional football, and making money."

On his vacation in 1964, Spiegel worked with Arthur Kinoy for a few weeks and then went down to Mississippi for a week. He came back, got a job with New York's Legal Aid Society, and quit corporate life.

"That was a fantastic experience. The negative thing was that the amount of work was so staggering. They'd assign you to a part of the criminal court, and you'd handle anyone who came in there and needed a lawyer that day. When the case came to trial, usually you hadn't seen the client before because they were often in the can, and lots of times you wouldn't even have time to talk to the client before the case came up. Sometimes I felt like I'd go mad or vomit on the bench, the pressure was so enormous. I used to feel that to do right I'd get up and tell the judge I wasn't ready for trial and that the defendant was being denied his constitutional rights to adequate counsel. But I knew I'd be fired in a minute if I did that, and they'd just hire someone who would go in and do what he was supposed to do."

Spiegel stayed there until November of 1966 and then went to the Mobilization for Youth (MFY) program, a multisocial service program with an excellent legal division, which was receiving OEO funds at that time, as it still is.

"I liked it there a lot better. I had full discretion over the cases I took. So I took ones that were rehabilitating, since MFY also had a full social work program going, or ones that needed lots of preparation or ones I knew Legal Aid wouldn't do right. The problem with Legal Aid or any public defender office is that they ultimately depend on funds from the same powers that run the district attorney's office and the judges, so they often cave in or coerce guys to plead out for lower charges. (In many cases defendants are promised lighter jail sentences if they will plead guilty to reduced charges. The rationale is that this will help to decongest the courts and thus speed up justice.) Harold Rothwax, now a New York City criminal court judge, who was the director of MFY, wasn't like the Legal Aid people. He wouldn't cave in. I stayed there until I just got sick of New York."

Spiegel had heard about Gary Bellow, who was then deputy director of CRLA, so he came out to California to interview with him and with San Francisco Neighborhood Legal Services.

"Bellow was very seductive about the program, and, after a few days with him, I had the feeling that I would not be the man I could be unless I came out to the San Joaquin Valley and worked with farm workers. After studying for the California Bar and passing it, I went to work in the Madera office in September of 1968. In December or January, I became director of the office. I couldn't stand living in Madera so, when I learned there would be a vacancy in the Santa Rosa office I applied for it, and went there in the fall of 1969 and stayed until June of 1971.

"It just never panned out for me. I'm an urban Jew, and I never got turned on by the farm worker thing. I also couldn't believe that CRLA's lawsuits made that much difference in the lives of the farm workers. The union [UFWOC] is much more important, and the only legal work that counts is the legal work that backs the union, which CRLA couldn't do because of the grant stipulation. But I must admit that I was in the minority in CRLA having this feeling. I also couldn't get turned on to the impact cases. I was most effective when somebody walked into my office, and I could do something for them. That turned me on. I enjoy just sitting and bullshitting with clients. I even get turned on to divorce cases because they involve human life; so I think, in CRLA, I was considered screwy.

"I also have a personal feeling that people from outside an ethnic group can't do much for that group. Urban liberals used to spend all of their time working with the Blacks; then when the

Blacks told them to get out, they went to the Chicanos. When the Chicanos get their own lawyers, the same thing will happen, and the liberal lawyers will find other groups. It's one of the weird things that happens in this field, and, for me, it's a fallacious scene."

CRLA did change Marty Spiegel's life. After he left, he stayed in Santa Rosa and opened a law office there, crossed his fingers, and hoped to get enough business to support himself. Most of his business so far has consisted of people who went to CRLA and were referred to him because their income was above that allowed in the OEO guidelines.

"That was another thing that bothered me there. I thought they were right about CRLA being there for the farm workers, but I found I had to turn away the people I identified with most and cared about the most. Now I can help them."

Although California Rural Legal Assistance, Inc., is one of the best and one of the most controversial Legal Services programs in the country, it is far from being the only one. In 1971 there were 265 Legal Services programs in the country, operating 900 offices and employing 2000 lawyers. Their annual funding amounted to $68.9 million, and they handled over a million cases for the year. There were Legal Services programs in every state in the country with the exception of North Dakota.

John DeWitt Gregory, the former director of Community Action for Legal Services (CALS), the umbrella corporation that oversees New York City's Legal Services programs, said, "I think many people in the New York Bar wanted Legal Aid [which the bar virtually controls] to have the whole OEO program. As a compromise, a Legal Aid official was placed on every local board. I guess they wanted to make sure that no radicals ran away with the program."

No radicals have, and in that respect the New York program is similar to most other programs. (There are radical attorneys who are or have been in Legal Services programs. They will be discussed in section II.) In most other respects the New York program, most likely because it is in New York, is unique. It receives $4.3 million each year which makes it the most highly funded program in the country. In addition to CALS, there are ten other corporations running the twenty-five Legal Services offices in the city.

"The middle corporations were formed as an attempt at decentralization, and the structure is abominable because with the autonomy of the local corporations it's very difficult to get uniformity of legal services throughout the city. Also, the funding we get is grossly inadequate. To have the kind of program that was intended we would have had to be funded at $5.1 million in fiscal 1968."

Gregory, a Harvard Law School graduate, began his career working with a single practitioner in Harlem in 1959. After two and a half years there and another year with a firm on lower Broadway, he went to work in the litigation bureau of the state attorney general's office.

"At that time I found no trouble with what I was doing, but, as I've thought back, I wonder how I could have done it. I'd have difficulty now being in a prosecutorial position."

From there Gregory went to Nassau County in Long Island where he was employed as house counsel for the welfare commissioner. When Nassau County started its Legal Services program, Gregory became director. He built the program there up to the point where there were four offices in poverty areas of the county, then came to CALS in January 1968, when it was just beginning.

"Although Mobilization for Youth and Legal Aid had been receiving OEO funds before, eight new corporations were starting up when I came here. Now the program employs about two hundred lawyers. We do have a large turnover because of the salaries. We also used a lot of law students until 1971 when the budget cutbacks forced us to cut back. Although the program has had impact on the lives of many people, at least in service cases, it has not been as effective as I wished it to be. Why? Part of it is just New York City. Part of it is the structure, the organization, the fact that some offices were never up to par. After three and a half years there I just felt that the frustration was unbearable. The funding was never enough. I spent a lot of time making sure I met the payroll. Every year there was a delay in getting our grant, and I got really depressed with the whole bureaucratic structure, writing reports that you wonder if anybody ever reads. We ought to be spending more, and not less, to see that poor people really do get equal justice in our courts."

After Gregory left the program, he joined the Law School at Hofstra University as an associate professor, with the hope that he could litigate as he taught.

The inadequate funding and bureaucratic superstructure that frustrated Gregory to the point of resignation are two problems that plague all Legal Services programs. Another problem common to all programs is that of the staggering number of cases with which they have to deal. Of the close to 300,000 lawyers in the country, 70 percent of them serve the 25 percent of the population whose median income is over $10,000 per year. There are fewer than 4,000 lawyers to serve the 33 million people (16.5 percent of the population) whose income places them under the poverty level while there should be 49,000 if the lawyers in the country (1 for each 640 people) were equitably split up.

To compound the problem, lawyers who have worked in private practice estimate that it takes five times as much time to deal with the problems of a poor client than with the problems of a middle-class client because communication is more difficult, there is less trust in lawyers and the legal system in general, and the client is likely to have more than one problem by the time he or she gets to see an attorney. This means that it would take about 257,800 lawyers to provide legal services to the poor in the same ratio as to the general population.

The author of the above estimates, Carol Ruth Silver, is currently trying to work out ways to deal with the problem. An activist since her college days at the University of Chicago, an

alumna of forty days in a Mississippi jail during the Freedom
Rides in 1961, and a graduate of the University of Chicago Law
School, Silver has been working with Legal Services programs
since 1965. She is now executive director of the Berkeley Neighborhood Legal Services program (BNLS).

"I came here after working at CRLA. The program had been
funded for about a year, but it had no credibility in the community and was about to be defunded. I wanted the program to
combine law reform and service casework since it was clear that
the community wanted the latter, and I had decided from my previous work that the former provided the greater good to the
greatest number. I chose to try expanding the service caseload
through the use of nonlawyers, law and other students, to permit
a system which would free up the lawyer's time for impact work.

"Basically the system we use is to have three or four students
interview all potential clients each day. Then, at the end of the
day one or more lawyers meet with them to discuss the cases in
detail and to assign further research investigation or other work
on the case. This way we expand the number of cases we can do
with appropriate levels of professional competence. I also started
working on expedited procedures, taking, for instance, divorce
cases—which constitute 40 percent of legal services cases—and
working out forms for them. I've been working on this for the six
and a half years I've been with Legal Services. We now have a
one-inch thick manual on how to handle default divorces, which
really is a manual on how to manage the office, the systems, the
forms, office machines, and necessary personnel. It even has a
script for the lawyer to use when he goes to court. Recently I
have tried to get a systems analyst to work on it to get it ready
for computerization.

"This expedited procedures notion—using forms and students
and eventually computers for things like divorces, bankruptcy,
some welfare cases, some landlord-tenant cases, adoption, guard-
ianship, name changes—saves the lawyers' time to work on impact cases. We have about fifty students working here for course

credit as volunteers or on work-study programs. A number of the programs in the Bay Area use these procedures, but they aren't used nationally yet. Many other programs let their attorneys get overloaded with cases or arbitrarily limit their caseload by various devices including refusing to do some cases, like divorces."

Berkeley, best known for the division of the University of California that bears the town's name and for the radical activity that has happened around the University, is, in fact, a mixed community. There is a middle-class community, a Black community which accounts for 40 percent of the population, and a student and radical community that is the smallest part of the population. BNLS takes on the cases of the eligible people from all communities.

The police department that gave the country the People's Park debacle has not changed its attitude, and with the May 1971 defeat of the proposal for community control of the police, BNLS is kept pretty busy with class actions to control the behavior of the police on the Berkeley streets. Because of the large number of rent strikes that began in 1970, BNLS has also brought several cases concerning the landlord-tenant relationship. It has also brought cases concerning redevelopment, welfare, consumer rights, social security, and bankruptcy.

To coordinate and develop the work of BNLS and all the other Legal Services programs in the country and to aid in the growth of a body of poverty law, certain back-up centers for research, consultation, and coordination do exist. Nationally there are the Columbia University Center on Social Welfare Policy and Law, New York City; the Berkeley National Project on Urban Housing Law; the Boston College Consumer Law Center; the UCLA Health Center in Los Angeles; the Harvard Law and Education Center; and the National Institute for Education in Law and Poverty in Chicago.

There are also urban law projects, partially funded by OEO, in New York City and Washington, D.C. The New York one is called the Project on Urban Affairs and Poverty Law and is attached to New York University's Law School. Steve Leleiko, the assistant administrator of the program, says that it has two constituencies, the law school and the community, and two goals, developing new curricula on urban and poverty law, and demonstrating the utility of the house counsel role to community groups. The lawyers in the program do both field work and school work. At the end of the twenty months they spend with the project they get a masters degree in law. Some of their projects have included work on decentralization of the school system, bettering housing law, and health care.

The Urban Law Institute in Washington was founded by Jean Cahn who, along with her husband, Edgar, is commonly credited with creating the structure along which the Legal Services programs have been built. The Institute had been associated with the National Law Center of George Washington University until 1971 when Dean Robert Kramer of the law school severed the relationship saying that the University was "not willing . . . to take responsibility for a public interest law firm." The Institute, staffed by about twenty lawyers, had similar constituencies and goals to those of the New York project. Apparently the University felt the Institute was concentrating too much on the house counsel role and neglecting school work for field work.

However, out of this severing came a very exciting new project. Antioch College in Ohio, a progressive school which has long operated on a plan of alternating campus attendance and off-campus field work, joined with the Institute in plans to launch a new kind of law school with a learn as you defend approach. This new school admitted its first class in September of 1972. Supporters of this program hope that out of it will come an increased readiness by traditional law schools to accept new programs.

In addition to these national back-up centers, OEO also funds statewide back-up centers in Ohio, Massachusetts, and Michigan. The Michigan Legal Services Assistance Program (MLSAP) is funded through the Wayne State University Law School in Detroit. It works with every Legal Services, Legal Aid, and law-sponsored Legal Aid clinic in the state; assists other poverty groups; works with the state OEO program to arrange legal assistance to individuals in parts of the state where no Legal Services programs exist; helps Legal Services attorneys with extended research and acts as co-counsel in cases where that assistance is desired; prepares background memos on new areas of the law; runs seminars; prepares legislation for indigent groups; and makes sure that the work of the national back-up centers is put into practice in Michigan.

The staff consists of five fulltime and one parttime lawyer. They have each attempted to take a specialty or two within the poverty law areas such as welfare, housing, education, student rights, consumer rights, migrant problems, civil rights, women's rights, and domestic relations procedures reform.

Alan W. Houseman, the twenty-seven-year-old director of MLSAP, has been active in civil liberties, civil rights, and welfare rights work since his college days at Oberlin. After his graduation from New York University Law School, he worked in Detroit, receiving a Reginald Heber Smith fellowship, commonly referred to as Reggie. (The namesake of these fellowships was a Bostonian, a legal theoretician, and the author of *Law and the Poor*. They are given "to recruit and train first-rate young lawyers to serve in local Legal Services programs." Other Reggies will be discussed in section II.) Houseman then became director of MLSAP.

"I conceive of this program as the equivalent of CRLA. We do perform the back-up function, but we also represent state and local welfare rights organizations except where there are good local Legal Services attorneys. We serve as lawyers to both the organizations and the people in them. We feel that the only way to buttress organizations is to serve only those people who are members. The only way an organization can function is to have ideas and goals and a conception of what has to be done to get to those goals, and the only way we can do anything meaningful is to relate to the organizations that we represent. We try to stay within the OEO guidelines, but at times we're forced to go into criminal court, and we don't hesitate although we do try to get the correct clearances. There is a difference between providing lawyers and obtaining justice, and the role of the back-up center is the latter. That can only be accomplished when groups of the poor become politically powerful, so we try to work with groups that are and ones that are beginning to grow in that direction.

"The only way you can find out the real legal problems of the community is to work with the people in it. You can't sit in this office and expect to get anywhere. I see this program as an aggressive kind of participation in the legal system. We're also into court reform itself. The middle class as well as the poor don't have the mechanisms to resolve disputes. The legal system has failed miserably, so new mechanisms have to be worked out. A lot of our housing work is involved with setting up arbitration boards to solve disputes instead of having to go to court. We'd like to work on getting domestic and school disputes out of the courts too.

"For Legal Services to be effective it must be part of the movements for change. Just how is not simple to say. I reject the Nader notion, although I use it a lot, that we as lawyers should decide what to do and how to do it. One must be related to the people affected by your decisions, respond to what they want and need. If indigent organizations didn't exist, you'd be in a bind about what to do and how to move because the OEO structure doesn't provide any kind of realistic guidance whatsoever. I don't trust the community action program structure because it doesn't reflect the currents of change, of what needs to be done to provide poor people with justice and redress. For instance, OEO Legal Services was set up to provide lawyers, not social change or justice or legal redress, and I don't think that idea, the storefront lawyer thing, is necessarily the best way to organize a Legal Services program. It's helpful to have lawyers in the community, but what counts is having lawyers who relate to community groups.

You can sit in a storefront for months and not relate to anything except the guy who comes in for a divorce.

"It goes back to what the function of Legal Services is. Is the thing to provide people with a lawyer or something else? For instance, if lots of clients are faced with divorce, maybe the thing wrong is the divorce system, and what you should do is alter that which requires court or legislative reform. You can accomplish more through divorce reform than through handling five hundred individual divorces. As I mentioned before, we're trying to set up an administrative court system that would not require lawyers for uncontested divorces where no children are at issue. We're doing litigation on it, and we have legislation pending. We're also attempting to lessen pressure on clients whom welfare forces toward divorces. Some welfare reforms have already come about through affirmative litigation, but the big changes will only come when welfare rights organizations have power.

"The lawyer first has to relate to people and organizations that are moving. That's where real change will come about, not through the courts. The courts are institutions of the society. More than anything else they sanction the practices of society rather than upset them, regardless of what the Supreme Court did in the sixties. Another fundamental thing a lot of lawyers and Legal Services people forget is that fundamental change doesn't come through court decisions. It comes through community pressure to enforce court decisions, and community support in the first place. Until we understand that, a lot of what Legal Services does is Band-Aid work.

"Although I have an independent role in welfare work because I'm not part of the welfare recipient community, and though I do have ideas I push for, I don't think that role is primary. What the people want is primary. It's for them to assert their best interests and for me to help them, always realizing that what welfare reform is all about is the economic redistribution of wealth and that until people focus on that, we won't be articulating the fundamental problem.

"I think the major legal problem is procedural. There are not vehicles for providing redress for people, and not many people give a damn about it. This relates to community control, corporate form, decentralization of courts, and setting up alternative mechanisms to the courts, and it would all bring people control over their lives. The second large legal problem is in the institutions that have the effect of continuing people in poverty, in racist discrimination. Those institutions have to be attacked, and the easiest one to attack is the government. That's why Legal Services launches a lot of attacks on government agencies and why there's a lot of question about Legal Services because, in effect, they're being paid to attack themselves.

"So far we haven't caused the state any serious problems. I don't think Michigan, under its present administration, would seek to terminate us. But I do see a problem of Washington's trying to control more when they find out what is really going on. They don't know, and the bureaucracy in Legal Services has tried to cover up as much as possible, not because we're doing anything wrong but because we're trying to get law reform through the court system by working with aggressive, militant groups."

Whether some Legal Services programs can continue to do creative, aggressive work for poor people in the country seems in grave doubt since Nixon announced the abolition of OEO in his 1973 budget.

It's likely that some of the Legal Services lawyers will continue working in a similar vein without government support. How and where the rest can be absorbed into some other part of the People's Law Movement remains to be seen. Some other alternatives for the individual rights lawyer will be discussed when we meet the lawyers who have taken them.

Consumer Rights Lawyers

At first glance it appears that all consumer rights lawyers are the fans and emulators of Ralph Nader, the young David who felled the Goliath of General Motors. And, although that appearance seems much too simple, upon evaluation it proves to be true to a very large extent. Nader began the consumer rights, or public interest, trend in law, and he continues to be the most flamboyant, internationally known symbol of this type of legal work.

A consumer movement, usually shrouded in conservation green, had been building in this country for many years before Nader came on the scene, but it wasn't until he showed people that you could fight city hall, or, in his case, General Motors, that it really began to move. Nader feels that his book *Unsafe at Any Speed,* which brought GM, eventually, to its knees, came out at an auspicious time, the midsixties: a time when the consumer demand created during World War II had been met, affluence had set in, and people were beginning to feel the loss of bargaining power that comes when most stomachs are filled, and bodies clothed. By the time his book came out the middle-class in the U.S. were beginning to feel that, if they weren't actually deprived, they were getting a raw deal. They were the ones suffering most acutely from inflation, planned obsolescence, sloppy workmanship. At about the same time that they realized this, and realized it gave them cause for complaint, the ecological crisis came to the fore and they realized that they were being kicked in the lungs and stomach as well as the pocketbook by those twins of free enterprise: big business and organized labor.

Although there were consumer and conservation groups that had been working on these problems all along, none of the people in them seemed to stand out enough to become the champion of the consumer, America's newly deprived victim. Then along came Nader, a young Harvard Law School graduate, the son of Lebanese immigrants. In his law school thesis he had started out to prove that cars were not safe, and he continued this project later, following the tip of a Fisher Body inspector who had become disgusted with what he had seen happening in those old automobile factories. Working on his own for several years, Nader, the Honest Abe of this century, prepared the book that so shook General Motors that it tried, in a wide variety of less than upright ways, to find some information with which they could blackmail him. But Nader's life was so clean that they could not find a thing. The book came out and Nader sued GM for invasion of privacy and eventually won a settlement that amounted to $280,000 after attorney's fees.

For a year after the publication of *Unsafe at Any Speed* Nader went into a retreat during which time he developed the theme of the book and began to work on auto safety legislation. Then he geared up for the summer of 1968 at which time, working with seven Harvard Law students, he brought out a report on the Federal Trade Commission (FTC), which eventually caused extensive reorganization of the agency. During that summer the term, and the concept, of "Nader's Raiders" were born. The next summer ninety students came to Nader's newly formed Center for the Study of Responsive Law (a tax-exempt, educational, and research foundation formed in June 1969 and staffed by a varying number of other lawyers, political scientists, physicians, and assorted professionals) to work as Raiders. Out of that group came a number of reports including *The Vanishing Air, The Chemical Feast,* and a report on the Interstate Commerce Commission (ICC).

By 1970, the Raider idea was so popular that the Center had four thousand student applicants, including one-third of the Harvard Law School, for positions that pay from nothing to $900 for the summer. Out of these, two hundred were chosen. They worked on a wide variety of reports on everything from nursing-home care to the Savannah River. Because of the number of unfinished reports and because the Center found that two hundred people were just too many, the number of Raiders in 1971 was reduced to thirty.

Nader's box score, both alone and with the Raiders, is totally impressive. Since he first came into the public eye he has—using his theory that the lawyer is a social engineer who should pick out those areas that should be attacked in the public interest—taken on just about every institution and industry in the country, including, but certainly not limited to, the automobile industry, the dental industry, television, meat inspection, mouthwashes, Geritol, the FTC, the ICC, the Food and Drug Administration (FDA), air polluters, medicine, nursing homes, coal mines, banks, supermarkets, think tanks, the antitrust division of the Justice Department, DuPont, citizen access to regulatory agencies, the Department of Agriculture, California (for its land use), the pulp and paper industry in Maine, tractor safety, airlines, Union Carbide, etcetera, etcetera, etcetera. In 1971 and 1972 most newspapers seemed to print at least one story each week about a new Nader project, making it impossible for anyone except a fulltime Nader-watcher to be fully up-to-date on what Nader is doing. In 1971 Nader also went to Canada, Britain, and Japan to attempt to get consumer movements going there.

He also advised some young lawyers, veterans of Campaign GM (which had attempted to give the public more access to Gen-

eral Motors by adding three public representatives to the corporation's board of directors), on setting up the Project on Corporate Responsibility, which extends the Campaign GM idea to
other corporations. Another function of this center is to take
"whistle-blowing" calls, a Nader term for corporate personnel's
calling corporate unfairness to the Project's, and thus, ultimately,
to the public's attention. In addition to this project he also works
with the Center for Auto Safety, which monitors the National
Highway Safety Bureau.

In 1970, perhaps sensing that he might be overextending himself, Nader opened the Public Interest Research Group (PIRG),
which is his privately financed action arm. The other centers with
which he works are considered tax-exempt, educational foundations. PIRG, which is now the largest public interest law firm in
the country, consists of thirteen lawyers, most of them directly
out of law school. For the 1970-71 year Karin Sheldon and
James Welch were both attorneys with PIRG. Since at this time
Nader is more of an institution or a symbol than he is a consumer
lawyer, their views on consumer rights law are more representative of the mass of consumer lawyers in the country. And, contrary to the press's illusion, there are other public interest lawyers
in addition to Ralph Nader. Like most of these other lawyers,
Sheldon and Welch were as enthusiastic about Nader as they were
about their work.

"The public interest thing started when Ralph began drum-
ming up interest in lawyers working for the public interest, rather
than working for the special interests of some economic interest
group," Welch said.

"Before Ralph there were lawyers who would be confronted
with a particular situation of consumer problems which they
would solve on a one-to-one basis but there wasn't anyone on a
nationwide basis. Ralph was the first person who looked at the
whole country and said that we have broad-scale public interest
questions that face all of us. He was the first lawyer to set up a
continuing monitoring function so lawyers could plan ahead, not

just react. The difference between us and the lawyers who used to do consumer cases on pro bono time is that we're trying to start a whole new element that acts rather than reacts."

"That puts consumers in charge and on the offensive so they're involved all the time, not just when they personally receive a defective piece of merchandise," Sheldon added.

"What we're trying to do is draft what we think is visionary legislation and get it passed. That has really been lacking in consumer or broad public interest questions until now. For instance, nobody had analyzed the impact of a corporation on society. Yet, when you think about it you realize that anyone can sign a piece of paper incorporating themselves and put an invisible shield between them and their acts, thus eliminating personal responsibility. The social impact of that fact is fantastic," Welch said.

"Obviously," he continued, "there's been a need for public interest lawyers for a long time, for lawyers who represent broad interests on a theoretical level rather than just represent a specific economic interest group and try to advance its cause."

At PIRG the lawyers do both theoretical and concrete work.

"We're a sole proprietorship of Nader. He finances the whole thing out of his own pocket. We do everything that is legal: draft legislation, bring court suits, participate in administrative rule-makings, help to organize public interest firms on a local level, write articles, write speeches and things for Ralph. With thirteen people we are the biggest public interest firm around, so we just took the world and divided it into thirteen parts so everyone has at least one area of expertise. Within your area what you do is up to you aside from specific projects that Ralph asks you to do," Welch said.

Karin Sheldon specialized in environmental questions and Jim Welch, in government subsidies to industries. Other people working there are concerned with federal subsidies to banking, setting up a public interest firm for retired people, the Civil Service Commission's role in "crushing" federal employees who put the public interest above special and bureaucratic interests, inequality in property taxes, the lack of genuine competitive bidding and other abuses in procurement in all levels of government, favored treatment from the Treasury Department, the FTC and advertising; the domination by industry of government advisory committees, corporate responsibility, professional responsibility or "whistle-blowing," food and drug regulatory matters, automobile safety, and the specific problems of Chevrolet Corvairs.

Because of the scope of their projects, Nader and the people at PIRG are actively trying to set up other public interest firms.

They waged a successful campaign in Oregon to have student fees raised by one dollar per quarter, the extra proceeds to go to a totally student controlled public interest firm. The success of the Oregon project, which was voted into being by referendum, sparked similar student movements in other states.

Welch worked on the project with Donald K. Ross, another PIRG attorney.

"After Oregon, the idea just exploded and is happening all over. A conscious project of our group is to try to see to it that more and more people do public interest law as a career. The obvious hurdle is money since public interest lawyers aren't collecting fees from anyone. So we've had several models we've tried to build. The student-controlled firm is one. Another is one we used in Ohio and Connecticut which is really a straight fund-raising campaign both at schools and in the community. A third model we've used is to have lawyers fund the firm themselves by going to the bar association and telling them to kick in a couple of hundred dollars each."

In June 1971 Nader tried another method of financing public interest firms by setting up a nonprofit corporation called Public Citizen to raise funds for his various projects. Through direct solicitation Nader hoped that the corporation would be able to raise $500,000-$1,000,000 in its first year to expand the work of his existing organizations and to help set up affiliated projects throughout the country.

Another method of funding a public interest firm is being tried by a group of Washington attorneys in a firm called Berlin, Roisman and Kessler. The three namesakes of the firm—Ed Berlin, Tony Roisman, and Gladys Kessler—and their associate David Cashdan were all government attorneys who had either become dissatisfied with what they were doing or were confused about what they would do when they left the employ of the government. They were personal friends and the original three decided to leave their jobs in 1968 and try to set up a public interest firm that would finance itself through fees.

"All of the public interest firms in Washington started organizing about the time that we did," said Kessler, "although some people had been proselytizing about public interest work for years. We decided not to go after outside funding because we feared that public interest law is going to be a short-term interest for the foundations that are funding some of the other firms. Also, we felt that foundation money cuts down on your independence. We had one small research contract and the people who gave it to us drove us out of our minds with instructions and interference. That made up our minds definitely not to do that again."

Their firm has been having financial trouble. They had intended to divide the income of the firm for their first two years but found that they didn't have enough income to make that worthwhile. Most of the members have spouses who work and this has allowed the firm to go on. They have hope for the future as more consumer groups who need specialized consumer lawyers grow.

The relationship between consumer groups and consumer rights lawyers seems a little nebulous at this time. While the Berlin firm waits for groups to come to them, Nader and his people seem to try to create issues that will eventually beget groups.

"The issues we have in our political campaigns now are really irrelevant," said Welch. "When was the last time a vigorous antitrust policy was an issue in a campaign? Yet, if you're talking in terms of free enterprise, which is the rhetoric we always hear, that is vital and we don't have it. If you're in power the easiest way to retain it is to keep everybody's attention elsewhere and that's what is happening, and what we have to counterbalance."

"Environment is a classic example of keeping attention elsewhere," Sheldon said. "Everybody can be for it. Nobody is for pollution. People can run around having antilitter campaigns instead of looking at the fundamental problem which is who is in charge. We have no control over that. We as the public have been locked out so long that we can't get in and make sure that good environmental policy is made at the top levels."

"The thing the whole public interest movement recognizes," Welch said, "is that there are whole levels of decision-making in the government that are unrelated to electoral politics. The courts, the administrative agencies which all make decisions for you are beyond your control unless you have lawyers, scientists, other professionals to testify for you. Right now nobody has analyzed these institutions and figured out how the public can have its input."

"When the public marches outside saying 'Stop Pollution' or 'End the War,'" Sheldon said, "they have to rely on parttime help, volunteers with good intentions but maybe not with the skills to do anything as have the people big business hires. For instance, Jim went to a hearing on oil shipments in New Orleans and on the side of the environment were 3 attorneys, on the side of the oil companies were 397. What kind of odds are those? With Ralph we're fourteen public interest lawyers, and we're the largest firm of the kind but we're working against the thousands of lawyers working for corporations and for the government."

"We all work tremendous hours here but it's not because Ralph orders us to do anything, although his standards are high," Welch said. "It's because there is so much to be done and everyone here is dedicated to it. This is the one area where you can honestly say 'If I don't do it nobody else will' and that drives you."

The PIRG attorneys make $4500 a year, hardly a lucrative salary. They are satisfied with the salary because they realize it "comes from the sweat of Ralph's brow," in other words from his GM settlement and from money he makes on lectures and royalties. They are also heartened by the example he sets. They say that he doesn't keep any money for himself and, in view of his highly publicized spartan lifestyle, that would seem to be true. Even now, five years after GM's original tricks, he still lives in an $80-a-month furnished room and he still uses the hall telephone.

The young attorneys who go to work for PIRG are told that they should only plan to stay there for one or two years. After this training or orientation period they are encouraged to go out and start up public interest firms in other places. This is another method by which Nader hopes to see the consumer rights movement grow. Both Karin Sheldon and Jim Welch followed this plan and left when their time was up to go to work for the consumer elsewhere.

Welch said that he found his work at PIRG very satisfying.

"I had a pleasant relationship with Ralph which is nice because I obviously admire him or I wouldn't have been there. Beyond that, I got personal satisfaction out of seeing the changes that have been made because of what I have done. Like the project in Oregon, just getting it going. Now there are fifteen openings for public interest professionals which would not have existed had Don Ross and I not gone out there."

"I can't think of anyplace else you could have done that your first year out of law school," Sheldon said. "Another thing there, was the people working with you. We didn't see Ralph all the time so if we had to depend on him solely for moral support it would be difficult, but the other people there are an incredible collection and that makes things good."

The solidarity in the office comes partially from shared dedication and partially because the people there seem to work at it. They eat lunch together every day and occasionally have meetings. The atmosphere is informal, with people making their own hours and chatting when they have the chance.

"The informality," said Welch, "which also extends to the other operations, has its pluses and minuses. A lot of people are doing their own thing which is pleasant for them, but once in a while you'd call a guy on the phone and he'd say 'Goddamn it, you're the fifth Nader guy who's called me today. Get out of my hair.' This overlap is sometimes unnecessary but sometimes beneficial. Besides the meetings we found out what everybody else was doing by reading the newspapers."

Although the PIRG attorneys, being neither tax-exempt, nor strictly education- and research-oriented, are free to go into court, they hesitate to do so. Some go into court more than the others, depending on their project.

Welch explains, "Our realization is that courtroom work is the most costly and inefficient way to do anything. So we tried to achieve change in as many other ways as possible, always with the threat that we had fourteen lawyers there who were sitting around just waiting to go to court. But we tried to use the media, hearings in legislatures, administrative agencies, and any other ways we could think of. Then, if all else failed, we could always go to court."

This distrust of the courts is shared by Gladys Kessler.

"My own view, which is narrow because I've only worked in Washington and a little in New York City, is that local courts are an abomination, and I've never even worked in the criminal courts. The caliber of judges is low. The indefinable sense of dignity, decorum, and rationality that is supposed to be in a court just isn't there. We have this myth that the government is a government of law and not of men. This is not borne out by any experience you have in the court system. It turns completely on the capriciousness of the judge. Each one is god in his own courtroom, but I don't know what we can do about it right now."

Because of this feeling and because of the issues with which they work, the Berlin firm doesn't spend that much time in court. A majority of its time is spent in trying to influence administrative agencies about their new rules, in administrative hearings, and in lobbying.

What convinces a person to go into public interest law?

For the people in the Berlin firm it was the work they had done for the government.

"We've seen the deficiencies," Kessler said, "and we wanted to be in a position to fight them. We wanted to do so in civil courts and in administrative agencies because none of us is experienced in criminal matters."

And they also wanted the opportunity just to do the work that they wanted to do.

Karin Sheldon traces her interest back to the fourth grade when she saw a picture in the paper of a woman about to be moved off her land.

"I talked to my father and resolved then that I was going to be a lawyer and rescue little old ladies. It somehow always stuck in my mind."

"I just felt," Jim Welch said, "that, on the gross level, as a nation and a world, we were not pursuing the right course. All kinds of things have to be changed. I know a lot of people think that, but I think that what I'm doing right now will most directly achieve it. I think what we are doing is incredibly revolutionary in the sense of the word that means new and unique. A lot of people say that what we're doing is counterrevolutionary, that we're not going to achieve any changes, that once we learn how to play the game under the rules that now exist, as we are doing, that they will simply change the rules. Well, that's a risk we'll have to take."

"In college," Sheldon said, "we were all involved in radical things in one way or another."

"But," Welch added, "if you're going to talk about power to the people I think the question is where is that power now, and how do you get the people into those powerful circles? What we're doing is aimed at doing just that."

Sheldon said, "I think the public has become timid because over the years things have gotten so complex and so removed from direct control that they know that they can't fight city hall most of the time. So they shrug their shoulders and say 'I'm not an expert. I'm not a lawyer,' forgetting that just going to law school doesn't confer on you any mantle of wisdom. It just gives you some skills. Anybody in the country essentially knows what is right and what is best and what needs to be done. It's just putting people together with people who have the skills. What we're trying to do as consumer lawyers is forge an alliance of those who feel they have no control over decision-making and get them into control. We do have problems at colleges when we speak with radicals who feel that we're counterrevolutionary, but I don't think that people who say that we're only working for the middle-class values have really thought it through.

"Environmentalists are getting this thrown at them all the time from militants who say ecology is only a fad, a diversion from the real issue of racism. But who is the greater victim of environmental contamination? It's not the white middle-class family in the suburbs but the poor people in the inner city or the people who have to work on farms and get pesticides dumped all over them, the people whose kids eat lead paint. These people are the environmental victims, and the consumer victims. What we're doing isn't a diversion, it's part of the total struggle."

"I believe that within the general framework of what we have, it is possible to work out a solution," Welch said. "We're optimistic. Because when you're talking about government responsiveness and efficiency and corporate responsibility you're getting at the root causes of racism, poverty, the war, and all of the rest. I'm not saying we'll solve them all tomorrow. An example of what's wrong that I use in my talks is that you hear so much rhetoric about law and order in this country. Yet, when you separate that from reality and see what the government's monetary commitment is to law and order you find that the federal courts' total budget is less than the cost of one C5A airplane. What kind of commitment is that? None. No wonder the courts are overburdened. On the one hand you're training lawyers in law school who know every procedural trick in the book in terms of tying things up for years in court, and on the other hand the government is unwilling to spend enough money to build a system that will respond to the needs of the people.

"Generally, I'm ashamed of my brothers in the legal profession. They've been trained in law school not to make moral judgments about what they do, and then they're thrust into a position where they have to make social policy judgments which is one of the things law school doesn't train you to do. To a large extent what is wrong with this country is that lawyers are running it, and they're not trained to do that."

"And people have this incredible faith in lawyers," Sheldon said, "that they can solve anything. That faith is misplaced. The law school is a medieval institution and it's backed up by an even more medieval bar which controls who gets to practice, who become judges, and who controls the law schools. It's a vicious circle."

"We have some plans in the works," Welch said, "to monitor the legal system. While at PIRG we all joined the bar association, and we were prepared to form ourselves into an ad hoc committee and make some changes that way in the bar exam, the character committee, and all of that junk."

"As the number of public interest firms increases in the country," Sheldon said, "there will be more of this happening to the bar associations, and to the law schools. I don't think anyone has really come to terms with the court system yet, seen how bad it is, how much has to be done."

"I think we'll make some changes," Welch added. "I think Nader as an individual has done a tremendous amount. He has awakened a spirit that maybe people can do something about what is happening to them."

"Because he did," Sheldon said. "Before he took on GM he had nothing: no money, political influence, or power. He was just a kid out of Harvard and if one person can stand up to the largest company in the world then the rest of us ought to be able to do it. Maybe not in the same way, but in small ways. And that's the way changes are made. One step at a time."

Nader, in the five years since he first published *Unsafe at Any Speed*, has taken a lot more than one step. An enigmatic person, compulsive about his privacy, albeit with reason, he has said that he was attracted to the concept of public interest law by reading about some of the leading American lawyers who were, historically, always on the frontiers of defending rights. He said that he felt that the same type of lawyer was needed to make institutions more responsive, and that his experience at Harvard, with its commercial orientation, developed that feeling further.

So, at a time that proved to be ripe, Nader came out fighting for the concept of the lawyer as social engineer, for organizing theretofore unorganized public interest. He dismissed the need for revolution by saying, "Who needs Marxist-Leninist rhetoric when you can get them on good old Christian ethics?" Since the time that he first appeared in the public view Nader has received a lot of praise and criticism, both of which were to be expected.

The most valid criticism is that he has taken on more things than one man, even with four back-up organizations, can do. Because of the number of projects he had by late 1971, the quality of some of them had deteriorated to the point where those institutions he was attacking could attack him back with equal vigor. Yet, with his attempts to start and fund other public interest law projects, he is trying to solve this problem although a final solution will come only when other as newsworthy consumer rights lawyers come into the public view.

Putting himself in the position of an incorruptible monitor of the public interest Nader has left himself open to punches from any direction. Yet, whatever final name he makes for himself, it must be admitted that this one man, by his own concrete example, inspired a lot of other lawyers to work for the public interest. Through Nader, a new type of rights lawyer was born. From the growth in the number of consumer lawyers that has occurred in the past six years it is reasonable to assume that this type of lawyer will have a great effect on America's future.

II
RADICAL
LAWYERS

New York City

New York City has an abundance of everything, including radical lawyers and radical organizations. Because of this abundance, the radical lawyers here do not tend to be very closely knit in any structural way. The NLG headquarters is here, and so is the first model mass defense office. While the Guild is not the only organization engaged in radical defense work, all of the radical lawyers are members of the Guild. But unlike other cities where the Guild tends to coordinate all of the political cases, in New York the Guild coordinates only those cases involving mass and major arrest situations.

The "big" political cases generally go to well-known radical lawyers and law firms or law groups such as the Center for Constitutional Rights and the Law Commune when it was still in existence. There is some friendly competition between these groups, but they do work together and cooperate with one another in times of stress. Yet there is always the awareness that they are in the Big Apple, the city that is the self-proclaimed center of the world. The intensity, the speed, the competitiveness, the aggression, the avant-garde ambiance of the city affects the radical law community, as it does all others, making it one of the most diverse and interesting in the country.

One of the pivotal people in the community is Mary Kaufman, a longtime Guild activist and civil rights and labor lawyer, who was largely responsible for the coordination and administration of the Guild's Mass Defense Office during its first three years of existence.

Kaufman was born in Atlanta, Georgia, in 1912 to a family of European intellectuals. Her father was a sculptor who moved his family of five to New York City when she was five years old.

"My early life was really one of poverty. My father was an extraordinary, versatile man whose primary occupation was sculpting, although he supported the family, with my mother's help, in every conceivable way from carving wood frames to being a small shopkeeper. From early childhood, I was very much attuned to the problems of the poor. Poverty was my economic level up until the time I finished law school. My mother led a rent strike during the early days of rent strikes on the East Side, and I also participated in things like that and the monumental hunger marches and organization of the unemployed in the 1930s. All this, of course, had a very great influence on my life.

"The other thing that influenced me greatly since childhood was the fact that in my family women did not play a secondary role. Both of my parents were strong personalities, and they participated jointly in the economic and home life of the family. So that although I grew up in a society where women were generally oppressed, I didn't have to battle my personal environment. Most of the young women I find today who are struggling for liberation also have to fight against the traditions in their homes where they were brought up to play with dolls and realize that their role was to be the assistant to whatever husband they got. We didn't have that in my family."

Kaufman got her bachelor's degree in political science from Brooklyn College and then attended St. John's Law School at night while working on a Works Progress Administration

(WPA) project during the day. As a testament to the equality in the family, her sister also went to law school and became a lawyer while, of her three brothers, one became an artist, one, an engineer, and one, a businessman.

After being admitted to the bar in 1937, Kaufman got a job with a labor lawyer since "that was what I always wanted to be from the time I started studying law. It seemed to me the most significant thing to do in terms of the development of the country." For $5 a week she worked processing cases which were submitted to the New York State Labor Relations Board, preparing charges against companies engaged in unfair labor practices or in interfering with union attempts to organize. She also continued her organizing work with WPA legal projects.

She became a member of the National Lawyer's Guild (NLG) when it was first formed, in 1937.

"I was not one of the principal organizers since I was heavily involved in the Lawyers' Security League, an organization of lawyers on WPA projects, but I was a member of the Guild from its inception. The Guild played a significant role at that time not only in helping to formulate many of the programs which were adopted by the Roosevelt administration but also in supporting Roosevelt in combating the reactionary trend of the Supreme Court which was invalidating many of the social measures that were passed."

In 1940 Kaufman went to Washington to work with the National Labor Relations Board, but she left after only one year to join her husband in New York when she became pregnant.

"I yielded to my husband's feelings that the woman's place was in the home, and I tried that until the end of 1944, when my son, Michael, was three. By that time we were in the war, and I found it absolutely essential to become involved in productive, creative work. I went back to Washington to work with the War Labor Board. My husband and I separated and I took Michael with me. After the War Labor Board became defunct, I worked for the Wage Stabilization Board."

After World War II ended, Kaufman was sent to Nuremberg as a prosecutor in the case of I. G. Farben, a German cartel
with economic connections in seventy-eight countries throughout
the world, which was one of the major supporters of the Nazi
government.

"Because of Farben economic influence in countries all over
the world, it provided a vast network for espionage and propaganda. My job was to establish proof that I. G. Farben used this
vast network in support of the Nazi aggression. Because I was in
Nuremberg from the beginning of 1947 until the end of 1948 I
did not see the gradual development of the cold war back home.
The loyalty oaths, the witch hunts against the Hollywood Ten,
the listing of so-called subversive organizations, members of
which were not eligible for government employment, the attorney
general's lists—all of these things took place while I was in Nuremberg.

"But there were incidents in Nuremberg which gave us
glimpses of the cold war. I remember two particularly. A man
from the American consulate in Frankfurt had uncovered many
of the documents that were used against Farben. In the natural
course of events I sent an assistant to see this man so that he
could authenticate these documents. He refused to do so saying
that the people on the board of directors of I. G. Farben were
very good people. When the assistant questioned him about what
appeared to be a reversal of his own position, he said, 'I uncovered this evidence during the war. Now we have a totally different
picture. We may need these people. Today our enemy is not the
Germans; it's the Russians.'

"The other incident occurred toward the close of the presenta-
tion of my evidence in the case. I learned that a band of sabo-
teurs, trained by I. G. Farben, who had landed in the U.S. during
the war and who had been captured, convicted, and sent to jail,
were being sent back to finish their sentences in Germany. I
ordered their appearance at Nuremberg. When they arrived I received a phone call from my superior who told me to send them

right back because the State Department was kicking up quite a fuss. That closed the door to proof of Farben's role in this sabotage effort.

"The group of lawyers I worked with on that case was all dedicated to the high moral principle of eradicating once and for all the possibility of a repetition of war. We were idealistic, we tried very hard, and we felt we had produced some very damaging evidence. I'll never forget the day when we sat and listened to the Tribunal's opinion and judgment. It found I. G. Farben not guilty of the crime of aggressive war although it did find some of the board members guilty of crimes against humanity and of war crimes. When we listened to that decision we were terribly depressed. I sat there and that was the first time I had a sense of shame for my government. I think that feeling was shared. We knew that the decision was politically motivated.

"I left Nuremberg and came back to the U.S. in September of 1948. I came back to the cold war atmosphere I hadn't watched develop and was appalled by it. I had been living in the past of the Nazis' rise to power—a rise which began with the elimination of the Communists and the use of anticommunism as a pretext for suspending the constitutional guarantees of the people—and came back to see what appeared to me to be the same development taking place in this country."

Kaufman began working on the Dennis case, the case in which twelve leaders of the Communist party of the U.S. were indicted under the Smith Act on a charge of conspiring to organize the Communist party of the U.S. and to teach and advocate the duty and necessity of forcible overthrow of the government. The trial, before Judge Harold Medina, lasted for nine months, with five lawyers doing the courtroom work.

"I worked in the office but did not go to court. The lawyers who did—Harry Sacher, George Crockett, Abraham Isserman, Lewis McCabe, and Richard Gladstein—did a brilliant job before Medina, who was one of the most sophisticated baiters of lawyers one could find. His actions were comparable to those of

Julius Hoffman in the Chicago Seven conspiracy case. It was said that the Dennis lawyers provoked the judge but the shoe was on the other foot, namely these were courageous lawyers who resisted the attempts of Judge Medina to prevent them from representing their clients as courageously as they could.

"At the end of that trial, I was in the courtroom seated at the counsel table when the verdict of guilty came down. Right after the verdict, Medina said, 'I have some unfinished business.' He asked the five lawyers and Dennis, who had represented himself, to rise and then charged them with contempt, summarily found them guilty, and sentenced them to prison terms. As I sat there all alone at counsel table while the others stood, I was again profoundly ashamed of my country.

"The atmosphere of fear already had its firm grip on the American people. The trial lawyers in that case had performed brilliantly and courageously. But I'm ashamed to say they did not get the support of most of the members of the bar. All of the lawyers served time in jail. In addition, Harry Sacher and Abe Isserman, great lawyers and men of profound principle, were hounded in a variety of ways, including disbarment. But both were eventually vindicated and reinstated to the bar after many hard years and lengthy litigation."

For the next few years Kaufman traveled around the country defending other people who were indicted under the Smith Act. She was trial counsel in the second New York Smith Act case, the case against Elizabeth Gurley Flynn and other leaders of the Communist party. She then went to St. Louis for the Smith Act case there, and then to Denver and back to a third New York Smith Act case. She also did appellate work on all of these cases.

In Denver the court had appointed twelve of the city's leading lawyers including the dean of the Denver bar to defend those indicted. Kaufman went there to help because of her previous experience in such cases, and was greeted by a newspaper headline that proclaimed "Redheaded Lady Lawyer from N.Y. Comes to Denver to Take Over a Million Dollars Worth of Legal Talent."

"Naturally, that did not ingratiate me with the lawyers because they thought I was coming in to take over. Despite the initial hostility this headline generated, we became a close working team. The key to the business of being a team is that no particular lawyer thinks of himself as the leading lawyer. Some lawyers do, but that is not my style of work. My style is to decide how best the case can be won and to work cooperatively with other lawyers to get there. My role was recognized by the judge in Denver because at the end he publicly acknowledged the assistance I had given to all of the lawyers in the case."

During the time when she was working on these cases, various defense committees saw to it that she had enough money to maintain herself and her son, who usually went with her to the places where she was engaged in trial work. Although she was engaged in Smith Act cases throughout the McCarthy period, she was never summoned before a congressional committee. She was once called before a federal grand jury in New York when a bail fund for political defendants whom she represented was under sharp attack by a variety of government institutions. These institutions succeeded in destroying the bail fund.

After the Smith Act was watered down by the Supreme Court in the Yates case in 1957 (in which it was decided that it only applied to action-inciting advocacy, and not teaching of abstract ideas), Kaufman did a variety of things including handling contempt cases arising out of the Smith Act and defending people called before congressional committees and the Subversive Activities Control Board during the McCarthy period. After that era she was in private practice for a brief period until 1966.

"At that time I decided to take stock and consider where to go next. I was terribly troubled by the racism in our society and the war in Vietnam. I spent a long time researching and reviewing the Nuremberg war crimes trials. I was overwhelmed by the similarity of the patterns of the Nazis with our own. I knew we were as guilty of genocide at home and in Indochina as were the Nazis. I wrote on the subject. I then traveled to Europe, the Soviet

Union, Czechoslovakia, and the German Democratic Republic to lecture and to study their legal systems.

"When I came back, the protests against war, racism, and poverty were in full bloom. I had been active in the Guild since the late fifties, and on my return the Guild for the first time undertook direct representation of people arrested in political actions. During Stop the Draft Week in New York, December 1967, the Guild chapter here set up a Mass Defense Committee which I chaired. Because of the number of arrests that ensued, the committee became an institution. At the time of the Columbia protests during which at least one thousand people were arrested, the parents of the Columbia students raised some money and set us up in an office. We got volunteer lawyers to handle those cases. After we completed work on the Columbia cases, we started to take other cases coming out of things like demonstrations or political activity around school decentralization, protests on welfare cuts, cases arising out of racism as well as the continued resistance to the war.

"Fundamentally, I assumed responsibility for training many of the volunteer lawyers who defended the people. I also participated in the actual representation of people and helped to set up collective strategy discussions. We'd have older lawyers, younger lawyers, law students, legal workers working together with movement groups at all stages of their activities—before, during, and after arrest situations. For some time we had a twenty-four-hour on-call arrangement. When we knew of a possible arrest situation, we placed lawyers either on the scene or on call. Many of the lawyers who trained with the Mass Defense Office have continued doing political criminal work. Some of the former Law Commune members, for example, had previously worked with us and continued to cooperate with us after the Law Commune was formed.

"I think in the beginning of this present period of history there was a trend among young radical law students not to finish law school because they believed that if they became lawyers they'd feed the illusion that equal justice could be obtained in the courts. But I think that trend has been reversed. The dominant trend now is that there is some point in being a lawyer because the need for radical lawyers is so great. I think the greatest service a lawyer can perform at the moment is to perfect his legal skills.

"In appraising what we can expect from the courts and, from there, whether it's useful at all to be a lawyer, one must recognize that the courts do not act in isolation. They respond to the same political pressures which are put upon all of the institutions in our society. But there are fortuitous moments in history in which a talented expression and development of the law in a particular case can bring a momentary major concession that becomes useful to the radical movement.

"For instance, the popular revulsion at McCarthyism and the easing of the cold war tensions paved the way for favorable decisions in the witch hunt political cases. But skillful legal work was needed to obtain these decisions. One of these was Yates, the California Smith Act case which was then before the Supreme Court. The lawyers there gave the court what it needed to reverse the convictions. And, after that, a host of convictions in Smith Act cases were reversed. Did that advance the radical cause? I would say yes; if you free political prisoners, you advance their cause.

"I think right now there is such an intense breakdown in our society that it's almost impossible to think in terms of any meaningful change in the courts. I think things will continue to deteriorate and people, especially the minority groups, will be struggling more against these deteriorating conditions. The oppression of the Black, Puerto Rican, Chicano, and Indian boggles the mind. I think if we continue to struggle hard enough, we may be able to replace the old forms with new ones. We're in pretty bad shape right now. The problems we have—racism, imperialism, poverty, economic breakdown—are pretty awful. We've got eighteenth-century institutions to cover a period in history of twentieth-century technological advances. That, plus the destruction of our environment, makes it very rough. We don't have all that much time really. The process of resistance and change of the system of our society can't wait another hundred years. It's got to take place soon. I'm naturally an optimistic person or else I wouldn't be participating in the struggle. I'm the sort of person who thinks each day you are alive and fighting is that much to the good. But that doesn't mean I am a Pollyanna. I have optimism that we can in time change the system, but I know it can't be done without hard and persistent organization."

In March of 1971 Kaufman left her post as coordinator of the Mass Defense Office and was replaced by Elliot Wilk. She is now involved as a laywer in the rank and file struggles within the labor movement. She considers the rank and file struggles important in politicizing the trade union movement.

"It's the working class which will be decisive in effecting change."

Probably the best-known of the radical law organizations operating out of New York at this time is the Center for Constitutional Rights, originally the home base for attorneys Arthur Kinoy, William Kunstler, and Morton Stavis. Now, after five years, it has become a major legal institution within the movement and is the outlet for the work of a whole staff of younger lawyers, as well as a center which coordinates the work of many lawyers outside of its own staff.

The Center has three other senior attorneys—Benjamin Smith in New Orleans; one of the originals, Peter Weiss; and Doris Peterson—who are recent additions to the New York staff, plus a changing staff of young attorneys. In spite of this diversity of legal talent, the Center, at least outside of the legal community, is best known as the work place of William Moses Kunstler who, according to popular legend, typifies as well as inspires the new breed of radical lawyers.

Kunstler is the best-known lawyer in the radical left, a folk hero to many in it and a nemesis to many outside of it. He is an emotional, flamboyant, well-spoken, photogenic man who wears his mantle of media stardom with both an awareness of its responsibility and an obvious relish.

Born in 1920 to a Jewish family of professional people who lived in New York City, he attended Yale, served in the armed forces, and then went to Columbia Law School. After graduating in the late 1940s he worked for a while as an executive trainee with Macy's in New York before going into small business and family law, in partnership with his brother Michael. Kunstler was not "discovered" by the media until he went to the South with the civil rights movement in the early sixties, although he had hardly lived the ordinary life of a lawyer in the preceding period. Besides lawyering, he has written ten books, numerous magazine articles, television and radio scripts; lectured; appeared on radio and television; and taught. Legally, though, he was going along the normal civil liberties route until he encountered Kinoy, Stavis, and Smith.

Arthur Kinoy, who is the same age as Kunstler, was born in New York City, attended the Fieldstone School, then Harvard College, went into the armed forces during the war, and later attended Columbia Law School, graduating in 1947 a member of the *Columbia Law Review.* He was admitted to the New York bar in the same year and began practicing law as part of the legal staff of the United Electrical, Radio & Machine Workers of America (UE) until 1950 when he became a member of the law firm of Donner, Kinoy & Perlin. Working out of this firm he continued to represent the UE but also began to work in important nonlabor civil liberties cases.

Through his work with the electrical workers he came into contact with Morty Stavis several times during the 1940s when Stavis was representing New Jersey locals of that union. Stavis, also a native New Yorker and a *Law Review* graduate of Columbia, entered the practice of law after his graduation in 1936. Following some unforgettable exposures to anti-Semitism while looking for a job in Wall Street law firms, he went to Washington,

D.C., as a lawyer for the Social Security Board and in 1938 spent almost a year working for Senator Robert Wagner. In 1943 he decided that he wanted to be a labor lawyer, so he came back to New York and practiced with another attorney for a while. He then moved to New Jersey where he began practicing on his own.

Until 1951, when the split in UE took place, he practiced labor law almost exclusively. After that, he turned to commercial practice, but always maintained a keen interest in civil rights and constitutional law, representing people called as witnesses before congressional committees, working in a range of civil liberties cases including dismissals as a result of government loyalty charges, and litigating a major perjury case in the midst of the McCarthy era.

Kinoy and Stavis got together in the early 1960s around the Willie Seale case. Charles S. Conley, a Black lawyer who is now a judge, came up from Alabama seeking help with that case. Seale, a Black man accused of raping a white woman, had been six hours away from execution when Conley obtained a writ that saved him. Kinoy and Stavis began to work with Conley on the case. The trio zeroed in on the issue on which Conley had obtained the stay of execution, that of exclusion of Blacks from the grand jury. They finally won on this point in the Court of Appeals for the Fifth Circuit, using procedural techniques of pretrial discovery which had never before been tried in comparable situations. Seale was later tried again, and his second conviction was also reversed. In 1968, after ten years of imprisonment without any valid conviction, he was finally released.

After that trial, Kinoy and Stavis began to team up on other cases. They then met Kunstler, with whom Kinoy had worked before, and, together with Ben Smith, they became a four-man team working in the South.

They were actively consulted by the late Martin Luther King in some of his early bouts with Alabama officialdom. They aided him when he was charged with a state income tax violation for failure to count as his own moneys of the Southern Christian

Leadership Conference (SCLC), and when he was involved in a libel suit that arose from publication by *The New York Times* of an advertisement of Dr. King and his supporters.

With the onset of the Freedom Rides and sit-ins of the period, they found themselves catapulted into work in an area ranging from Danville, Virginia, to Halifax County, North Carolina, to Lowndes County, Alabama, to New Orleans and Mississippi.

Recalling those early days Stavis said, "I think the team concept became a full reality in our work in Mississippi in 1964 and '65. We were counsel then to the Mississippi Freedom Democratic Party and were involved in the congressional challenge to the seating of the five congressmen from Mississippi. It was a massive undertaking which involved coordinating the work of more than 125 volunteer lawyers who came to Mississippi, contributing not only their own time but also even their travel expenses, to take depositions and establish the facts relating to the exclusion of Blacks from the electoral system. Thereafter, we had to deal with congressmen and their committees. The debate on the floor of the House in the opening of 1965 was historic; and though the five congressmen from Mississippi were seated, it was the beginning of the end of the exclusion of Blacks from the electoral machinery of that state."

Kinoy at about the same time was working on the *Dombrowski* case, in which Ben Smith was a defendant, together with James Dombrowski and the Southern Conference Educational Fund. This was the case which decided that if a state law (in this case the Louisiana Subversive Activities Law) had a chilling effect on the exercise of First Amendment rights and was unconstitutional or was being used in bad faith, persons prosecuted under that law would not have to submit to prosecution and seek vindication by appeal. Instead, they could enjoin their prosecution in federal court.

This decision had far-reaching effects on what is commonly termed "affirmative litigation." It meant that the federal courts could be used to enforce the Constitution affirmatively, to protect movement people, instead of just being employed as a defensive weapon. The practical consequences of this difference of approach were enormous. State and municipal legal harassment of movement workers was one of the key devices used to throttle organization. Before this decision, the Constitution might ultimately be enforced through slow-moving appeals that could take two to four or more years, but, in the meantime, organization of the movement could effectively be stopped. With this decision there was the chance that the state court prosecution could be stopped dead in its tracks!

The four lawyers began to wonder whether there was reason to formalize what they were doing. "At that time," Stavis remembered, "we were sustaining all of our work and expenses out of our own pockets. Bill, Ben, and I still had our private practices, and Arthur was a professor at Rutgers Law School. But the calls upon us were increasing.

"We thought if we could institutionalize, we would increase our effectiveness and have a chance to bring in young lawyers to work with us. We had some friends and relatives who were impressed with the work we were doing, who shared our views and wanted to encourage us. At first we thought we could set up something with Rutgers, but it became evident that if we became a branch of the law school we would be subject to faculty controls and that just wasn't our style. So, with the help of friends who were satisfied that we were introducing imaginative and aggressive approaches to civil rights law and who promised seed money, we organized our own charitable and educational institution. The original group of friends has remained loyal supporters of the Center and they, together with the senior volunteers and a few others, are the board of directors.

"We formed a New Jersey corporation originally called the Civil Rights Legal Defense Fund, but later changed the name to the Law Center for Constitutional Rights to avoid the possibility of confusion with another organization. We applied for and obtained tax-exempt status. Dennis Roberts was the first staff member and we opened our office in Newark in November of 1966. We embodied some pretty fundamental ideas into the operation of the Center and though the Center has undergone many changes, those principles govern us today. We decided that the Center would clearly not be attached to anyone's private office; that none of the funds would ever be used to compensate any of the senior attorneys (although we all contribute up to 100 percent of our time to its work); that we would immediately begin to train young attorneys, not as brief writers for the seniors, but as active and responsible lawyers; that we would disseminate our materials to help attorneys throughout the country; and, above all, that we would continue to explore fresh ideas, especially in the area of litigation, so that law may be affirmatively responsive to changes in our society.

"We stayed in Newark for two years and built a staff of people recently out of law school. Then, as our work expanded, we moved to the space we now occupy in New York, and dropped the word 'Law' from the name of the Center to meet New York State registration requirements. In time we moved from our concentration of work in the South to a broad involvement in all major civil rights and civil liberties litigation in what is generally referred to as the 'Movement.' In the beginning much of our work involved expanding the concept of affirmative litigation but as repression of movement leaders heightened, we became increasingly involved in the development of litigation techniques of a defensive nature."

The list of cases in which the Center has been, and in many instances still is, involved reads like a *Who's Who* of major movement cases: the Chicago Eight, Catonsville Nine (the first Berrigan case), Harlem Five, Rap Brown, John Sinclair (the wiretap case which the Supreme Court accepted), Bobby Lee Williams, the Harrisburg Berrigan case, Ocean Hill–Brownsville decentralization cases, etcetera, etcetera, etcetera. The Center has worked on cases relating to criminal prosecutions coming out of ghetto uprisings and campus disturbances; suits against congressional investigating committees; minority groups; the peace movement, including cases involving the GI movement; jury prejudice; discriminatory bail practices; immunity in front of grand juries; legality of grand juries; women's rights, including abortion suits; military justice; prisoners' rights; the concentration camp section of the McCarran Act; harassment of "unruly lawyers"; and representation of an amalgam of peace organizations in negotiating and obtaining the permit for the 1967 Pentagon demonstration.

The Center has a strong policy of cooperating with other legal organizations—the ACLU, the NECLC, the NAACP Legal Defense and Education Fund (Inc. Fund), the NLG, and so on—and with individual attorneys also interested in the constitutional questions of the day. A good example of this is the roster of lawyers who were drawn into the appellate briefs in the Chicago conspiracy and contempt case. While Kinoy, Doris Peterson, and Helene Schwartz had major responsibility on the substantive brief and Stavis and Jim Reif on the contempt brief, really active inputs came from Anthony Amsterdam from Stanford, David Bogen from the University of Maryland, Alan Dershowitz and Charles Nesson from Harvard, Herbert Reid, Sr., from Rutgers, Mike Tigar from UCLA, and individual practicing attorneys William Brackett, James B. Moran, Thomas P. Sullivan, and John C. Tucker, all of Chicago, and Len Weinglass and William Rossmoore of Newark.

The Center's ability to carry its large case load is explained by the enormous time contributions of its five senior attorneys and a staff of concerned lawyers, office workers, and law students. Their staff attorneys in 1971 were Father Bill Cunningham, an attorney as well as a priest and law professor; Jan Goodman; Mike Ratner; Jim Reif; Rhonda Schoenbrod; Nancy Stearns; and Mark and Carol Amsterdam, who work in Okinawa.

"Graduates" of the Center staff include: Dennis Roberts, now practicing with the San Francisco firm of Kennedy and Rhine, and a co-counsel in the Angela Davis case; Bill Bender, who is running a Constitutional Litigation Clinic at Rutgers; Beth Livezey, who is with the Bar Sinister in Los Angeles; Carl Broege, who is with the Newark Legal Collective; Mike Sayer, who is with Neighborhood Legal Services in Auburn, Maine; Harriet Van Tassel Rabb, who is teaching at Columbia Law School; Rita Murphy, who is in private practice in New York City; George Logan III, who is with the judge advocate's office, USAF, in Glendale, Arizona; and John Warren, who is now in Cleveland, Ohio.

Because of these younger attorneys, the Center is very different now. While Kinoy, Stavis, and Kunstler are still very much in evidence, the staff of young lawyers and legal workers are taking on increasing responsibility and are being recognized throughout the movement for major contributions in their own names to the legal issues of the day.

"The Center selects its cases," Stavis explained, "by a judgment of its board that a particular area of work fits into the major constitutional issues of the day. Of course that is not a very specific standard but it at least gives us the flexibility to recognize that the important constitutional questions are ever-changing and that the essence of our work is to identify how one applies the fundamental precepts of the Constitution to current developments.

"Now we are witnessing the development of wide-ranging prosecutive techniques which, though they have antecedents, are in fact totally different from those heretofore employed. The Chicago conspiracy and contempt case was in a sense a turning point for the political use of the courts by the government. After all, the facts as to what had occurred were the subject of widespread TV coverage. The President's Commission on Violence and Disorders had issued the prestigious Walker report which, after reviewing all the events surrounding the 1968 Chicago convention, concluded that there had been a riot by the police, substantially sanctioned by municipal officials.

"Despite pressure from Chicago city officialdom, Ramsey

Clark, the outgoing attorney general in the Johnson administration, had refused to let a prosecution go ahead against the demonstrators. One of the chief signals that the Nixon administration intended to change the role of the courts was the Chicago indictments, issued but two months after Attorney General Mitchell took office, the object being to rewrite the history contained in the Walker report.

"In other words, the Department of Justice hoped that through the device of a trial, with the government lawyers carefully selecting the story that they would tell the jury, and with the hope that the judge would also circumscribe the defense that could be developed, perhaps a jury verdict could be obtained to negate the reality of what had transpired. To a substantial extent, the government succeeded."

In 1972 both the contempt and substantive convictions of the defendants in the Chicago case and of their lawyers were overturned by the U.S. Court of Appeals. The overturning of the contempt convictions was a rather Pyrrhic victory since it was done on a procedural point—that the contempt trials should have been held in front of another judge—and since the Appeals judges condemned the behavior of the lawyers and defendants, but not that of the prosecution and judge. The other victory was sweeter since the higher court ruled that a fair trial could not have taken place in the atmosphere of Judge Hoffman's courtroom, and that he did not follow correct procedure in jury selection, or just about anything else.

Yet, although no one will serve time in jail, the government was successful, because few people will remember the coverage of the Appeals court case, while few can forget the immense coverage of the original trial, staged by the government.

"The Harrisburg Berrigan case, the Seattle conspiracy case, the Panther Twenty-one in New York, and other cases are the progeny of the Chicago case, and each involved the use of conspiracy charges against political dissidents, often with little regard to historical reality," Stavis continued.

"It is really much worse than even the period of the Smith Act prosecutions in the late forties and early fifties. Many of the groups that are being attacked now have no consistent political identification. The prosecutors go out of their way to generate out of political rhetoric a taint of criminality, and the old techniques of paid informers and even provocateurs are being employed on a stepped-up basis.

"The Center has done a great deal of original and creative work in fashioning protections against the abuses of the grand jury, which as a suppressive tool is being expanded in an unprecedented way. Historically the grand jury was intended to protect the citizenry against overzealous prosecutors. It is now being employed full-scale as a device to terrorize people, essentially as congressional committees were used during the McCarthy period. Federal grand juries are sitting throughout the country, pursuing young people who have attached themselves to various communes which may be engaged in one or another form of political dissent. In Tucson, Arizona, for example, several young people spent several months in jail for refusing to talk to a federal grand jury. But perhaps one of the clearest examples of grand jury abuse went on in Boston, where a large group of the leading intellectual dissenters against the war in Vietnam were called before a federal grand jury and threatened with contempt if they did not disclose their knowledge as to how the Pentagon Papers were finally made public.

"We also made a major commitment to the area of military law when Peter Weiss joined our staff as a senior volunteer attorney over three years ago. To date, this commitment has involved us in the defense of GIs whose constitutional rights have been denied, in affirmative litigation aimed at extending more of those rights to military personnel, and in legal action attacking the war and exposing the criminal manner in which it is conducted.

"The Center is also deeply involved in the legal work of the women's liberation movement. A major effort was undertaken in the abortion area, but work is also being done on the issue of equal pay and promotion, maternity leave for husbands as well as wives, and on an attempt to end arbitrary termination of employment by employers upon discovery of pregnancy. Serious consideration is also being given to the special problems facing women in prison, a long-neglected issue.

"We're also concerned with Nixon's packing of the Supreme Court with people who reflect his ideology. This threatens not only the American people but also the institution of the Court as the forum which maintains the continued vitality of the Constitution. We feel that the role of the Center has to be to continue to press for the recognition—if not by the courts, by the people—of the durability of the principles upon which this nation was founded: freedom of speech, freedom of dissent, tolerance for individual differences, acceptance of change, and respect for freedom and equality. We now may be losing more in the courts, but we will continue to do our bit to elevate the general understanding of the enduring values of these principles. We have had bad Supreme Courts before and their influence was overcome by the responses of the American people. It may well mean that we will have to place a heavier emphasis on the educational aspects of our work.

"The changing character of the Supreme Court and its necessary impact on the lower courts will probably lead movement lawyers to turn to juries to a much greater extent than to courts in seeking protection against oppressive use of the judicial system. This may mark a very significant change from the situation during the McCarthy period, when the American people were so brainwashed that during Smith Act prosecutions, defendants' lawyers sought to have cases determined by courts and waived jury trials. The government successfully claimed that *it* had a right to a jury trial! But today the increasing questioning of authority by significant sections of the population, which parallels the diminishing extent to which the courts are prepared to enforce the Bill of Rights, will require movement lawyers to concentrate their efforts on juries. The results in the Panther cases in New York and Connecticut suggest that a combination of first-class legal work plus a general suspicion that the state is engaging in political persecution place the jury in its traditional role of protecting people from unfounded prosecutions."

Center people are not sure as to how their work will unfold over the next few years. They hope to exercise continued aggressiveness and imagination in meeting the new constitutional problems that will emerge from the interaction among a changing Supreme Court, the repressive techniques of the administration, and increasing challenges from the young and the oppressed.

Since most of the major radical law organizations have their national headquarters in New York City, radical attorneys practicing privately are fairly few. The usual pattern seems to be that lawyers work here at one of these organizations and then carry the knowledge they gain with them to some other part of the country. An exception to prove that rule is Henry (Hank) diSuvero, former co-director of the NECLC and now an attorney who is in private practice.

DiSuvero, the son of an antifascist Italian diplomat, was born in Shanghai, China. He came to this country with his family in 1941 as a refugee and grew up in San Francisco. He attended Berkeley where he was editor of *Slate*, the pre-free-speech-movement radical paper. After attending Harvard Law School he worked for a Wall Street firm for nine months and then spent four years in a "liberal midtown firm." While there he did some volunteer work for the ACLU and the NAACP. He then became staff counsel of the New York Civil Liberties Union, and then executive director of the New Jersey ACLU chapter.

"I was a liberal until the time of the Newark rebellion in 1967. At that time I was working for the New Jersey ACLU and the whole thing had an immense impact on me. Right after the rebellion I found myself arrested and charged with a slew of crimes, including threatening the life of a policeman. It came about during a demonstration by Anthony Imperiale [the leader of a reactionary Newark Vigilante group] and off-duty policemen. That was a watershed experience for a white, middle-class professional liberal.

"It's one thing to visit inmates in prison but it is another thing to have to sweat it out until your own bail money is raised. I beat the charge because I was innocent and a white middle-class person who obviously did not go around threatening the lives of police officers.

"That incident, plus the clients I represented when I was with the ACLU began to make me change my views. I just began to feel hopeless about the chance of any significant reform that could be achieved in the context of existing forms. It seemed that every social movement I had been involved in had been, in effect, thwarted. While doing civil liberties work it became clear to me that whenever people tried to take advantage of the rules of the game the system had laid down in order to achieve peaceful change, the rules of the game tightened up. That demonstrated to me the truism that everybody recognizes today which is that power never yields gracefully. It only yields when it is forced to yield."

From the time that he left his New Jersey civil liberties post until he started in private practice in May of 1970, Hank worked with Romana Ripston as co-directors of the National Emergency Civil Liberties Committee (NECLC), a more radical civil liberties organization.

"Of the four of us practicing together now—Daniel Meyers, Gretchen Oberman, and Lewis Steel, and myself—three of us consider ourselves radical lawyers and the fourth thinks of herself as a classical good lawyer. Although we're not really set up along commune lines we agreed to do half of our work for free, and we have been able to meet that standard to a large extent. We do cases for groups like the Weather Underground, the Young Lords, and other political groups in the area."

For a period of time, both when he was with the NECLC and in his own practice, Hank spent a good part of his time working on military cases, an area which, with the number of desertions from the armed forces and the increasing instances of insurrection within them, is of vital interest to people in the movement for social change.

"I spent one summer in the early sixties in South Carolina, and going to a military court reminded me of going to courts in small towns there. Both the military defense and prosecution are heavily interlocked in the relationship they've had in the past and expect to have in the future. They're all members of the white officer class and they feel vastly superior to the defendants that come before them. They look upon civilian lawyers as interlopers trying to upset a formal structure that seeks to preserve the appearance of judicial procedure while denying its substance. And because the civilian lawyer has an expertise generally lacking, they feel threatened by him. Normally they go all through the ritualistic forms of criminal procedure with the underlying assumption that the defendant is really guilty so that their only real decision is in the disposition of sentence.

"Until recently only soldiers who came from families with money could afford to have a civilian attorney, but now there is developing a feeling of special obligation among radical lawyers to do military work because there is such a dearth of capable attorneys in the field. I'm not so sure that a person has a better chance of winning with a civilian attorney, but the fact that a civilian attorney comes with a kind of authoritative sense to people who are trained to respect authority does work for the defendant.

"Military courts aren't different from other courts here, except that they are worse. Judge, prosecutor, defense, everything comes from the officer class. If you had a jury system in the military, a real one with a cross-section of the population at any base, you would have a system of possible justice. Instead you have just a system of discipline. I think that they should just give up and give the power to try people to the federal courts, or at least give a person charged with a military crime the option of removing his case to a federal court. Then they would quickly find out how many people feel that the federal court is fairer than the military court.

"Not that the federal courts are much better now with the way that the government is using them to repress political activity by charging people with classical crimes—arson, murder, and the like. Out of the fifties and the use of congressional committees and subversive control boards came a revulsion and a rallying of the liberal community to the side of the people being persecuted by these means. So now the system has decided to press movement people into the category of classical criminals and therefore alienate them from society and from the liberal community. For instance, the government insists that Angela Davis was not prosecuted for her political beliefs, as she would have been under the Smith Act in the fifties, but for her alleged classical criminal activity.

"What I see happening is that the government is taking all of the tools they have developed for fighting ordinary crime, and using them against people in the movement. Political people are being prosecuted for bad checks, fraudulently applying for a housing loan, providing false information, all kinds of what we consider nonpolitical activity. It's much harder to engender public sympathy and support for these kinds of prosecutions.

"One of the mistakes that we have to watch for is that, as the state moves on the movement and drags people into the courts, we don't allocate a disproportionate amount of time, energy, and resources on legal defense. Although legal defense is important, the movement is never going to be successful in the courts, and it is a mistake to turn a lot of cases into political cases when that means a large diversion of resources. A case should be treated as political when it almost reaches archetypical proportions—like the Chicago conspiracy case, Bobby Seale's case, the Panther Twenty-one case. But not every case is that and many political busts should be treated as nonpolitical because, by heightening the political nature of the case you only bring down worse consequences on your client. That is not to say that every conceivable legal thing should not be done for every case. It should. One of the obligations of a movement lawyer is to be as skilled as possible so that every time the state moves on the movement it knows it will have its hands full. The one classical case where I think it's worthwhile to be political is where the penalty is very very low. For instance, if every political disorderly conduct case, with a penalty of two weeks, was treated politically, it would show the state that harassment-type busts are going to cost a lot of judicial machinery and manpower.

"Another thing the movement has to deal with in terms of its lawyers is not to let them lead it. I feel very strongly that legal leadership was one of the mistakes that happened in the civil rights movement. Lawyers became too essential to it. Because lawyers become funnels for a lot of information, because they can talk, negotiate, mediate, contend, they tend to be projected or to project themselves into positions of leadership that they really don't deserve. They have no base nor are they able to move great numbers of people, and they tend to be conservative and very conscious of the risks people are running so they have a distorted sense of what actions people should engage in. Also, they don't run the same quality of risks that people in the movement do.

"It is true that the system is now moving on lawyers with contempt citations and threatening disbarment, but the risk of those sanctions is nowhere near the risks that other people are willing to run for the movement. I think the system is going to continue to move on lawyers though. What's happening is basically that the lawyer is supposed to be kind of window dressing for the machinery the system sets up and is supposed to be someone who sympathizes and identifies with the establishment and performs its functions. But when the lawyer begins to identify with his client and say that they aren't criminals or that if they are it's only because of what they believe, then those lawyers are no longer part of the establishment and no longer will be tolerated.

"In the fifties we went through a whole bout of repression against lawyers and, to a large extent, those lawyers were deserted by the rest of the bar. I don't think that will happen as easily this time. Too many lawyers have encountered arbitrary judges and realize that, even if their politics aren't those of a Kunstler or Lefcourt, they should not be badgered for doing their job. It is true there are lawyers like Louis Nizer who'd like nothing better than seeing Bill and Jerry disbarred and are proposing felony convictions for lawyers who persist in 'disruptions of trials,' but I don't think they will necessarily win out.

"One of the reasons they won't is that I see a whole generation now growing up that is just not going to take a lot of the crap that a lot of people have been dishing out. By and large we are seeing a complete destruction of any kind of traditional authority because these kids realize that any so-called rational authority is really irrational. All the norms that are the underpinning of society are disappearing. The one thing that disturbs me about the whole thing is that I'm old-fashioned enough to believe in the work ethic, and I'm distressed by a movement that wants to succeed not working so hard to succeed."

While some younger people in the movement might not agree with diSuvero's emphasis on the work ethic, others do, especially young movement lawyers. A group of such lawyers got together in New York three years ago and worked very hard to create something totally new in the legal scheme of this country—the first law commune.

The idea for the commune began to take form in the spring of 1968 when hundreds of students were arrested during the disturbances at Columbia University. Young lawyers started getting together with the Guild Mass Defense Office in defense of those arrested. After several months of working together on those cases, four lawyers met again at a conference sponsored by a group called Movement for a Democratic Society, and began to discuss alternative forms of law practice that could meet the needs of the movement for social change. Formal discussions among these lawyers and nonlawyers interested in legal defense work began in October of 1968.

There was general agreement that there was a need for some type of law firm that could both service the movement and reflect its values. In the beginning of 1969, four lawyers and four non-lawyers found office space and opened the doors of the first law commune.

By the time the doors opened, those participating had set up a number of ground rules for the operation of their firm. They did away with the traditional seniority system in law firms—there were no senior partners or junior partners. Pay was determined by need, with lawyers, nonlawyers, and legal workers all sharing equally in profits. A salary ceiling of $10,000 per year was set. No fees were to be charged for movement cases, regardless of the movement group's ability to pay. Fees from paying cases were to be used to support this free work, to expand the commune, and to support the legally related outside projects of the organizers who were working with the commune.

Secretaries were supposed to be both good legal technicians and politically involved people, and they were to have an equal voice in the running of the office. Clients were supposed to have an equal voice on decisions relating to their cases. The professional lawyer-client relationship was supposed to be broken down by that method and by demystifying the legal terms and traditions that have historically been used to keep the layman from understanding what is actually happening within the court system. And the people working within the commune were expected to struggle continually against their own professionalism, elitism, chauvinism, and individualism, and to affirm their political role as primary and their legal role as secondary.

In addition to the above, the commune was trying to set up a viable alternative to traditional methods of practice that could be followed by other radical attorneys.

Nineteen sixty-nine was a year of political arrests in New York, and the commune was kept busy in its first few months defending such groups as SDS and its various factions. They also began to expand their staff.

One of the lawyers that joined them during the first expansion, Jerry Lefcourt, brought with him several clients who helped to shape the future of the commune. The most important of these, in terms of the commune's growth, were three of the defendants in the New York Panther Twenty-one conspiracy trial. The other defendants in that case had been having a difficult time finding lawyers who would represent them, and so two other commune lawyers eventually took on some of their cases. This all happened in the fall of 1969 and no one, at that time, had an accurate idea of the commitment that these cases would entail.

As it turned out, the pretrail hearings on that case lasted from January to June 1970; and the trial itself lasted from September of 1970 until May of 1971, when all defendants were acquitted of all charges. With a commitment of three lawyers to that case for that length of time the resources of the law commune were severely strained.

Nonetheless the commune continued to operate and expand. In 1971 twenty-one people—Bob Beasley, Carol Birnbaum, Bonnie Brower, Eunice Burnett, Fred H. Cohn, Susanne Cohn, Bill Crain, Ann Garfinkle, Hersh Katz, John Kornbluh, Veronika Kraft, Carol Lefcourt, Jerry Lefcourt, Robert Lefcourt, Susie Orbach, Carol Ramer, Gus Reichbach, Steve Sandler, Ruth Silber, Marty Stolar, and Susan Tucker—were working there in capacities that ranged from lawyer to law student to secretary or legal worker to clerk to writer in residence.

Aside from working on the Panther case they were working on other movement cases, and they divided up into teams to handle the fee-generating work which ranged from matrimonial cases to hip corporate cases, with an emphasis on draft and dope work.

Those lawyers not working on the Panther case were forced to do a bit more hustling on fee-paying cases because of the financial strain of that case and because their original offices had been burned down in early 1970 by an "unknown arsonist." They had lost all of their equipment and much of the work they had done thus far on the Panther case in that fire, and it had taken them six

months to find another office. One of the commune members recalls that many landlords would not rent space to them when they
found out who they were.

While these external influences were at work putting the commune under financial and psychological stress, they were also experiencing internal problems. Two of the original organizers left
to work fulltime in movement organizational work. The remaining two continued their relationship with it, but only in an indirect
way.

The lawyers found that it was not a simple matter to change
the professional lawyer-client relationship. Clients, in many cases,
expected the lawyer to make all of the decisions and were resentful when the lawyers would not do so.

The concept of a secretary being an equal member with full
voice in the running of the office also presented problems. As one
legal worker said, "The concept that there wouldn't be any secretarial role, that the lawyers would do their own typing and filing
and answer their own phones was kind of an idealized notion. By
definition a legal commune exists within the establishment, and
you are required to do certain things like file motions at the
proper time. You can't say, 'Well, we have a law commune and
we were busy on another case so we couldn't run down and do it.'
So that original notion had to break down. It just wasn't functional.

"Here the employer-employee relationship did not exist in the
traditional form. We could all speak out at commune meetings,
but, to be honest, equal weight wasn't given to what the nonlawyers said. And I don't see how it could be, again, functionally.
You can learn certain things about the law by the nature of your
involvement, and here you do learn more; but, again, that is limited by the pressure of the work that does exist. How can my
opinion based on no knowledge, no experience, no expertise of
how to handle a case be given equal weight? On issues like
whether to take a case it's different. Then everyone's opinion
does carry the same weight."

Perhaps the most serious internal problems arose from each individual's struggle with his or her own sense of individualism and professionalism. Although the factor of competing for money can be, and was, successfully eliminated, it is more difficult to eliminate the factor of competition itself. With the profit motive out of the picture, the people in the commune found that the lawyers were competing for the big cases, and the ego-satisfaction that their attendant publicity could bring.

The two original women attorneys were most acutely aware of that particular problem since the competition syndrome seemed to present itself more visibly in the men. Several months after the commune began, the problem became so oppressive to the women that they considered splitting off and forming a women's legal commune. However, after talking with other female radicals, they decided to stay and try to work out the problem within the commune. From that point on all cases that came in were allocated at the weekly commune meetings so that when the competition syndrome reared its head it could be dealt with by the group as a whole. Still, to some degree, it persisted.

The whole question of male chauvinism also plagued the commune.

One of the women attorneys said, "Things improved but it still presented problems. The real trouble came when it fitted right in with my own insecurities. If I was worrying about not being capable, and then I was told that I was not quite capable it was hard to distinguish whether it was because I was a woman or whether it was because I couldn't quite fight back.

"But at least here everybody admits that there is such a thing as chauvinism, at least verbally. Other places I've worked, well, some tried to deal with it, but in most, either the men would say 'Forget it, I'm not a chauvinist' or 'I am, but it doesn't matter.' "

One of the men in the commune said, "Male chauvinism is a serious problem in any group of men and women. It's below the surface if women are outside of the movement or not into women's liberation. We've improved some here. The men are more aware of their own chauvinism, and the women realize that part of the problem comes from their own backgrounds. It's hard for them to be on the same competitive level as a man. Men are told all along that the best possible thing for them is to be famous, to be a star. It's a big step not to believe that in practice as well as theory. It's a particular problem for lawyers. The profession offers an incentive to be a male chauvinist. You get points as a lawyer for being competitive, aggressive, famous, for destroying the other side—so it's hard to be schizophrenic, to be one way in court and another outside of it."

Because of all of the problems, both internal and external, that the Law Commune encountered they decided, as a group, in July of 1971 that it was time to change their form. They dissolved the group as it had been, and the individuals who composed it set out to search for other alternate forms of practicing law—and living.

Their experiences, in their two and a half years of existence, provided them, and the other dozen or so law communes in the country, with a rich supply of material about what does and does not work in this type of legal practice.

"There were real limitations upon us because we were trying to alter our whole lifestyle and workstyle, and yet we were not all living together," said one of the commune members. "I think if we had been we could have totally immersed ourselves and had a really good thing. We needed more personal and political cohesion. From now on I want to be very sure of how people I'll work with in this way feel about politics and about each other. While we in the commune all agreed generally about politics we did not have a clearly defined political view. It would have been easier if we had all started at the same point—in time and in politics."

Another member said, "If I said I was satisfied with how the commune worked out I would feel that I was probably not being critical. And if I'm not critical then I'm probably being lax so I can't say I'm wholly satisfied but, relative to anything else I have been in, it's been fabulous. Talking in absolute terms I think the way we tried to work on things and the way we worked on them is the way you have to do it if you're a radical and a lawyer.

"We took cases for political, and not any other, reasons and we tried to give clients the best possible defense consistent with their political positions. I don't think there is a lawyer from the commune who could now practice law any other way. Some of us might stop practicing law, although I think very few. But I think all of us have totally rejected the lifestyle, the image, the professionalism, the superior kind of self-satisfied image that lawyers usually have."

Newark, New Jersey

Newark, New Jersey, is a city nationally known for battles and corruption. It burst into headlines in the summer of 1967 when, shortly after the Detroit rebellion, it, too, became a racial battlefield. It next came into the headlines when its longtime mayor, Hugh Addonizio, was indicted, and later convicted, on sixty-three counts of extortion.

Aside from these indications of its own special problems, Newark also suffers from the general maladies of urban rot. Newark has long been a city of ghettos—first Italian, then Black and Puerto Rican. The inner city has spread to include most of the city. The middle class has fled to the surrounding suburbs. The nonwhite population of the city is approaching 75 percent. Housing, schools, services are all inadequate. While everything deteriorates around it, the money interests who control the city from their plush suburban homes, continue to rebuild and renew the downtown business district.

Newark now has a Black mayor, Kenneth Gibson, who is trying to clean the city up, but it is a steep uphill fight. The corruption of the Addonizio administration permeated deeply.

Few people who have a choice seem to stay in Newark for long, radical lawyers included. One exception is Leonard Weinglass, a lawyer who rooted himself in the city ten years ago, and is now helping other radical lawyers to plant their roots there too.

Even if Leonard Weinglass was not involved with the formation of a legal collective he would still be a lawyer whose actions and philosophy indicate something of the future of the people's law movement. Catapulted into media stardom through his participation in the Chicago conspiracy trial, he has firmly rejected the results of that projection and has remained what he has been for the past ten years, a community lawyer whose first allegiance is to the people of the community he serves.

Len, whose tall, husky build, wry smile, and casual attire give him the air of a young, somewhat absent-minded professor, is a native New Jerseyan who returned to practice on his native soil. Born in Belleville, New Jersey, in 1933, the grandson of an orthodox rabbi who also ran the Empire Burlesque in Newark in partnership with Jimmy Durante, he moved with his family to Kearny when he was six years old. He went to public school there —"loved it, wouldn't miss a day"—played football, was elected president of the National Honor Society and vice-president of the student council.

From there he went to George Washington University in Washington, D.C., where he majored in political science, philosophy, and history and worked on Capitol Hill as an elevator operator.

"I became the operator of a private elevator car for Nixon when he was vice-president under Eisenhower and for Johnson, who was then majority leader and had an adjoining office. I was only there for a month when Johnson had his heart attack so I didn't know him very well, but Nixon and I used to talk a lot. He was very nice. After the Chicago trial some of the reporters asked Nixon if he remembered me, and he said that he did."

At George Washington, Weinglass was a member of ROTC, an honor cadet (a major), a member of the Pershing Rifles and the Arnold Air Society. He was commissioned when he graduated and went to preflight school with the intention of becoming a pilot, but when the requirement for pilot was raised from three to five years Len dropped out to go to law school.

"From the time I was twelve or thirteen I wanted to be a lawyer. My uncle was a lawyer, a bachelor, an amateur golfer who used to drive an old Pierce Arrow and I used to ride in the rumble seat. Of all of the people in the family he just seemed the happiest to me and the most fulfilled. He had a sense of freedom I really liked. He got me interested in reading Darrow when I was thirteen, and I made up my mind to be a lawyer and never questioned it until I got to law school."

When Len went to Yale Law School in the midfifties, he was not pleased with it. He remembers that the school was so conservative at that time that during his first year they didn't want to hear Adlaï Stevenson and prevented him from speaking by shouting him down.

"I just wasn't into the ivy league idea. It seemed to me no one was into doing anything except a lot of strutting and preening. Law school was very accommodating and easy, with an ironclad assurance that no one would flunk out, so I took advantage and spent a lot of time running around New York City."

In his second year at the law school a new teacher appeared—Bailiss Manning, who is now dean of Stanford Law School—who caught Len's fancy. He took all of Manning's courses which were in the corporate law field.

"By the time I got out I was really qualified in that area although criminal law was what I was really interested in."

At that time it was necessary to clerk for nine months in New Jersey before you could take the bar exam so Len got a job for $27 a week with a law firm in Newark, turning down a $5000-a-year clerkship with a judge to do so.

"That really amused me to go to school for seven years and then make $27 a week. I really wanted to have that."

After he passed the bar he was called to active duty in the air force and assigned to Dyers Air Force Base as a legal officer. One court martial he was assigned to involved a Black airman who had been charged with a crime by a sergeant from Georgia who had the habit of calling the men in his unit "nigger." Len brought out this fact in the trial to impeach the sergeant. The airman was convicted so Len took an appeal to Washington where the conviction was reversed because the racial issue had been injected into the court proceedings.

Shortly after, the base commander called Len in and told him he would be off the base within three weeks, reassigned to Iceland which, by treaty, did not have Black GIs. "See if you can win a case up there," the commander told him.

Weinglass spent a year in Iceland and loved it. It was the first time he had been outside of the U.S. He also spent a month in Israel during the Eichmann trial. He returned to New Jersey and "spent about seven months wrestling with the problem of reentry. Everything here seemed not worthy of any particular effort."

After that period he started traveling around New Jersey. "The thing that had really impressed me about Iceland and Israel was that the people I met really knew their country intimately. I wanted to really know New Jersey and feel closer to it. I went to every town in the state. And also I thought if I found some town I liked I would begin practice there."

Eventually he met an old friend from high school who was doing social work in Newark. This friend told Len that Newark was the place he should be, a place that really needed a lawyer. Len started writing briefs on a parttime basis for a Newark lawyer who was president of the Yale Law Society there, and continued doing so for seven months. Then he joined the firm, Shreiber, Lancaster and DeMos, for a year and a half until an old injury recurred that put him in the veteran's hospital for six weeks.

"During that period I was able to think of my situation, and I decided to open my own practice in Newark."

With the $200 he was given upon his release he made the

down payment on a leased office in what was then a run-down section of Newark on Bleeker Street, near the downtown area. The office consisted of three rooms on the first floor of an old townhouse. Len used the two front rooms as his office and lived in the back room. During his nine years of residence there, the office/dwelling was broken into six times. He was there to meet the burglars several times, once with Tom Hayden. He used undergraduate students from Rutgers as secretaries.

"The new parts of Rutgers weren't here then and this area hadn't been selected for urban renewal yet, and it was a very run-down neighborhood but I really liked it. My thoughts at that time weren't political. It was 1961 and there were no political organizations you could relate to. To me it was a personal decision. I wanted to work in a neighborhood and in a community and to just be a lawyer available. When I came here I preceded public defenders so I'd just go to the courthouse and try cases free. I was kind of always on call. Being without a secretary I had virtually no overhead and I did have one or two cases that paid me. Later I did get some clients—like *Look* magazine—as a result of my earlier work with the Schreiber firm."

It's conceivable that Len could have spent more time as a prepublic defender taking whatever cases he could get, most often for free, had he not become involved in the John Butenko case, in the federal district court in Newark. Butenko was an American engineer who was charged with espionage. Ray Brown, a very successful trial lawyer, was made his chief counsel, and he asked Len to assist on the case. Len closed up his office to participate in the trial, which was the longest espionage trial in the history of the country. After that, he began to be involved in larger criminal cases in Newark, but, more importantly to him, he began to be more deeply involved in the community.

He was working with men like Father Dresel, who had a church in Newark and was organizing tenants back in 1962 when Tom Hayden came to Newark to form the Newark Community Union Project (NCUP). He had met Tom but had no involvement with him until a rent strike leader, Ida Brown, was charged with atrocious assault of two policemen. The night before the trial, the lawyer who was going to handle the case quit, and Len received a frantic phone call from Hayden. He agreed to take the case and won it. From then on Len defended NCUP. He later defended most of the VISTA group that came to Newark, and represented radical Newark residents like Imamu Baraka (LeRoi Jones). He has also represented Kennth Gibson, now mayor of Newark, most notably in a case known as the Ken Gibson suit which kept former Newark mayor Hugh Addonizio from giving away $280 million worth of real estate that Newark owned in the northern part of the state to a corporation to administer at a cost of $1. The Gibson suit stopped the transfer, ultimately resulted in the indictment of Addonizio, and possibly helped Gibson to be elected.

By 1969 Len had a booming community business with "eighty cases always kind of pending." Tom Hayden had left Newark after the 1968 Democratic convention. In 1969 he was indicted along with seven other men for conspiracy to incite a riot at the convention. After his indictment he called Len and asked him to represent him.

"I went to several meetings and saw that I shouldn't get involved in the case, that there were nine very competent lawyers involved, and that there was no reason for me to go away. I was reluctant, then decided not to bother until Bill Kunstler got in touch with me and said that there was difficulty arranging the defense, and they needed someone who would take time off and work on the case. At a meeting in New York, Bill persuaded me to do that. So I got involved in there and I would say it was my first major involvement in a political case."

That involvement kept Len in Chicago for five months and earned him a twenty month and nine day contempt sentence, which was overturned on appeal. It also, as mentioned before, made him a media star of the people's law movement. As a result of that case he agreed to take on the John Sinclair White Panther case in Detroit, which began and abruptly ended in the beginning of 1971 when the trial judge ruled that the wiretapping evidence against the White Panthers was inadmissible.

He also became chief defense lawyer for Anthony Russo in the Pentagon Papers case.

"After Chicago a lot of people were telling me to leave Newark, but I just don't want to leave a place with people I like and with whom I work. I don't want to become severed from my personal relationships and become a national, movement trial lawyer, which I find very difficult for me to personally adjust to. I like the feeling of being in a community and working on local cases. I find that I cannot move into a city like Chicago for five months and live, then Detroit for three months, then Los Angeles. I just get very disoriented personally.

"The star system is ridiculous. There are good local lawyers almost everywhere. I'm willing to go out to a community and work with local lawyers but they have to do all of the courtroom work. Whatever we learned in Chicago, and whatever we know about political trials, we'll lend, but the trials should be by local people."

When Len returned to Newark after Chicago he felt for a while that he couldn't continue to practice. His cases were backlogged; he was tired; he had developed a nervous cough.

To cure the last problem he moved to a communal farm in a rural part of Jersey. To cure the former problems he began meeting with some recent Rutgers Law School graduates, some of whom had worked with him on the Chicago case, with the intention of starting a legal collective in Newark.

"We tried to form a group in March and April of 1970 but it just didn't work. We were asking too many questions of each other, going through the same process that everyone goes through when they collectivize. You begin to examine everyone's position intellectually; you begin to want clear guidelines of what's going to happen, what's going to be, a definition of the group. All those are impossible questions that can be debated endlessly. So it didn't work.

"Then an interesting thing happened around May or June. The group formed a basketball team and played together twice a week. We all began to know each other better and like each other more. We decided to sit down and talk about it a second time. This time none of those problems were present. They all seemed to have disappeared, and everybody was saying 'We'll be able to deal with that.' So we started to practice together out of the old office on February 1, 1971, and we moved into our new building on May 1."

The basketball team, the Red Raiders, is still going strong. The members of the collective, aside from Len, are Philip Ahlberg, Stu Ball, Carl Broeg, Mike D'Allesio, Jeff Fogel, and Roger Lowenstein. While the ages range from twenty-five to thirty-nine, most of the collective members are in their twenties. At present they are all bachelors although five of them have been married and divorced. Except for Len, all of them live in Orange, New Jersey, within a block or two of each other.

As a collective they represent the expected political groups—the Panthers, the Young Lords—but they also hope to be able to provide legal services at a reduced rate for those people in Newark who aren't rich but yet earn too much to qualify for the Legal Services program. They all agree that they want to serve the community and stay out of the movement star trip.

"We want to hang loose and not get hung up over form," said one of the members. "We'll have women in the collective, but we don't want to get into having to watch every word we say for chauvinistic undertones. And as far as male bonding with the basketball team, well, the women can join it if they can play as well as we do."

"We're not your normal movement collective," said another. "We're just starting and getting to know each other and we don't want any ironclad rules. For example, one of the largest areas of discussion we had in the beginning was about our new house. It had a hole going from the first to the third floor. Now some people made a political argument that we should cover it up so the office wouldn't look 'fussy.' Others made an aesthetic argument that it looked nice uncovered. These arguments gave us a chance to see how we worked out problems together. We ended up leaving it open because it would have cost a lot to cover it up."

None of the members of the collective are worried about Len being a star. They feel that he just doesn't want to be. And the media stardom he has obtained has come in handy for the collective since Len makes enough money from speaking engagements to keep the office going.

And Len is very happy to be working in a collective since it fits well with many of his philosophies.

"What is needed here is a total revolution on the scale that China has had, more than Cuba. By that I mean a revolution where people just begin to have a more full and complete understanding of what their life is about. I've lived through the 'Age of Pinter,' the fifties, the 'Age of Estrangement,' and, apparently, under our system the most successful individuals are the ones that achieve a large measure of economic security and can have whatever they want, travel wherever they want, do whatever they want. Yet, these people are not particularly happy or satisfied individuals especially as opposed to the people in other systems, such as China, who seem to have a larger sense of themselves and a greater sense of their own lives' worth. I kind of agree with the Maoist thought that in order to achieve a true sense of individuality you do not remain in an alienated state but rather you proceed to the group, and it is only in the group and through the group that you achieve a true sense of being an individual and a full human being.

"So if you're going to look at it personally, why struggle in a system where, if you achieve success by that system's definitions, you will have achieved unhappiness? I think we have to reorient the way we look at the way we are living, orient our lives around different goals and values. To that extent, I'm a kind of revolutionary I guess.

"But, as a lawyer, I'm kind of conservative and cautious. I had an awful lot of criminal practice in this state before the Chicago case, and the lawyers here couldn't believe the accounts that they read about me. Basically I think that the court system is a good structure. I think if there were a revolution tomorrow I'd probably still be in favor of jury trials, of judges as finders of law and juries as finders of 'the fact, and of the appellate process that we have. But the judicial system is such a sensitive instrument that when you have social and political upheaval, such as we have now, it's impossible for it to function. Consequently, we have a breakdown now, but there has been a breakdown every time there has been a major social or political shift in the country. But, with its sensitivity, the judicial system usually responds.

"But, as Adams and Hamilton correctly foresaw, it responds by the judges pulling back into the establishment in order to protect it. That's why they absolutely insisted on the independence of the jury, as the only insertion of the community into the courtroom. They saw that the jury would give defendants the measure of protection they need at a time of crisis. But that was before the media. Now you have juries that are so heavily influenced by the media that the protection they give is also being compromised.

"But I think there is nothing wrong with the system that a change in personnel wouldn't correct. If there were Justice Douglases sitting on every one of the twelve thousand judicial spots that there are in the country, I think the court system would be pretty good. But the fact of the matter is that the method and manner in which judges are selected in this country is designed, not consciously, in such a way that it produces the least qualified men. The people we select as judges, by and large, are men who are alienated from the communities that exist in this country, and, consequently, they are totally unable to come to grips with the realities of what the country is, so they turn and run in fear.

"Justice Oliver Wendell Holmes said it correctly when he said that law should not be based on logic, but, rather, on experience. But the men who are reading the law and interpreting the law have nothing but logic because they have virtually no experience in the communities that are impacted by the law enforcement agencies in this country.

"I also think we have an economic system totally off the track. We have produced a huge surplus and a huge store of resources and a gross national product annually of $1 billion, but all around you every day you see the evidence of economic failure. States, cities, schools, even medicine are hindered by a lack of money. There isn't even enough shelter in the country. Fifteen million people are below the poverty line, and over three million people under the age of twenty-one are undernourished. You can go on and on.

"The fault lies in the primacy of private property, and in the distribution system, and I think we won't even be able to begin to deal with the basic survival problems we have now, including the ecological, until there is an entire revision and shift in our thinking toward the role of property and the priorities of human needs. Here, again, we need the revolutionary change I spoke about before. I don't think that changing the economy around a little and redistributing the wealth a little differently is going to address itself to what the basic human problem is, and that is how to live in a large society, and in a community within that society with a sense of self-worth and individual freedom."

9

Chicago, Illinois

The People's Law Office (PLO) in Chicago, which began in the late summer of 1969, is now the oldest existing legal collective in the country. The people in this collective have found that, by going with the tides of history, and of the movement, they have been able to stay together, expand, and grow.

The People's Law Office was started by lawyers and law students working for the Legal Services program in Chicago, with the help of a somewhat older lawyer who had obtained experience in radical cases by working on the many trials that came out of the 1968 Democratic convention.

"There were two or three lawyers in Legal Services, and two or three law students who got turned on to criminal political cases. We had started to know Fred Hampton [a Black Panther party leader in Chicago who was killed by the police during an alleged shootout at a Panther apartment in 1969], and some of those people, and they had a very great influence on us.

"In Legal Services Daley controlled the money and he didn't want any criminal or civil rights cases done, or suing police officers or anything like that. So each month we'd continue doing these cases, and each month the lawyers would be reprimanded, fired,

and then rehired. At the beginning of the summer of 1969 we just
had to get away from Legal Aid because we just couldn't function
and keep up any personal sense of existence. So we all started
thinking about going somewhere else."

By this time both those with Legal Services and the older lawyer with whom they associated had worked for the Panthers, and
desired to do more work for them. During that summer, local police and the FBI focused on the Panthers both in Chicago and
elsewhere. Many Panthers were arrested, and several shootouts
with police occurred.

"All of this contributed to moving us away from being liberals
or liberal lawyers who wanted to help poor people into people
who wanted to relate to the political movement."

At that point of time, the collective idea was in the air. The
New York Law Commune was functioning, and other radical
lawyers and law students were beginning to wonder whether that
form of practice would be viable for them. The people in Chicago
decided to give it a try. They found an old sausage shop on
Halsted Street, a street that is the boundary between one of Chicago's few integrated neighborhoods, a Latin neighborhood, and
a Black neighborhood. There were—and still are—a lot of political offices in the vicinity, so the PLO along with these other
offices have always been subject to window-breaking by right-
wingers or whoever doesn't like left people at the time.

The building chosen by the PLO'ers was dilapidated, so they
rebuilt it and opened their doors for business in August. At that
time there were four lawyers and several law students and
political women involved in the collective. As with many lawyers
in the movement, the philosophy of the groups that they serviced
had an influence on their philosophy.

"When we began, the city was full of Panthers and other
groups that belonged to the Rainbow Coalition [a coalition of
third world and some white radical groups]. We were relating to
them and to what they were doing. During that time we were also
representing SDS. When that organization split, we began to rep-

resent all of the factions. Then the Weather Underground had their 'Days of Rage' in Chicago. For legal defense they had their own legal collective, and we weren't part of it. But we did advise them, although they preferred to train people to do their own cases. A lot of people involved with them had been law students, and so that was feasible. There were one hundred and fifty cases that came out of the 'Days of Rage,' and we did take some of them so we talked a lot to the people in their legal collective, and we were also forced to listen to them. The subjects they brought up we usually found ourselves discussing. Although most of the cases were over by February of 1970, what we were talking about continued, and their kind of analysis hung on.

"We began to realize that we couldn't take the case of every Black person. We began to see the internal imperialism of the country, how Black ghettos were really colonies, and we had to deal with the question of violence because we were representing violent people. We began to realize that we would have to make conscious decisions about whom we would represent. We learned to make choices. We decided not to sue the police on things like brutality because people primarily needed defense representation.

"While we appreciated that the Weatherpeople had pushed us to have an analysis, none of us ever became Weatherpeople, or even Weatherpeople lawyers. What they did for us was stimulate a lot of thinking and talking and changing of lifestyles. We did reorder our lives a lot. For instance, a lot of us who were married then aren't now. So they did stimulate us, but they also brought us a lot of repression because people did not understand our relationship to them and thought we were more connected than we actually were.

"Out of that period we did come to an analysis. We know that America is imperialist both abroad and at home, and that the pigs are the knowing, evil instruments of that. This led us to understand why there are more Black people in jail. It let us understand the influence of junk in the ghetto, and why Black people are picked up by the police three times before they are twenty so that if they are then picked up on a heavy charge they get three times the sentence that a white person would.

"We also began to understand what we could and could not do. Out of our analysis we decided that the main thing that oppressed people want is not to go to jail, and so we decided to do mainly criminal cases. All notions of legal aid disappeared from our heads."

"We had thought that we would be a community law office, but it never turned out that way because there were so many political people who needed our help when we began. When community people come in with noncriminal problems we either send them to a place that will help them, or tell them how to take care of the problem themselves. We've turned out to be neither a community office, nor a straight political office. We represent people who don't belong to a specific group, along with people who do. In large part we represent Black people who get fucked just because they are Black, and we do this because it fits in with our political analysis, but we also represent freaks and students because that fits our analysis too.

"For instance, we had a prison case of a guy who had stabbed a guard, which no other lawyer would touch. This happened before Attica and we were just so outraged by it that we took the case because it fit with our analysis of imperialism, and we won it. Without the collective life and the struggles that go along with it, you couldn't make a decision to take a case like that one. That decision came from our previous political background, and our previous work."

"Our work in Carbondale, Illinois, was another good example of how our analysis has affected our political growth. In February 1971 there was a shootout between the Panther chapter there and the local pigs. The Chicago Panthers asked us to go down and see what we could do. We were busy here, but our politics told us that it was an important thing to do. Carbondale is down near Cairo, six or seven hours from here, and it has a branch of the University of Illinois in it. When we went down it soon became apparent that we could help the Black community, do a good law job, and continue our work with freaks and students, whom we consider important. It also provided a chance for one of our lawyers, who did not want to work in Chicago, to live a slower, more together life.

"A year before, when we considered only street gangs and Panthers important, we never would have gotten involved in such a thing. But, by May, we had a house, and an office there, and a large group of people who gathered around the collective. We all went down at times and got involved, and it was great fun and politically important. We changed because of it, and so did the Carbondale scene."

"Another example of us at work comes from our reaction during the Attica rebellion. When it happened, we were stunned and felt that we had to do something. We sat as a collective and decided that, since we relate to the country, and to the movement nationally, it was our problem, too. Collectively, we discussed our needs versus the national ones, and we discussed professionalism. Then, together, we made a decision that someone should go, and we decided who that person should be. Although we had been told not to send a legal worker because it was felt that there was nothing legal workers could do, we did send one along with a lawyer because it fit our philosophy, and they both found things to do. That's how we work. We decide where we fit externally and how we feel internally.

"One of the things we have learned is that white people are serious revolutionaries. They are not irrelevant. We could see, when hippy collectives started in Chicago, that these people were making a political statement, and that it was an important one. We stopped looking down at ourselves for being white and being lawyers. We came to realize that good legal work is really important. We also realized that white people had a role to play, that of fixing up the white world."

"Legally, we became specialists in criminal law, both because of a conscious decision and because of the forces of history. All along we had been doing criminal work because the older lawyer with us had been a community lawyer for three years before, and he was able to teach us a lot. Plus, we all had a predilection for that work. When we started, Dennis, the older lawyer, had a lot of experience and a lot of cases. He'd give us some of the cases to do, and tell us how to do them. We also had good help from the older liberal bar in Chicago because the Panthers and SDS had organized them to help with all of their cases. They gave us advice and tutoring. Now, 98 percent of our cases are criminal ones. The majority of these cases are for Black people because the majority of people who are busted on criminal charges are Black. We take everything from disorderly conduct to murder, and we have a heavy felony practice.

"We take free cases when we think it is politically important to do it—for instance, when it is a major case or an obvious frame-up. In Carbondale six people had been busted on fifty-six counts and it would have cost them $7000 to $8000 for defense which they couldn't begin to pay, so we took that case for free. We do that in a very small percentage of our cases, where people have to be represented and don't have the money. Otherwise, we ask everyone to contribute something. We are no longer bleeding hearts. If we have to get up at nine in the morning and contribute, we feel that our clients should contribute something too.

"Where we differ, in that respect, from other lawyers is that we'll get the person out of trouble first and then ask about money. It is a question of humanity. But we know that most of our clients can have access to money, and we need to be paid because we support ourselves through our criminal practice, unlike other collectives. Because we take our work and our own lives seriously, we don't have a problem asking for pay, and we'll lean on people if we have to because we have to eat too. Our fees are generally only one-third or one-fourth of what the fee would usually be."

"Each lawyer has twenty-five to fifty ongoing cases. The people who have been in practice or like to go to court more take more cases. We do substitute in court for each other if it is more convenient that way. It is a total miracle but we have no competition now for cases, although we did have that problem before. If we see competition beginning, we stop it. Unlike other collectives, we don't decide collectively on all cases we'll take. We trust each other and have faith, from the past, in each other's judgment so we don't feel that that is necessary.

"We also don't have weekly collective meetings. We meet when we need to. It's all very informal. We found the strict collective form very far out in a lot of ways but we found, after we'd been together for a while, that it got oppressive. Now we have fewer rules and more flexibility about who does what and who lives where and why, although we are still bound together by our history and our work."

The PLO does, however, still follow the usual collective rules about finances. People are paid according to need. Salaries run from people who work free because they have other income to about $9000 a year for people with several dependents. Around half of the people in the collective live in a communal house. Through being together, the people in the office have come to a new view about legal workers, women in the office, and the women's movement in general.

"We went through the same kind of splintering that the women's movement did. At one point we saw men as the enemy, in much the same way we saw the state as the enemy. Then we realized that we were wrong, that the men weren't the state, and that there were a lot of valuable men in the office. We came to realize that you don't develop women's leadership by yelling. You do it by the women being leaders, by their doing the work.

"We came to see that women in the law office have an important role to play, particularly the women lawyers. They can show the men that there is no need to compete, to yell, to have the idea first. We also found that the legal workers had a lot to contribute, but we found that everyone does not have to contribute in the same way. Here, again, our progress paralleled that of the movement. When we began, the legal workers all typed pretty much. Then, they all got assigned to cases. But some of them found that they didn't like that sort of work. So now whatever they want to do, they do. One woman, for instance, administers the office, but she also does speaking work on prisons, which is what she wanted to do since she has been in prison herself. Now we also get volunteer secretaries from downtown law firms who come work with us because, when they do, we include them. When a lawyer gives something to someone to type, he or she tells them what it is. That simple act turns them from typists into participating human beings."

"Because we are part of the movement, and not just lawyers, we go through the same changes and political growth that the movement does. This has resulted in some changes of personnel at the office, but there always has been a core of continuity. As people grow, some feel they want a more individual practice, that the collective idea and the casualness that goes with it are not for them. We've had moltings when a lawyer leaves and the people closest to him or her go too. Also, we have law students who work while they are in school then leave when they graduate. Even with all this, though, we have generally five lawyers and six legal workers or law students in the office at any one time, plus one lawyer in Carbondale, with a group of five or six other people also working there.

"For a long time, our idea of a collective was working six or seven days a week and having a lot of meetings. Then we wore out, and so now we have slowed down. Lawyers try not to go to court more than three times a week and we all try to go to the country on weekends sometimes so we can just sit and think.

"Now, too, everyone in the office has a life apart as a political person. We go to school and we organize, depending on our preferences.

"We have also found that political growth is an important, ongoing thing. In the beginning we spent enough time in analyzing what we were doing. Now we work, and integrate our politics into that work. We have very few political discussions because we feel that everything we do is political, and that political education is integrated into the other decisions that we make. We also put no labels on our politics. The movement is going through so much that we can't afford to be sectarian."

Detroit, Michigan

Riding around Detroit is like riding around a cheap set for a bad movie version of Aldous Huxley's *Brave New World*. The people there don't say "Praise Ford" but the buildings, the street signs, all the inanimate objects in the city seem to. Everything is a constant reminder that Detroit is the center of the automobile industry in this country. The automobile is the vehicle that carried us into the Technological Age and the automotive industry represents much that is negative about the age. The car is the consummate example of man creating a machine for his use and then finding that he loves his creation so much that his creation owns him. It is one example of how, through technology, a lot of man's humanity has been lost. Something about Detroit makes this constantly clear.

Like Newark, Detroit is an ugly city. Highways, byways, and expressways are continuous altars to the auto. Houses, in some degree of decay, spread with a sameness that makes it difficult for a stranger to tell one part of the city from another.

The people who populate Detroit come there, for the most part, to work in the automotive industry. Polish and Italian immigrants were the first to go into the factories to work long hours at repetitious work for small pay. Then, as white immigrants were "melted" into other positions in the society, the majority of workers became Black. In 1970 the Black population of Detroit was around 47 percent, and Black workers made up the majority in most factories connected with the automotive industry.

Workers in this industry have always been at the forefront of the labor struggle in this country. The struggles around the formation of, and later within, the United Auto Workers (UAW) pointed the way for the organization and demands of other unions, and the UAW has remained one of the strongest unions in the country. To many of Detroit's Black workers, however, the UAW seemed to be, for all its social democratic ideology, insufficient to their needs. The main reason for this insufficiency is that the racist strand that permeates most of America's institutions is quite evident in the UAW.

In 1968 a wildcat strike occurred in the Dodge main factory in Detroit. The organization leading this strike was the Dodge Revolutionary Union Movement (DRUM), an organization composed of Black workers, Black students and intellectuals, and the Black street force. Most of the people connected with DRUM had histories of radical activity in Detroit, and many of them were connected with a newspaper called the *Inner City Voice* which had begun to publish in 1967 following the Detroit rebellion.

Out of DRUM came an organization called the League of Revolutionary Black Workers which encompassed DRUM and other revolutionary movement unions that began in different automotive plants in the Detroit area. The League is a Black Marxist-Leninist party which, according to its general policy statement, has the short-range objective of "securing state power with the control of the means of production in the hands of the workers under the leadership of the most advanced section of the working class, the Black working-class vanguard."

In June 1971, three years after the founding of the League, the organization was irreparably split by the resignation of three members of its seven-member executive board. The members who left declared that henceforth they would only work under the direction of the Black Workers Congress (BWC), a revolutionary workers' organization, begun in November 1970, which now has chapters in twenty-two cities. Those people who left the League had always seen the formation of a Black workers' congress as the goal of their work, but they had wanted to strengthen the League first. However, severe ideological differences caused them to leave the League when they did.

The BWC has thirty-two objectives, stated in their manifesto, which range from workers' control of their places of work, to "a rational planning of a world economic system that will eliminate racism, wars, hunger, disease, lack of housing, oppression of women, class antagonisms, and big nation chauvinism," to "the creation of a genuine revolutionary workers' party in the United States under the leadership of third world workers, men and women, employed and unemployed, who will be guided by the accumulated wisdom of all revolutionary thinkers, and who will work untiringly to implement the objectives of the International Black Workers' Congress."

Kenneth Vern Cockrel, one of the founders of both the League and the Black Workers Congress and now a member of the organizing committee of the BWC, is a brash, bold, brilliant young attorney who has done much to reshape the Detroit legal community. He is flamboyant, exceptionally well-spoken—in a rapid speech pattern that combines elegant sentence construction, run-for-your-dictionary words, Black and hip slang, and a radical sprinkling of obscenities—and he should, by all rights, be one of the stars of the national legal movement. He isn't because he doesn't choose to be.

Cockrel was raised in the Royal Oak Township suburb of Detroit by his relatives since his parents died when he was young. He moved around among his relatives attending different schools until 1955 when he quit Central High School in Detroit and went into the air force where he was trained as a nuclear weapons mechanic specialist. He spent part of his time stationed in Germany. When he got out, with the high school equivalency diploma he had received, he decided to "do a school thing." He was admitted to Wayne State University as a "conditional adult" until the end of his first semester when he was regularly admitted. He worked all of the time he was attending school—as an orderly in a hospital, as a bricklayer's helper, as a jumper in the *Detroit News* circulation department, and as a worker in the Great Lake Steel plant, among other things.

"I don't know how I decided to be a lawyer. There was no cataclysmic occurrence in my life that caused me to focus on it, you know? I probably started out to be a doctor when I was working at the hospital, but I had a low aptitude for math, so I fell out of love with it and decided to go to law school."

While he was in law school, he worked as a research director for a community project in Detroit's Northend and he also ran for state representative in 1966, as a Democrat. After he passed the bar in 1968, he became involved in the formation of a new law firm that was being started by Harry Philo. It was here that he met Justin "Chuck" Ravitz, now his comrade and often his co-counsel.

Ravitz was born and raised in Omaha, and went to Babson Institute in Massachusetts, intending to become an accountant.

"It was a horrible business school and I became a rebel there, basically off on an Ayn Rand kick. I went to law school at the University of Michigan not at all sure I wanted to be a lawyer and with an application pending with the Central Intelligence Agency (CIA). I got cleared by them and left law school after my first year to go to Washington. I wanted guerrilla training and I wanted to go to Vietnam. I left after four months cause I wasn't getting the experience and training that I wanted.

"I was like a 'good guy' who believed in the concept of building a mechanism whereby people could better control their own destiny and combat the deficiencies and hopelessness of bureaucratic state welfarism. I thought that 'creeping socialism' was the cause of problems that could be solved by some abstract and moral joinder of laissez faire capitalism and the enforcement and realization of equal opportunity rights for all persons. I was probably the only Randist in civil rights marches. Obviously, I was really an aberration.

"While in Washington I met Allyn, my wife. She was very active in left-liberal politics, and she played a dominant role in my liberalization, encouraging me, for example, to leave the CIA and attend the University of Pennsylvania, where I obtained a masters in International Relations in December of 1964. I had planned on then going to India to march with Gandhi's successor, Vinoba Bhave, but, fortunately, passage was never cleared on the freighter. After then rejecting academia, I returned to Michigan and completed my law degree.

"During the summer of 1965, I clerked in Detroit with Sheldon Otis, and after graduation I returned to practice with him. Shel was my mentor and whatever legal competence I have acquired is in large part attributable to him. Radical politics came to me as a direct result of my experience as a criminal lawyer practicing in recorder's court. Revolutionary politics evolved out of continuing struggle and was materially advanced by interrelationship with my law partners and my political comrades in the Motor City Labor League (MCLL), a Marxist-Leninist, white cadre organization of which I am a member.

"This firm was born July 1, 1968. It was essentially the creation of Harry, who is a nationally renowned products liability lawyer. He has always struggled against monster corporations in a way that is beneficial to workers and he has always done this with a keen sense of its political import. Harry came to Detroit in the early fifties after HUAC harassment in New York, and he had a heavy history of involvement as a worker in labor struggles. Thereafter, he carried the rank and file vote in Local 600— the largest local in the country—but lost the presidency of that local because of the retiree vote. He attended law school in his midthirties and was with what was the original left law firm in

Detroit, the Goodman firm, which was a firm that came out of the UAW split with Reuther axing the so-called Commies, et cetera. A leading figure in that struggle was Maurice Sugar who started that firm, and later George Crockett, who is now a judge in recorder's court. Harry left the firm in 1966 and went up to Muskegon and started practicing with a large firm up there.

"After the rebellion of 1967, he thought that it was improper for him to be there. He wanted to be in Detroit, and he felt the necessity of starting a firm that would have a revolutionary concept, so he started this one.

"This firm does not typify the 'new left law firm.' There is a hard division of labor. We all know what we are about and we all respect one another's politics. When we formed there were a lot of lawyers in Detroit interested in the struggle but they always got strung out over economics, especially the young guys. I was in Legal Services for a while, and I saw a lot of good people come through it but they'd disappear because there wasn't anyone out there who could provide them with a place that would fulfill their needs, while allowing them to do relevant law and allowing them to grow politically.

"At the time that Harry approached us, we recognized the need for the formation of a strong, revolutionary law firm that had the resources and power to be more than just a legal arm for the struggle on a case by case basis.

"In late 1969, both because of our success as well as our limitations, in terms of growth, I wrestled for a while with the unrealistic notion that we could possibly merge a number of left law firms in Detroit without impairing the financial motivations of a few rather wealthy liberals. The idea was based upon an economic analysis of the optimal size of workmen's compensation units, et cetera . . . but it was politically myopic and unworkable—or premature, anyway. We then turned to the idea of opening a staffed Guild office. Detroit had played a major role in the Guild for many years but, at that time, the Detroit Guild was doing very little. So, in February of 1970 we opened an office and out

of that we started to educate young lawyers and to refer cases to
ones that needed support, and to involve a lot of lay people and
law students in the operation of the office. We organized the lawyers in the city, got monthly pledges, bought a house for the
Guild with some other political groups, and now we can double
the number of lawyers employed in that office.

"So this firm is really growing in a number of ways. We're
trying to complement the Guild's growth, our own growth, and
we're trying to get people into other left law firms so that they
may relate to the struggle fulltime. Within the past two years
there has been significant growth of the legal arm here in Detroit,
but it is still embryonic at this point."

"In those first two years," Cockrel said, "Chuck and I did
primarily criminal defense work. But now things are evolving in a
whole other way. In the firm people are now engaged in activity
that relates itself to structuring organizational forms quite apart
from engaging in individual criminal defenses although we still do
all kinds of cases. We defend a lot of murder cases because we're
very competent lawyers, but we spend a great deal of time in organizational activity."

In a recent and very political case handled by Cockrel and
Ravitz, James Johnson was charged with murder after shooting
and killing a foreman and two white workers at Chrysler's Eldon
Avenue Plant, a plant noted for its militancy and wildcat strikes.
Johnson, born and raised on a Mississippi plantation where,
among other things, he discovered the dismembered body of his
cousin who was killed by the KKK, worked for months on the
"ovens" at Eldon before finally being transferred to the cement
room. Upon refusing to return to the ovens, the hottest, hardest
job in the department, he was summarily fired. He went home,
got his carbine, and returned to the plant to stalk and kill his
"symbols of oppression." Cockrel and Ravitz successfully defended Johnson, who was acquitted on grounds of temporary
insanity while Chrysler, in turn, was "convicted." The testimony
of workers and a psychiatrist disclosed the brutal and unsafe

working conditions, the speed-up, the racism, the unwarranted firings. These same conditions placed Chrysler on trial again a short while later when Detroit attorney Ronald Glotta, also a member of MCLL, pursued the case of *James Johnson vs. Chrysler Corporation* in a workmen's compensation hearing.

"I spend probably 60 or 70 percent of my time on BWC business, and Chuck spends a good deal of time in organizational activities relating to the Guild and other political structures, such as MCLL. We also spend time in developing legal forms that will facilitate certain organizational development, and in running classes for and developing law students and young lawyers that we want to bring in here or into the Guild office. It's a full schedule. Then my other thing is that I play 'political celebrity'—I perform, speak, write, tape. You do the whole bit you have to do. What I'm trying to say is that apart from the fact that we do a lot of legal work and have a high involvement in criminal cases, and others, there is a whole other level of responsibility that flows from the political involvement of ourselves individually as well as the firm and that takes a whole lot of time.

"We draw what we need from the firm and the firm gives us time to do all of the other stuff. But we are not a collective firm. We take the position that there is a point beyond which discussion is an inappropriate response to the resolution of certain problems, and that they'll be resolved in practice.

"We know what happens," Ravitz said, "in the Bay Area, say, where left lawyers and legal workers have spent so many hours fighting with one another and, we believe, probably too little time creating organizational forms that can relate to masses of people, particularly workers. We recognize, of course, that we have the advantage of being in Detroit where there is greater class consciousness and revolutionary consciousness. We recognize too that we have been socialized in capitalist America and are not free of the last vestiges of counterrevolutionary stigma. Nonetheless, while we struggle with our deficiencies, we place greater emphasis, I am sure, on organizing necessary and vital preparty forms; on engaging in practice that will build and preserve cadre, educate and promote mass revolutionary consciousness, neutralize others, and serve masses of people. We do not fight a sometimes hopeless battle of seeking to purify liberal lawyers.

"We have in the past given considerable attention to the criminal law and developed many young lawyers in that area. Because of objective conditions and greater political understanding and organizational growth, we are placing increased emphasis upon supporting wildcats, and independent unions, and on developing many more lawyers with labor and workmen's compensation skills such as Ron Glotta possesses.

"We always are looking to make the institutional attacks that will expose this system for what it is. We have learned the hard way—from a 'dynamite' police receivership suit in 1968 that was summarily dismissed after months of collective work—that this is not the time to initiate affirmative litigation unless it can be structured in such a way, politically, so as to see to it that we are not reliant upon the courts. We have a very heavy jail suit that has been going on since January 1971; but, before we could commit ourselves to the litigation, we advanced our apparatus so that we would be in a position to fight the jail struggle on a higher level recognizing that it would not be 'cured' by the courts. We created the Labor Defense Coalition which engages in labor struggles and also serves to centralize the attack on the six-armed apparatus of the so-called administration of criminal justice: the police, prosecutor, judges, lawyers, bondsmen, and jail. This gives us a central repository in Detroit that materially assists us in serving jail inmates and all accused persons, assisting lawyers with problems in any of these areas, documenting the myriad stream of abuses, and engaging in crisis organizing when appropriate. Meanwhile, the jail suit continues and it's having a heavy impact—but, we're not dependent on it.

"We have learned a great deal about police brutality litigation and how to handle cases so as to extract money from the enemy for our clients and ourselves, and how to expose brutality in a winning way. We have an empirically developed approach that is both principled and pragmatic. We know that people victimized by brutality every day cannot, in the vast majority of cases, get any kind of justice in this system. So, we litigate only a minority of cases, and in all other instances we talk reality to people: we teach what experience has taught us about the courts, and we tell people how to move and jam the man's machinery if they at least wish to give expression to justifiable wrath."

Another important political case in which Cockrel and Ravitz "jammed the man's machinery" was the New Bethel case which actually was two separate cases of people accused of the assault and shooting of two policemen in the vicinity of the New Bethel church. During a preliminary hearing when Judge Joseph Maher tried to raise the bail of one of the accused to $50,000, Cockrel called him "a pirate, bandit, racist, honky dog fool." A contempt case was brought against Cockrel whose defense was that everything he said was stone true and that his right to speak was protected by the First Amendment. That case was won, and both New Bethel cases were won. Several months after the second victory, which was followed by a bombing of the firm's law office, Clarence "Chaka" Fuller, one of the three acquitted defendants, was assassinated.

"In the second New Bethel case," Ravitz said, "we completely overturned the racist jury system, exposing how wholesale numbers of Blacks were excluded from jury service by the commissioners for recorded reasons, such as, 'Afros,' 'community organizers,' 'chewing gum,' 'obesity.' To a significant degree as a result of that victory several hundred more defendants now struggle, demand their right to a jury trial, and a great many win. We recognize that the enemy will, we think, in this decade revoke the 'right' to a jury trial, and that is but a part of the ongoing process that will both heighten and alter the form of struggle and strip away the facade of the truly criminal criminal administration of injustice."

"Of the other people in the firm," Cockrel said, "Harry does, as we said, products liability work and major personal injury; Tai Maki does a lot of bread and butter stuff and so do Barbara Robb and Clarice Jobes, both of whom are also counsel for women's groups. But you can't say these folks are into a prosaic kind of money-making operation to sustain the firm—not that that is to be disparaged—but there are political consequences that flow from the kind of work that they do. They are all political people, they are all conscious of the fact that there is a political context within which their work can be comprehended and they all do relate to the strains and tendencies that are part of the generally progressive tendency operating in this country. The women who work here as secretaries do caucus about decent wages and meaningful work, but whether or not a person participates in a decision about what will be done ought to depend on his capacity to make a meaningful contribution to the resolution of the problem that is under discussion and not about whatever subjective feelings he has about being Black, being a woman, or so on.

"See, I'm only concerned with the subjective state of people's minds as they externalize it in such a way that causes you to feel oppression, that causes you to be hungry or fucked up. Then we begin to deal with things. But the state of mind? Fuck it! That's t-group shit, you know what I mean? Send them to Esalen. I could spend the rest of my life running my Black thing; a Chicano could spend the rest of his life running his thing on the gringo. You know, you could do that or you could go on and get down. When people are running this thing about the women do the dirty work I just don't get it. Know what I mean? What work ain't dirty?

"My definition of myself flows from my membership in the BWC and my commitment flows from that fact. We have a division of labor and I happen to be a lawyer. Whether or not I will take a case flows from how it would affect the BWC. I am a member of the central body of that organization, and we discuss things collectively and my decision comes from that.

"If I go into court I go in to do one thing. I've called the judges pigs. I certainly don't give a fuck what they call me. I go in to win. There is no other reason to be there. It is a waste of time if you don't win. The people I'm concerned with is the jury. We all know that judges can influence the outcome of a trial, but that can be dealt with. When somebody starts fucking with you, you start fucking back with them whoever they are—cops, judges, prosecutors, whoever. You simply deal with that.

"The position that the BWC takes with relation to the court system is a very clear position, you know, that the court system is simply the functional appendage of a larger system of racism, capitalism, and imperialism; that it exists to serve two functions: (1) it is structured to facilitate the economic transactions that underlie the maintenance of the system of capitalism and imperialism; and (2) it also tends to isolate, possibly incarcerate, those who haven't already been killed who represent a sufficiently serious threat to the continued existence of things as they are. For us it is a very simple thing. There is nothing mystical about the court system at all. We know we're not going to litigate or elect ourselves to liberation in this country.

"Any trial that goes down in this country represents to me the illegitimate exercise of power by an illegal state mechanism. All trials are political trials. The way I justify my participation in the legal process is the same way I would justify my participation if I were a plumber or anything else. We need every skill that the enemy has.

"Apart from that, the responsibility of a lawyer is the same as that of anyone else who operates in one of these bourgeois institutions and has the responsibility, by definition, to do all that is possible to discredit that institution, to disabuse persons of the fact that they ought to repose confidence in the operation of that mechanism for the resolution of their grievances in any meaningful, just, and deliberate way.

"When we go into a court, we never defend. We're always attacking the American legal system, and we're also trying to get the client out. You have to deal with people where they are and you have to deal with their problems in such a way as to delegitimize the system. The only way you can do that is to demonstrate its bankruptcy and also accomplish positive results. That is what New Bethel was all about. To demonstrate to people rather graphically that armed attacks on the Black community by police are not going to go without a response being forthcoming; to demonstrate to the courts that you are not going to be able to call in the whole bullshit establishment and win. Then we went on to the jury challenge, and demonstrated to people that people were being kept off of juries cause they had Afros, cause they wore miniskirts, cause they chewed gum, literally. We kicked their ass at every level in that case, and that is the approach we take.

"I don't relate to this thing of being a radical lawyer. There's this whole popularization now of the young radical lawyer. It's a good thing to be. They even have those programs on television. It's a hip thing to be, like it's hip to be a rock artist. I'm serious now. There's this whole stereotype—this white dude, with long hair, wire frames, colored shirts, boots, all that shit—and there are all kinds of people interested in adopting it. But the truth of the matter is that it is really hard work. To me the responsibility of people with legal skills is the same as the responsibility of people with all other skills, if they are really real. To be a radical lawyer is important but I think they have to take it a step further. A revolutionary lawyer is a person who is a member of a revolutionary organization who happens to be a lawyer. It's hard because of the paucity of organizational development in the white left and the amazing degree of factionalization there. The struggle isn't about personal charisma. It's about collective leadership. There is nothing romantic about it. We've had bombs placed in the law office, and we've been attacked physically.

"Few people outside of the BWC have any understanding of the scope of its activity, know how many people are cadre, or anything of that sort. We're not a secret organization, but there has to be a difference between activities of a mass character and activities of a cadre character. The BWC has the classic vision. We know that the form of the struggle in this country will come from material conditions in this country. We know that there is no one-to-one correspondence between what happens in Vietnam and what is going to happen here. We're Communists explicitly.

"We are about the business of trying to organize workers at the point of production. We have plant organizations and not solely in Detroit. We have members throughout the country and we are a national organization, but that concept is deceiving. Usually it has to do with the incidence of media coverage. Fortunately we haven't been enshrined in the pages of the underground press to our detriment. There have been writings but we haven't become media heroes and I would be hopeful that we don't, although it would appear inevitable that we will.

"We have had organizational inputs of a national character. The Black Economic Development Conference (BEDC) was held here in April 1969, and out of that came the Black Manifesto and the Black Star Publishing Company which is a component of the BWC. We are a national organization based on our concrete organizational ability to service the needs of persons to whom we relate, wherever they might be. It will be international in scope because we have comrades throughout the world. We see the struggle as being a protracted one, and we don't want to move prematurely. Fascism is not yet at its apex. The enemy hasn't even really released one arrow.

"What we want to do is develop an organization that has the capacity to function systematically around the organizational objectives, consisting of well-trained, disciplined cadres capable of accepting the overall analysis of the organization and of discharging the tasks of the organization which have been collectively arrived at within a democratic centralist frame of reference, and of discharging those tasks with competence. What we have to build is people who have the ability to analyze the situation and move correctly in that situation.

"We're not media-oriented or white-left-oriented. We're not interested in outlefting anybody. We are not interested in the acquisition of power as such. We are interested in the acquisition of that power that will strengthen our organizational ability to take another step toward liberation.

"The BWC is constituted only of people who are Black, but we have very good relations with white persons who have the political approach and proletarian consciousness to try to do mass organizing or even a sufficiently sophisticated cadre that could be about the task of organizing that we can see. We're no longer into waging meaningless struggles with people in the left—ideological struggles. We don't have time for it. We're concerned with what people do. We are in solidarity with any people who tend to even hint at a direction of progressive politics and in opposition to the ruling class. I once thought there was some hope with white youth, but their commitment is tenuous and subjective. Youth is not a class, to put it another way, and it is hard for me to see them as serious allies in a protracted struggle. If they do struggle, they will be allies.

"I don't see operating anywhere in America any observable tendency that would suggest that there is the likelihood of the resolution of the kinds of contradictions that are extant in this society short of persons being confronted with the necessity of engaging in what we regard as the highest form of struggle— armed struggle. I see that as being inevitable. I don't say that as any kind of gleeful predictor of dire consequences. I just don't see operating any tendencies that argue to the contrary, and I do see tendencies that are rushing us to the brink of the ultimate fascist dictatorship.

"I suspect that a great deal depends upon the capacity and ability of whites to demonstrate to the vast majority of the white population in this country that their interests are not served by the maintenance of the interests of the ruling class and the instrumentalities employed by the ruling class to perpetuate themselves in power. There are small signs. Whether or not they will be able to reverse the operation of the racial contradiction in this society in time to prevent Blacks from being forced to conclude that the task at hand is survival, remains to be determined. We know that we're trapped and that armed struggle is being waged against us, and we are certainly not going to go peacefully. We don't have that choice. But a lot depends on what whites do, not for us but for themselves. I'm neither optimistic nor pessimistic. We'll take it as it comes. We don't have any choice."

Along with Cockrel and Ravitz, a community of very serious, dedicated, radical young lawyers has emerged. These, in combination with the older radical lawyers who have been in Detroit since the labor struggles of the 1930s, make the Detroit radical legal community a serious and aggressive one. In some ways this has been the case throughout this century. Because the automotive industry has always been pivotal in union organizing, because many legal struggles usually arise out of such organizing, radical lawyers have had to be present in this city, and so have radical organizations. Therefore left organizations in Detroit have a relatively long and stable history.

The National Lawyer's Guild has always been strong here, perhaps stronger here than anyplace else. Before the McCarthy period it was the second largest bar association in the city. Many of the judges on the circuit bench were members. At that time it was advantageous for anyone who wanted to practice labor law in Detroit to be a Guild member. Then, with McCarthyism, the Guild here, as elsewhere, was wiped out. Yet, at a lot of the critical points of the Guild's history, the Detroit chapter helped to hold it together. In 1963 the national office was moved to Detroit for a time, and Ernest Goodman became its president. When the Guild decided to open an office in the South, George Crockett was the lawyer willing to take the assignment of opening it, and many Detroit lawyers went to the South to work. Then, in the midsixties, with the reawakening of a nationwide movement for social change and the influx of young lawyers into the Guild—

with all the generational dissension that caused in the organization—the Detroit chapter was still able to hold it together
because of the long and stable history of left organizations in the
city.

Because of the presence here of radical organizations with
histories of strong views, radical lawyers in Detroit did not have
to look to new national movements to find places where they
could aid in the struggle. They had to look no farther than their
own city, and that is where they largely did, and do, look.

Their newly reconstituted Guild regional office functions in a
variety of ways: as a mass defense office, as a clearinghouse for
cases, as a place where Guild organizational and administrative
work happens and where political priorities are set. The lawyers
who work out of this office also try some cases. The chapter now
has several hundred members, and up to one hundred of them
could be called on any given project within a twenty-four-hour
period. There are also student chapters of the Guild at the law
schools of the University of Michigan, the University of Detroit,
and Wayne State University, giving this office an additional one
hundred members who are willing to do work. Tom Meyer is the
office's staff attorney, and Hugh M. "Buck" Davis, Jr., is the directing attorney.

Buck Davis, also a member of MCLL, was born in Rocky
Mountain, North Carolina, son of a railroad worker who, in
working his way up to middle management levels, moved his
family all over the South. Davis went to public schools and then
to Hampden-Sydney College in Hampden-Sydney, Virginia.

"It was a private college for the not-so-bright sons of not-so-
rich southern pretenders, located in Prince Edward County where
the schools were shut down for seven years to avoid integration.
I was there then and it bothered me not a bit. I was considered a
liberal by my friends because I took the position that there were
arguments on both sides, not just one. Through a series of fortui-
ties I went to Harvard Law School where I was among the worst

students they ever had. I had no interest in the law school, the law, or anything except experiencing the rather strange northern culture.

"By the end of three years there I had come to a position, because of my imminent entry into the armed services, against the war in Vietnam, which was the only political position I had ever reached. I decided against the war in the whole range of ways war could be condemned. I was an armchair liberal.

"I graduated in 1968, joined VISTA to avoid the service and was, fortunately for me, and, eventually I hope, unfortunately for the government, sent to Chicago to begin my VISTA training in the middle of the Democratic convention. I hadn't been there a few minutes before I was gassed for the first time. In the next few days I experienced a lot of street action. It was the most exhilarating thing that I had ever experienced. I became an instant revolutionary. I was afraid to remain in Chicago so I got a transfer to Detroit.

"When I came here, I became associated with a group I now know to be radical lawyers although, at the time, they were just people I worked with. I found them the most humane, sincere, dedicated people I had ever dealt with. Ron Reosti was my boss at the Community Legal Council office, and he taught me some fundamentals of political analysis. I was a VISTA lawyer for a year then I got a Reggie, the national OEO glamour boy scholarships wherein they attempt to interest persons who otherwise would go into corporate practice to spend a year's conscience time in some sort of relevant legal experience.

"I'm not sure that Legal Services does that much good for poor people. The Legal Aid idea seems to have started in Chicago around the turn of the century. The organized bar would take politically favored but incompetent attorneys and put them in Legal Aid offices with guidelines that precluded any real work being done. It stayed that way until the 'Great Society.' When the first OEO offices were opened, people realized that poor people had a lot of legal problems. For the first few years Legal Services were just expanded Legal Aid offices. The staffs would be well-intentioned but not particularly political young lawyers. Then Legal Services started doing test cases which helped some, then they went into the third stage, representing groups and acting as a service unit to organizational groups. That was politically more sophisticated and a step forward, but then the government tried to break it up because it was too threatening. And there was also the problem that, because the financing was meager, helping one group meant that you couldn't help another. I finally came to the conclusion that you next had to teach the groups to work together, teach them that the government, not the other groups, is their enemy and aid those groups willing to undertake the task of a socialist revolution. Then the final step now for an attorney is to decide that one group is correctly addressing itself to the problems that exist, and to service that group, which may mean giving up the practice of law if that is what that group decides you should do.

"Toward the end of my Reggie, a decision was made to open up a Guild office here and I was asked to run it. I said that I would. I got to know Ken and Chuck, and Chuck told me that it's said that it takes five years to make a good trial attorney but that it could be done in six months if I was willing to work. I met with him for long sessions two or three nights a week. We talked over the problems of the office every day, and I never made a move without consulting him. He was wrong. It does take more than six months to make a good trial attorney but I was still learning enough to be able to deal with the problems. Chuck is an extraordinary attorney.

"That's how the office started. We got enough pledges to support the office, send money to the national office, and act as a clearinghouse for a hell of a lot of cases. We had eleven hundred cases offered to us during Cambodia week in 1970.

"And we continue to function well because the big three radical firms here—the Philo firm; the Goodman firm, which now consists of Ernest Goodman, Mort Eden, Dean Robb, Robert

Millender, Richard Goodman, George Bedrosian, Bill Goodman, Charles Barr, Paul Rosen, Jim Tuck, and Marijana Relich; and the firm of Jim Lafferty, Ron Reosti, Abdeen Jabara, Victor Papakhian, Dennis James, Marc Stickgold, Judy Munger, and Dick Soble—are all united in their support of us along with some other firms, individual attorneys, and the Legal Services establishment. While the radical law movement has political differences, it is closer than many others, and it is able to unite around big issues. Because of this closeness, and because of the community's chosen course of minding its own city, it is sometimes accused of being too insular.

"The radical law movement here, as well as the left, is accused of a lot of things. One of them is provincialism. I think that might be true even though, whenever we travel elsewhere and come in contact with other groups—either legal or political—in other areas, we invariably realize that we have widely differing views on the practice of law, the direction of the movement, and the relationship between lawyers and revolutionary organizations. So the charges of provincialism are true but somewhat muted by the fact that we understand this is not a national movement at this time. The movement is fragmented, and our task for the present time is to take care of business in Detroit. We intend to do so. We think things will grow organically and dialectically, and we think there will be national fusion after a number of years, and we think that we won't have trouble expanding our vistas when reality corresponds with that expansion and it's possible to do so on a well-organized basis.

"We are also accused of Detroit chauvinism, and I think there is truth in that charge also; but, in many ways, the refutation of that charge has to do with our sense that we're correct, that if we are Marxist-Leninists, then Detroit and the working class—especially the Black working class—will be the vanguard of a socialist revolution in this country and that, very likely, the mainsprings of that will be in those production cities that have high Black populations. So I think while we have to establish stronger and better communication with other sectors of the left throughout the country, and while we have a terrific amount to learn from what people are doing in other parts of the country, that we are correct in our attempt not to become nationally visible.

"I think we are correct in maintaining a low profile, in making ourselves financially viable, in attempting to build the sort of cadre and peripheral organizations which will sustain us through the period that is about to come which will be worse than now. We aren't in a fascist era yet, and people talk about repression and it is real, but the fact is that we're operating in what is still a quasi-democratic era. The other might come, I think, and we must be prepared to resist it, to survive it. I think that by doing too much, by going beyond our organizational capabilities at this time we'd create a disaster, so we're proceeding in a rational, planned way. What I'm saying is that we're serious. We aren't fucking around. We think we'll be here more than a minute; we think we'll be able to make ourselves strong enough to survive the physical and financial attacks. We are going to build a reservoir of personnel, programmatic analysis, front groups, organizational forms, feeder organizations, fund-raising operations, and all of those sorts of things that will enable us to survive a long-term struggle.

"I guess the watchword for what we try to do is competence. It simply is considered not political in this city to undertake any task organizationally that you can't do. If you decide to do it, you'd better do it. That's really our position.

"In our legal community we aren't awfully concerned with lifestyle. Few make much money. Some have income limitations, and we do use our money for mutual support. But we do feel that there are limitations to the amount of lifestyle implementations that can realistically be made at this stage of history. We have to support ourselves and build a financial base. To do that we have to be able to get money, and to do that we have to be able to get it from people who have got it. To do that we have to be able to operate somewhat schizophrenically and somehow in a traditional way. We like to not have to beg for our money and not to have to depend on the largesse of people who can arbitrarily or whimsically cut us off. We'd like to build bases that are continually viable for the work that we have to do.

"We attempt to live in a collective way insofar as we attempt to be democratic. We happen to feel, by and large, that the added personal strains and the internalization process which you get into when you get into collective or communal living can drain off energies from essential work. That has happened with a number of communes here, and I think it is a recurring pattern. It is a more economical way to live and will therefore be increasingly common, but communes can burn people out very swiftly because most of us are fucked up behind our class backgrounds.

"And we think it is necessary to maintain, for purposes of getting money and stability, a front which is not easily attacked whether from publicity or from a landlord who has been put under pressure. We want to avoid being smeared with low-level attacks devoid of political content. Many of the advanced experiments with living and practice on the Coasts have a lot to teach us. However, the objective circumstances in those places differ from those of a Black, industrial, production city, and it is unclear how transferable those experiences are.

"We believe that lawyers should relate to the courts any way they have to. You're dealing with a judicial funnel by which predominately poor and Black defendants are fed through from racist cop to racist judge to racist court staff to racist jailers, to racist lawyers, to racist bondsmen, to racist prison keepers. It happens all the way down the line and it works like a charm. So the only reason to go to court is to win. If my client or political question is politically valuable enough for me to be in there, within very wide limits there's almost nothing I wouldn't do to get my client off. The only real tactic is to win and if that means I cut my hair or kiss the judge's ass or play ball with the prosecutor or do any of those things that I find abhorrent, I'll do them.

"One of the things you do to win is to politicize the case and that isn't always done around the court system itself. Every time there is the opportunity to expose something consonant with winning the case, you do it. Your own personal welfare should not be a consideration. If it's necessary for you to take a contempt, you take it. If it is necessary for you to make it absolutely uncomfortable for you to operate because of the hatred that you engender in normal court personnel, then you do that.

"I guess I attack whenever I go into court, even though I am a great deal softer than either Chuck or Ken, and I've been criticized for it. If you realize that trials are games and have absolutely nothing to do with the truth or the finding of the truth but have only to do with winning, then you play it as best you can.

"If we're right in our analysis that courts arc a functional appendage of a larger system of oppression, then we're going to have to assume that their attitude toward those of us who are trying to change the very substance of that system is going to be one of attack. Both Ken and Chuck have been cited for contempt, and the state bar initiated disciplinary proceedings against Ken. In the state bar proceeding we faced them again, head-on, attacking their investigation for what it was—just another example of the system's institutionalized lawlessness and racism— citing numerous and dramatic examples in a very political and important document. We mounted mass support and were grateful for the response of scores of Guild lawyers around the country. And, as in the contempt cases, we won again. In fact, in Ken's contempt case, with the full support of lawyers from all around the country, we let them dismiss the case and avert proofs that Judge Maher was a 'honky,' et cetera, only on the condition that they reduce the New Bethel defendants' bond from $50,000 to $10,000. They did so.

"I take it that the best defense against attack is strength. Consequently I take it that our ability to make ourselves so powerful that they can't attack us is the only real way to do it. Which

means that we've got to have so many lawyers, so many comrades, so many defense organizations, so much personnel, money,
and publicity that we can draw on that it is not feasible to attack
us. That won't keep them from doing it, that hasn't kept them
from doing it, but it has enabled us to kick their ass every time
they have tried, and we continue to operate in that way."

Los Angeles, California

Los Angeles may well turn out to be the archetypal American city of the post–World War II period. With its sun, smog, super-super highways, continuous suburbs, with a population on wheels shopping in its multitudinous shopping centers, eating from its seemingly infinite variety of drive-in plastic food places, going home to amazingly alike garden apartments, it seems to embody most of the current silent majority values of this country. There are ghettos, but the good folk only see them from car windows at twenty or sixty miles per hour. The downtown section, where it is not being renewed, is run-down, but, with all the shopping centers, who but the people from the central city see it? The city is a myth, really, that only those stuck in it are forced to believe. For the rest, the city is a series of neat little suburbs.

In such a city, establishing a community of any kind is a difficult task. Everything is so spread out, that it is hard to know where one should begin. Given these conditions it is not surprising that the predominant radical political form in the city is the collective, nor is it surprising that the radical legal community is closely knit. The National Lawyers Guild chapter has around five hundred people on its mailing list, and many of the approximately one hundred and twenty active members attend some or all of the Guild's weekly luncheon meetings. With the Guild's decision at its 1971 Boulder, Colorado, convention to admit legal workers, it is likely that both of these figures are now higher.

In the 1930s and 1940s Los Angeles was a center of union organizing. In the late forties it was the first city out of which came a blacklist (the Hollywood Ten).

Because of this early organizing activity the Guild chapter is composed of both lawyers from that period and the "new breed" radical lawyers who came out of law school in the sixties. Although there are differences of opinion between these two groups, they seem willing to learn from each other.

The firm of Jean Kidwell and Frank Pestana is composed of two lawyers who are husband and wife, are both in their fifties, and, as lawyers, date back to the early organizing period. Pestana is the son of working people who immigrated here from the Portuguese Islands in 1916 and settled in Oakland. He dropped out of high school and traveled the country on freight trains for three years before the labor struggle impressed him enough to send him back to school with the intention of becoming a labor lawyer. He went to Berkeley as an undergraduate, and then to Boalt Law School at Berkeley, graduating in 1940. He immediately joined the firm of Gladstein, Grossman, Margolis & Sawyer in San Francisco, opening an Oakland office for them.

When the war came he went into the army's judge advocate corps. Following that he became an attorney for the Federal Employment Practices Commission, which was trying to work against discrimination against the Black manpower that was coming from the South to help in northern defense industries.

After he left the Commission he went back to the Gladstein firm for a time, then came to Los Angeles to work in the law office that represented the motion picture studio unions.

"There was a terrific labor dispute in those unions from 1945 until 1949 when they were destroyed. In the strikes that accompanied the disputes, real repression came down. As many as fifteen hundred people would end up in jail at the same time for picketing, or allegedly violating court injunctions limiting the number of pickets in front of the studios. Jeannie and I were both arrested for taking the messages of people arrested to their families.

"In 1949 when the unions were destroyed by McCarthyism, we had to build up a whole new practice. We did some labor work, but, in that period, the unions would not take lawyers who had had any sort of leftist political careers. During the early organizing period all the CIO unions had had left-leaning Guild lawyers, while all of the AFL unions had had old hacks. But in the McCarthy period, left lawyers were fired right and left by unions, and the lawyers who went with the unions then were the ones who had been on the outs with the CIO unions before. So I went into straight work—whatever labor I could get, civil rights, police brutality, immigration, and work that stopped deportations."

Kidwell, who did not become Pestana's legal partner until 1950, had come to the legal profession in a roundabout way. She was born in San Francisco in 1917 and was brought up by her father, who was a trade unionist. She went to the University of California at Berkeley majoring in mathematics because she felt, because of the pressure of the times, that that field or teaching were the only occupations open to her. She met Pestana in 1938, when she was still an undergraduate, and they ultimately married. When he went into the army she worked for the army. On their return to Oakland, she worked for the government as a statistician, but found that she was bothered because of her own, her father's, and Pestana's politics.

"I knew it would continue if I was in statistics, so I decided to go to law school. I had thought of going to medical school but I was twenty-nine and there were undergraduate courses I would have had to complete first. So it was law school; I don't even know how."

She began attending Boalt, but, after six months, Pestana moved to Los Angeles and, after six months of a long-distance, commuting marriage, Kidwell went there too, completing her law courses at the University of Southern California.

"Originally, we had thought we'd go to the San Joaquin Valley and establish a legal service for the farm workers, but we ended up working here. My first partnership was with Stanley Fleishman, but eventually he had an accident and, at about the same time, I became pregnant. I had my first child when I was thirty-two and two others after that. I tried to work, but we had no money to have someone watch the kids. After the unions collapsed we were lucky if we made twenty-five dollars a week from legal work for the next few years. We did a lot of free work—all of our immigration cases were free—and we had no people giving us financial backing.

"I was a member of the Communist party from 1938 until 1962, but my relationship to it was strange in that I was never considered one of the lawyers who should be compensated for doing political work. I ultimately left the party because of a disagreement over their saying not to engage in the movements of the sixties because we could hurt those movements if we did. I went to the Mississippi Freedom Rides anyway. A friend from CORE had come to me and told me that they needed publicity because of the number of young people disappearing into the prison system down there. They wanted doctors and lawyers to go there to get them publicity.

"I tried to get other lawyers from Los Angeles to go there but none of them would. So I went with another female attorney. We got arrested and they wanted to bail us out right away, but we decided to stay in and go through the state penitentiary so we could see where people were and what the conditions were. From Mississippi the two of us went, by invitation, to Cuba. We had discussions there about the international Communist movement and a lot fell into place.

"When I returned to L.A. I went back to the group and, in the proper way, started asking questions, but got no response so I left the party."

It was in the late forties and early fifties that Kidwell was involved in a serious struggle within the local chapter of the Guild.

"Frank and I had always been Guild members and I felt that the Guild should not be a mass organization. At that point of time there was a faction who wanted to turn the Guild into that. It was a protective thing that they wanted. But I felt that we had to be a group of radical lawyers that had the right to take a political position without being a political organization, or else the organization would have been pointless. We eventually won, if only by default. The Guild was placed on the attorney general's list and that killed any chance of its being massive then. It moved even more to a bar association orientation and a lot of energy was expended getting it off of that list.

"Actually I think the Guild was practically gone by the sixties. If the southern thing hadn't started, if young people hadn't entered, forcing it to change its direction, it probably would have folded. It really wasn't until the Santa Monica convention in 1968 that I felt it definitely would survive.

"By that time the old Guild lawyers were getting old. I believe that lawyers for the most part come from a bourgeois background and, if they don't, law schools do a good job inculcating this into them. The system generally doesn't have to worry much about lawyers when they've done their education and then become part of the arm of government. So, if they manage to fight all of this and get to be fifty or sixty and are still involved in struggle, that's pretty good. As it happens, it also seems to be pretty rare, so the Guild needed some new blood."

Occupying the second floor of the same run-down, but comfortable, pink house in West Los Angeles that holds the Kidwell and Pestana firm is the Bar Sinister (BS), a collective entirely composed of the new breed of lawyer and legal worker.

The Bar Sinister, which can be taken to mean the literal "left bar" or the "evil bar" (since that is how they feel they are viewed by the establishment) or, from its initials, the "bastard of the system," opened in June of 1970. By the end of that summer ten of the people who now compose the Bar Sinister were working there. The political atmosphere and economic conditions that helped to form the ideas of these young people also led them to choose the collective firm. Looking at their backgrounds helps one to understand why collectives came about when they did, and the types of lawyers attracted to them.

Joan Andersson was born in Los Angeles in 1942. Since her father was stationed overseas she spent her childhood with her mother and her father's relatives in a suburb of Chicago.

"I always felt separate from the people in the suburb. My parents were working-class and had given me a different attitude than that around me to things like racism. Eventually we moved to California because my parents didn't want me to go to a ruling-class high school. We settled in the San Fernando Valley and I went to a white, working-class high school where I was a cheerleader and interested in my image but never did things like join a social club because I didn't like the elitist attitudes they had.

"I spent my first year of college at the University of Oregon and again felt out of place because it was a party school and I basically just studied. Then I transferred to UCLA and there I realized that I was a radical. I had an Indian professor who was a Socialist or Communist and who was able to voice the opinions I had always had.

"I decided to become a lawyer because a lot was happening in the South, and I wanted to be there yet I wanted to continue with school, and law seemed a way to relate to people on a practical basis. I went to Yale Law School, with most of my thoughts on civil rights, although it seemed that I was becoming more radical than the civil rights movement, and left after three weeks. I spent the next year as a social worker here in Los Angeles, but I realized I was no more than a policeman administering money so I went back to law school thinking again that that would let me relate to people in a more meaningful way even though, at that time, I did not have much faith in the court system as a way of changing things. My two years at Yale were the time when I most consciously became a Marxist-Leninist-Maoist.

"I spent most of the first year doing community work in a Black ghetto near Yale. I became involved in a police brutality case which kind of clinched it in my mind about the absurdities of American justice—the Black people I had seen beaten up were convicted of assault. That summer I went to work for CRLA and began to see how the court system treated Chicanos and those organizing among farm workers. The next summer I worked for Truhalf, Walker & Bernstein in Oakland and did some work for the Black Panther Party which was just beginning to emerge, and some free speech cases. I saw then that classical political cases were the only thing that interested me if I decided I wanted to be a lawyer at all. I spent my last year of law school at UCLA doing a lot of political work.

"After I graduated I spent a year working for the Guild as a student and lawyer organizer. Then I came here and worked for some Los Angeles lawyers for a while before spending three months in Cuba with a *Venceremos* Brigade. When I came back, the Bar Sinister was beginning."

David Epstein is also a native of L.A. He was born into a middle-class Jewish family that moved to Venice, California, when he was twelve.

"Moving from a solid middle-class community to a mixed one really had an effect on me. By the end of high school I had real questions about the institutions and values all around me. I went to Berkeley and was there for the free speech movement which began my radicalization. But I think that I am in the generation that tailed right on the beginning of the whole thing.

"I came down to UCLA Law School in 1966 and found it very traditional and quiet. I had decided to become a lawyer because of the momentum of my background and history, and because it was also the time of the civil rights movement when there wasn't a contradiction between being a lawyer and being in the movement. Between my entering and finishing law school my radicalization really occurred. I became involved with people who wanted to do community work in Venice and with people who were working on the formation of a student conduct committee which wound up being almost an advocacy procedure. Then, in my last year of law school, about a half-dozen of us who saw we wouldn't be comfortable going into a straight law office began to have discussions, and these were the seeds of the BS."

Carla Forteney was born in West Virginia and her family then moved around ending up in California in "a typical middle-class situation."

"I went to high school in Sunnyvale, then I went to the Art Institute in Chicago. I started to change there, got into the beatnik thing, then I went to the University of Illinois where I became involved in their free speech movement, antiwar stuff, S.D.S. It was a typical student involvement.

"Then I moved to Los Angeles with a guy who was going to law school at UCLA, and that is how I began to get involved in legal stuff. That's how a lot of the women legal workers get involved. I was involved with the Guild student chapter and some college politics, while I was going into and out of school. Eventually I broke up with that guy but, by that time, I knew David Epstein who was then working in the Guild office and I began working there doing legal defense work, getting lawyers, putting out publicity, going to meetings.

"I went on the Third *Venceremos* Brigade and that was a real turning point. It gave me faith that the things I wanted were necessary, and that there is a worldwide movement trying to get the same things. When I came back the people here, who I'd known from the Guild work, wanted me to join them. I thought, after Cuba, that I wanted to be in a direct organizing role so I felt some contradictions about working here but the needs of the movement are so broad, and I had had a lot of experience doing legal things, plus I had built a relationship with the people here, and so I decided to join them."

Karen Jo Koonan was born in Savannah, Georgia, then raised in New York until she was fifteen when her family moved to Venice. She was a dance major at UCLA and into the bohemian scene until the summer of 1964 when she went to Mississippi.

"Some friends told me about their experiences there the previous summer so I went down and became a Freedom School teacher and worked on voter registration. Needless to say it was a radicalizing experience. The school was burned out after I had been there for seven months so I went to New York, deciding I wanted to be a dancer and ending up working in a bank. Eventually I came back to UCLA and stayed there for two and a half years. Then I realized that being a dance major was politically irrelevant, and I moved to San Francisco where I worked for a movement newspaper for two years and did organizing for draft legal defense work. I got to know the lawyers in the Bay Area and one of them, Dick Hodge, trained me to be a legal secretary and I worked for him parttime for a year. Then I became a secretary at the Guild regional office in 1969, and I stayed there for six months.

"During this time I had been involved in other political things — I went on the first SDS trip that was supposed to go to Hanoi in 1967, but we ended up going around the world in a month and meeting with NLF representatives in Cambodia; I was involved in the Oakland Seven case; I was on the streets for People's Park and then Joan and I organized that defense committee. In December of 1969, when I was still working around the San Francisco Guild office and doing temporary legal secretarial work, I wanted a vacation so I came here and spent some time with Joan and Dan. They talked about the BS and I got turned on by the idea so I moved to L.A. Then I went on the same *Venceremos* Brigade that Joan did and, when we came back, the BS was beginning. I went to Cuba again in December of that year on a special lawyer and legal worker trip."

Barry Litt, a native of Pittsburgh, moved, with his "upper middle-class Jewish family," to Los Angeles when he was fifteen.

"The notion of success in monetary and scholastic terms was stressed heavily in my family. In high school I had a teacher who could get people to think in political terms, and I started doing so. Paula [now his wife] and I met in high school.

"I went to UCLA for a semester then I finished up college at Berkeley, where the free speech movement was going on. I defined myself as a fringe radical, which meant that my ideology was undefined. My wanting to be a lawyer goes back to all kinds of Jewish things like being articulate, not wanting to be a doctor, and still having a strong sense of wanting to be a professional. So, after Berkeley, Paula and I and our first child moved back here and I went to UCLA Law School.

"My main focus during both undergraduate and law school was reading, especially fiction, with an unclear notion of whether I wanted to be a lawyer or writer. After I took the bar exam I wrote for three months but I wasn't pleased with the results. I had known Dan and David in law school, and I knew about the idea of a law commune so I decided to try that. I started going to meetings in January of 1970 and continued going. In those first six months of meetings I found that I had to define myself politically, and I came to the idea of being a Marxist-Leninist, although I am still defining."

Paula Litt was born in Chicago and raised in Los Angeles.

"I came from a wealthy family, but we did not have the trappings of wealth. I went to University High School where I met Barry. By my last year there, I was alienated and my grades started to slump. I was interested then in social action related to my religion but, by the first year of college, I'd lost that interest too. I went to UCLA for a year, then dropped out and went to Berkeley where I went to secretarial school and worked for the University.

"Barry and I got married after his second year there. I worked for a while, went to school for a while, kept bouncing back and forth. I had a child and that gave me some feeling of definition, but it was a disastrous one although I related positively to having children. While Barry was in law school we had two more. Then, when Barry started going to the meetings for the BS, I began going too. I had always had an intuitive sense about politics which crystallized at this time.

"When the BS began I started working with it. We had sitters come in for the children, and we each stayed home with them one day a week until the collective where we now live, which is based upon freeing parents to work while giving children adequate care, came into being."

Beth Livezey is a midwesterner.

"I was born in Oklahoma and grew up there, in Norman where my father was a history professor at the University of Oklahoma. I went to the public schools there and then went to Pembroke College in Providence, Rhode Island. While I was there I became involved in tutoring and in some of the recreational programs in the poorer sections of the city. I was also involved in such issues as open housing, which was before the Rhode Island legislature while I was in school.

"When I was a senior it seemed like lots of people were either getting married or going to graduate school, neither of which was appealing to me. I had gotten increasingly interested in the civil rights movement so, upon graduation, I went South and did civil rights work for two years. During that period I decided that more movement lawyers would be helpful, since there were very few at the time. So I went to Vanderbilt Law School in Nashville because I felt it would be more important to stay in the South than to go to a northern school where there would be people who thought and acted more as I did.

"While I was there I helped to start the Law Students Civil Rights Research Council group and I did some community work. After my first year I worked for C. B. King in Albany, Georgia; and, after my second year, I worked for the Center for Constitutional Rights which was then in Newark. During my last year of law school—from August through January—I worked in New Mexico on some of Reies Tijerina's earlier cases and also took some courses at the University of New Mexico.

"When I graduated I took the New York bar and began working for the Center. I both worked in New York and traveled around doing case work in Ohio, in Chicago for the conspiracy trial, and in other places. After a year of that I felt the need to work in more of a collective form, and in one geographical area. Through the Guild I met the BS people and discussed their hopes of establishing a collective. It seemed like many of our plans and needs meshed. I came out here during the summer of 1970 to see how it was working, and I decided to stay."

Dan Lund is a North Dakotan. At the Guild's 1971 convention he was elected national vice-president of that organization.

"I was raised on a farm near a small town in a parochial atmosphere. I never saw anyone who wasn't a Norwegian or a Swede until I was fourteen years old. But, in spite of that, there were some radicalizing influences. My grandfather was an old world progressive who hated the banks and Wall Street; my great uncle was a lumberjack and a Wobblie; and my mother and grandmother were very active in the Presbyterian Church which was then strongly influenced by a social gospel notion.

"We moved to Culver City, a working-class suburb of L.A., in the early fifties and, while I was in high school, I began to define myself as a socialist because I knew it was sure to terrify and offend everyone around me. I took some kind of perverse satisfaction out of doing typical things well—like sports and getting good grades—and still having a self-defined notion as an iconoclast.

"I went to Pomona College in Southern California where I met some people active in the civil rights movement. I never did go South though. During the summers of my last two years at college I was a grape worker around Fresno and did some work with the California Migrant Ministry and with the pre-Chavez agricultural workers' organizing committee.

"I saw there the conditions under which people worked and the power of the bosses in labor. The strikes were viciously broken and the organizers were helpless, so the workers' solidarity broke and fragmented. It had a great effect on me. I wanted to go out and organize yet, at the same time, I felt cynical about the nature of labor organizing. Finally I decided to be an academic because I thought it was pretentious and paternalistic for me to try to organize farm workers. I went to Yale in graduate work in radical church history for a while but I choked on the cloying atmosphere of the East.

"I quit and came back to California in 1964 and began to do parttime support work for Chavez's union which was then beginning. In the fall of 1965 the grape strike began and I spent a good part of the next year working for the Emergency Committee to Aid Farm Workers, which was trying to mobilize middle-class political and financial support for Chavez. That was a critical time between the beginning of the strike and the time that the UAW gave its support to the organizing work. But, when they got the UAW support, they had to go along with the liberal anticommunism that went with Reuther's money, and so I became more cynical about the process of organizing workers in this country.

"So I decided again to retreat from organizing but, this time, I decided to become a labor lawyer so I could work with groups like Chavez's and give them the kind of assistance they needed so that perhaps they wouldn't be forced to make the kind of unholy bargains they had had to with the UAW to get their lawyers and their money. I went to UCLA Law for a year then I began to work with Jim Lorenz on the proposal for CRLA. I was inspired to do this from what I understood the history of the thirties to be when young, radical bureaucrats were able to creatively use many of the government agencies. I thought that OEO might give us an opportunity to do that if we were really serious and if it were done on a big scale.

"I took a year off from law school and served as one of the administrators of CRLA, and I fought for a radical approach to support local organizers and organizations, particularly those that tied themselves to the farm workers' union even though I was somewhat cynical about their tie to the UAW and what that portended. It was a concrete, day-to-day education in bureaucracy and radicalism. While the radical spirit in CRLA was predominant at first, it soon became the minority view. CRLA took a sophisticated turn to the right and became what it is today—the most effective, well-organized legal services program in the country. They are technically probably doing the best legal job in terms of law reform, class action, and sophisticated advocacy for rural poor people, but they have no feeling for supporting local political organizing or mass organizing. In fact, they have a fear of it. Instead of building a base among the people, they've built a base among the liberals and the young creative bureaucrats of Washington who liked the idea of that program and who took a great deal of their own identity as bureaucrats from the fact that programs like that exist.

"After a year I left them to return to law school, sobered and determined that it didn't make much sense to be a labor lawyer and that I didn't know what I was going to do. That was 1967 when there was an intensification of the peace movement. I became active in SDS, and was arrested at the Dow demonstrations at UCLA.

"In the summer of 1968 I was introduced to lawyers and law students who were with the Guild and, while this didn't provide all of the answers, for the first time I felt that I had found a community of people who were good to work with, who could combine being a professional with a revolutionary perspective. My last year in law school I spent a lot of time working with the Guild and, when I graduated, I took over the regional office here and worked at that for a year organizing law students and lawyers and trying on many things for size in terms of what kind of legal work made sense in terms of serving the movement. At the end of that year, the discussions about the Bar Sinister began and I decided I wanted to join in."

Carson Taylor was born in Pennsylvania and raised in Rhode Island.

"My family was upper-middle-class. I went to private schools after the fifth grade. I went to Governor Dummer, a boarding school, for my high school years and then to Amherst College. Ever since I was a kid I had wanted to be a lawyer so I went to Duke Law School.

"While I was there I began to get more radical. Going down to the South, a lot of the contradictions in the society became clearer to me. I thought of staying in Durham after I finished. There were discussions about starting a law commune there, but it didn't look like it would come off.

"It was June of 1970 when I graduated, and my wife, Gwen, and I decided to come out here for a vacation. I knew some of the people from the BS from the Guild so I talked to them when we got here. We never left."

Earle Tockman, a Chicagoan, went to the University of Illinois in Champaign/Urbana.

"I'd always wanted to be a lawyer because of the glorification of lawyers in society and because I had a talent to articulate. However, I took up accounting in college because I thought I wanted to be really rich. Then I decided I could be even richer if I became a tax lawyer so I went to Northwestern Law School. I was a liberal through college and thought I was in the vanguard of the struggle even though I was playing the game. After my second year I worked for a corporate law firm and hated it, but I still couldn't break my bourgeois hangup about money.

"I had this unsophisticated hangup about capitalism and what it did to people, including me, and I really felt the frustration of the contradictions in my life. The last year of law school I decided I wanted to be a poverty lawyer. I got a Reggie and came out here to Los Angeles. I was sent to Compton, a Black area of the city. I began to enter an identity crisis about what it meant to be a lawyer. I joined a group called Lawyers of the People where I met a lot of the people who are now with the BS. Eventually I decided to join them."

Joining the Bar Sinister is one way for Earle, or anyone, to get over their bourgeois hangups about money since the salary scale at this collective is so low it is nonexistent. When the collective has money, people take what they need to pay their bills and to subsist, but there is no minimum or maximum draw as there was at the other collectives discussed thus far. Part of this is by choice and part is because the Bar Sinister began with people who were, for the most part, inexperienced. No one had a client list they could bring with them to the collective as has happened in the others. And, because of their inexperience, the collective is very careful in the cases they undertake. When they take a case they study all of the areas of law involved and consult with more experienced lawyers like those in the Kidwell firm, Michael Tigar, Oliver Wendell Holmes, Jr., and Ben Margolis. So, as of this writing, it takes them a good deal of time to handle their cases.

To cut down on expenses, five of the people from the collective live in a big house in Venice in a working-class, Chicano neighborhood, three others live in the child care collective of which Paula spoke, and the remaining two, at the time of writing, lived alone.

From its beginnings, the Bar Sinister has viewed itself as a political collective first, and a legal collective second. Instead of being the legal arm of the movement, as the Guild tries to be, it wants to be a legal arm *within* the movement.

"Especially in the white left here, we are considered a political collective, just like a collective that does organizing or runs a bookstore."

From their beginnings this attitude has given them a unique set of problems. Following the six months of discussions when it was decided that those interested would give the idea a try, they got an offer of free office space and decided to take it.

"Suddenly, there was the Bar Sinister. Then problems began, like whether people should have individual offices and right on down the line. Then came the question of secretaries. Not all the men could type then, although they all can now. Then we came to the question of collective responsibility for child care which led to the question of efficiency. What is it? What is efficient in terms of a lawyer's time? All of those were important discussions that led us to challenge ourselves with the notion that we were a collective of people all of whom were equal.

"There were monumental struggles about things like whether to have secretaries. One woman was going to come here and be a semi-legal worker and a semi-secretary. But some of the other women pushed that idea aside. Some of the men, however, had expected to set up a commune like any law commune in the country which has secretaries even if they do have equal pay. To get the women to not go along with that, they had to struggle through their own slave mentalities. It's rarer now that outward chauvinistic acts will happen, but they still do and we will stop a meeting to deal with a chauvinistic remark. The struggle against chauvinism is the very foundation of our existence, but we deal with it as it happens.

"In the beginning the women met separately, then we realized it wasn't necessary because that struggle was so incorporated into our existence that those meetings seemed artificial. That isn't to say that the women don't have separate things to talk about, but we do that every day and, if a separate meeting is necessary, we meet. And four of us attend weekly women's meetings with women from other collectives in the city."

The legal workers in the Bar Sinister do a good deal of legal work—interviewing, researching, preparing witnesses for examination—but they don't feel that they are doing it to become lawyers themselves. They are doing it because they feel it is politically important, because they feel that their own understanding of it leads to a better understanding on the part of their clients.

"At one point we had to deal with whether we felt that political work was just like legal work. If it isn't, we would have been saying that lawyering is the only work and the rest is a luxury. So we came to the point where, in defining priorities, it's all work—that goes across the board from child care to legal work."

To emphasize this attitude the collective tries to spend one full day each week on collective studying. On this day called "Dare to Struggle, Dare to Win Day," they discuss books that they have all read on their own time. The reading is done in sections—one month they might study racism; another, the Russian revolution. Because of this practice, they often find themselves criticized by other members of the radical legal community for spending too much time in self-analysis.

"We're always in the position of defending ourselves from criticism. You're damned if you do and damned if you don't. We never said we had all of the answers, but we want to struggle with things and try to make them different.

"It can be true that collectives spend so much time on self-criticism that they don't get much law work done but I don't think this is necessarily a criticism. I don't think of myself as primarily a lawyer. There are more important things, and one of these is political development. We spend time in things like self-criticism because it is necessary, and one of the results is that we react pretty much the same toward things. It helps to have your heads together to have a good working collective. It's difficult to function collectively instead of individualistically.

"That sort of criticism is an easy one that can best be made by those who don't know what goes on in a law commune. If anything, we spend too much time working on trials and litigating because that is absolutely necessary, and too little time in self-criticism and developing ourselves as political people—although the time we spend is probably more time than most lawyers do, because, with a very few exceptions, most lawyers never develop as political people, although they occasionally develop as legal technicians. It's the lawyers who are defensive about their own lifestyles or economic needs or lack of political development who are quick to say, 'Well, they're just into developing some kind of self-satisfying hippie practice; and not into becoming good lawyers.'

"But, any person I've ever met in a law commune recognizes that, because of the people we represent, and because of who we are and how we are seen, we have to be better than anybody else just to hold our own in court. We recognize that we have to be as good as we possibly can. It's important to note, though, that we don't try to be good or great in every area. We try to discipline ourselves and limit the areas of law that we know and know well. I think, even now, that we've brought a seriousness and a thoroughness to our legal work which has already resulted in some significant courtroom victories as well as a good fight in every case we've undertaken.

"The frustrating thing is that we have received almost no support and very little interest from practicing lawyers. The people mentioned before who help us are the exceptions. Other lawyers either have a curious interest or are kind of waiting for us to fold so that they can say 'I told you so.' "

"The most excitement we've encountered comes from brand-new lawyers who are baffled by what they can do, or from law students who are looking for ways to be both radicals and lawyers. So not only are we struggling for ourselves and for the movement to prove we can work, we are also struggling because we feel that we have a real obligation to those people who we hope we can help to stimulate.

"In a capitalist country when you're trying to break down individualism and trying to learn to function in a collective way, a great deal of time is necessary because it's been so drilled into us by the system that one competes with other people, that a lawyer has knowledge he keeps to himself. Breaking all of that down is difficult but it seems, if there is going to be change in this country, that is the kind of thing that people should put time into. It won't do much good to have a power change in this country if the people who take over haven't tried to change themselves beforehand, and haven't learned that it is a constant struggle."

The Venice Legal Collective (VLC), in Venice, California, is different from the Bar Sinister. It is, in fact, different from most of the collectives in the country in that the people who compose this collective see themselves as people first, and political people second. They also seem to have a greater sense of the irony and humor in their own lives and work than do most collectivists. This is reflected in their office, which is disordered, chaotic, and, as likely as not, ringing with laughter or the sounds of five different conversations all taking place at the same time.

The idea for the collective began to germinate in 1970, when some of the people now in the collective were working for a legal health program of OEO that operated out of UCLA. The original plan had been to have a medical/legal collective; but, when the legal people were ready to begin, the medical people were finishing their education and/or in the planning stage, and so the two groups split off. The collective formally began in November 1970, although some of the lawyers did keep working with other projects through the beginning of 1971, largely because the collective needed the money.

"We decided to form the collective because life is short and dull; and we had great expectations and optimism that it would give us a chance for a new way to work and use the law, as well as deep depression about what we were going to do with our lives, and real alienation since the thought of going into the straight world really began to feel as alien as it looked. So, actually, we got together for both personal and political reasons.

"We had four goals when we began, and we continue to have those same goals. First, we wanted to perform legal work for the Venice community and other people in the Los Angeles area who would require the services of a low-income law office, and we wanted to do so at fees that would not rip off the people. We wanted to relate to the community, which is another one of those glorious and nearly indefinable words. Our first problem was in defining the community since it is made up of Browns, Blacks, Indians, working people, freaks, college people, old people, and just plain people. It is a highly disorganized community—of the attempts to organize it, most have resulted in failure—with multitudinous political beliefs, as well as social and cultural differences. Since we have had a hard time finding 'the community' we relate to the various communities with varying degrees of success. We do not feel that we have really become a part of the community, although we feel, with time, we will blend into it. It is only right that we become a part of the community just as everyone else does, by working and living in it.

"We are an office in the community, and we handle many clients from the community. We often handle quick 'freebies' involving phone calls, short paper work, advice, et cetera, for people who live here. Often these are people who just wander in from the street. And, often, they bring us cases which are for small amounts of money or property or small something else. Few lawyers will take these cases and the people are often stuck. In some instances we help them; in others, we direct them to the proper place for them to get help."

In the time that they have been together, the people in the collective have done just about enough orthodox legal work to support themselves, plus a minimal amount of political cases.

"There haven't been enough resources to do much political case work. We're learning, and it takes us sixty hours a week to get the work done because when we do something usually it is for the first or second time. It takes us a day to do something it would take another lawyer five minutes to do. But that has been a personally enriching kind of experience, and we think it will help us end up as a good law office. Our cases now are political in that people shouldn't be arrested for dope. They shouldn't have to pay money to lawyers for a divorce and they shouldn't have to put up with a quota system on the highway that makes them get picked up for a traffic ticket.

"We feel that the legal profession and the system of law weigh heavily on the poor, the minorities, freaks, women, and other groups of people. While we realize that this is not a shocking revelation, we wanted to approach the law with that in mind, and to deal with judges, court personnel, other lawyers, and even the clients in a way that would erode the traditional notions of the legal system. We dress as we feel comfortable, cut our hair as we like, talk to the people as persons to the extent that that is possible. Some clients, we've found, do feel the need to have a heavy-handed, authoritarian lawyer handling their case, but we try to change that when we can. We are trying to alter the mystique which the law contains for most people."

"We try to have a basic respect for people and the directions that they grow in. We don't see talking about being respectful and humane and then putting numbers on people to organize them. We seek to do these things on a daily basis. It is not glamorous, and the effects are generally only as far-reaching as the people we touch, but it is exciting to see the difference in some people when they leave here. Some seem to have a new feeling about casual people, or people with long hair. We believe as more people organize their working lives on this level, more and more people will be touched. Doing it the way we are is often painful and it is possible because, and so long as, the personal benefits are involved."

"Generally, we do not find legal work pleasant, and since we keep fighting the very kinds of ego-tripping it could afford one, we pay a price for our political view of the law. But we are paying that price, in part, because of some of our other goals.

"A second goal we have is that we are seeking to learn about and develop our personal selves. Since work is a large part of life, and since most of us feel we ended up in the law by accident, finding a nonoppressive place and way in which to do our work is very important in allowing each person to find his or her own way. Working, as we are, with friends, where the people are important and profit is secondary, we have the chance to let things out, to reflect, to question. Although it sounds trite, we feel that working in a collective can make it easier to 'know thyself.' We feel that life in our times seems to reinforce the difficulties in dealing with oneself. In our collective we are trying to set the conditions so that people can have a go at it. This is a difficult goal to work on, let alone achieve. Yet, we feel that we have all grown as people to a greater or lesser extent."

The third goal of the eight people in the collective—Mark Edelstein, Susan Edelstein, Dave "the Rave" Grabill, Peter Horstman, Chip Kurtzman, Sandy Nathan, Carl Schwartz, Barbara Young—is closely related to the second. They hope to build honest, productive, creative, understanding relationships among themselves, and then among others.

"We feel to do this it is important to work among friends and to help each other. We have built relationships, but not to the extent that we should have. In many ways this relates to the extent to which people have dealt with themselves. We need to love ourselves in order to love each other. These kinds of love are obviously difficult, but we have profited from our struggles. We feel that our size is important because, in a large group, your ability to have choice is cut down so far that it becomes a threatening thing, and your ability to see yourself is hampered because you're trying to deny yourself.

"While doing all of this, our other goal is to make a contribution to the political development and needs of that vague and difficult animal, 'the movement.' We are bound by a desire for radical change. We hope to have an entity that can do political work aside from the politicalness of being what we are. There are problems, in case you haven't noticed, with politics. We are not bound together as Maoists, Marxists, anarchists, or anything else. This poses problems because we do not unite behind any dogma. Rather, we are forced to unite on the bases that we've already discussed. We are trying to do things because they are right for us, not because they are 'politically right.' Some of us feel more attraction to political activism than others. Some of us are more skeptical. Some of us are very anti-intellectual and cynical of people who are deeply committed to rhetoric, of people who are very working-class-analysis and have to be 'right on' in everything they do and say. Those of us who share that opinion are cynical for two reasons. One, we don't enjoy it and we want to enjoy ourselves; and, two, it's bullshit, and most people aren't able to live up to the shit that comes out of their mouths."

"Yet, we all share the basic disdain for the quality of life nurtured by our society, and by the various forms of domestic and foreign oppression perpetrated by our government.

"In our work we are struggling to break down the oppressive attitudes we sometimes have toward each other. Male chauvinism, sexism, professionalism all represent attitudes with which most of us have been raised, and which we are now seeking to overcome. We feel that we must find new ways to relate, rather than lawyer to secretary or professional to nonprofessional. Obviously, this equally applies to the way in which the office relates to clients. There are many aspects of the law which can be dealt with not only by a lawyer, but by anyone who is knowledgeable in that area. We are attempting to expand those areas by study and practice, thereby helping the lawyers to struggle with their professional attitudes, and helping the legal workers to overcome their feelings of ignorance of the law. The jobs of typing, answering phones, et cetera, are spread out as much as possible so that when shit work is done, at least it is equally divided.

"Obviously, breaking down attitudes and gut feelings that have been built up for many years is difficult, and our office has had its share of difficulties in these areas. At times the tensions are almost overwhelming, and the pressures seem unbearable. Too often we store up our grievances only to explode at a collective meeting instead of discussing our feelings, if possible, at the time of the incident. Recently though, private discussions are becoming more frequent and, if nothing else, this keeps the lines of communication open, which is the only real chance we have to continue to develop as people and as a collective."

"Taken all together, what we have said should indicate that we care about our own lives, that we seek to participate in a radical change of the society, and that we are trying to create our own small community within the larger one. We are part of the movement, although we don't have an interest, necessarily, in leading it. We feel that our lives reflect that we are just part of the small kernel of dissatisfaction festering in the corn fields of America. We hope to join with other kernels to create a better field for us all. Above all else—the politics, the rhetoric, the movement—we are people, with all of the strengths and weaknesses that people have. Some of us are afraid to open ourselves too completely. Others at times need help that the rest of us feel unable to give. But we continue to attempt to relate, and, to love each other."

12

San Francisco, California

San Francisco is the real melting pot of post–World War II American culture. Here people of the establishment, of minorities, of the counterculture physically live side-by-side in relative harmony, although each group sustains itself through its separate mental and cultural ambiance.

Perhaps because of the natural beauty of the environment, perhaps because, after the earthquake of 1906, people can never forget that they are the encroachers liable to be shaken from their homes without a moment's notice, this city, even in bad times, seems somehow more friendly than most other American cities. It is a city of experiments and experimenters. The free speech movement, the Black Panther party, the hip subculture all began in the Bay Area, and the return-to-the-land movement had its full twentieth-century flowering there.

The diversity of the city, the sense of experimentation, extends to its radical law community. What movement lawyers are doing here now, other movement lawyers in other parts of the country will probably be doing in six months or a year, since San Francisco seems always to be that much ahead of the rest of the country.

What the radical lawyers there are now doing covers a wide spectrum.

San Francisco's radical law community consists of young lawyers, a little-bit-too-old-to-be-young-but-keeping-with-it lawyers, older lawyers, counterculture lawyers, lawyers-turned-organizers, organizers-turned-legal-workers, revolutionary lawyers, liberal-radical lawyers, and on through every permutation of radical lawyer, legal worker, or general political person.

Vincent Hallinan is an older lawyer, probably the oldest active lawyer in the community. He is seventy-seven years old and still as much a fighter as he has always been. Recently he was cited in *Ripley's Believe It or Not* for playing Rugby for thirty minutes when he was seventy-three.

He is, of course, an Irishman, and gives one the impression that he has tried to live up to the sprightly, cocky, pugnacious-in-a-friendly-way image that all Irish-American men seem to favor. He was born in San Francisco in 1897 to immigrant parents. His father was a streetcar conductor and was active in the early unionizing efforts of his occupation. Because a lawyer kept the family from being evicted from their basement apartment which the landlord wanted to use for storage space after the big earthquake, Mr. Hallinan decided that nine-year-old Vince should grow up to be a lawyer. Neither Hallinan ever wavered from that decision.

Vince Hallinan attended parochial schools, and, at fifteen, was declared bright enough to be put in the hands of the Jesuits. From that time through law school, he attended the St. Ignatius schools in San Francisco. He recalls that, at one point in his career when he was suspended from practice, he tried to go back to school at the University of California and found that all of his schooling, including law school, did not qualify him to be a freshman there.

While he was attending St. Ignatius Law School he worked for Daniel Ryan, a lawyer who let him handle most of his Justice Court work. He took the bar examination the first time it was given by a board of bar examiners, passed it, and soon went out on his own. His first year in business he made $20,000 as the result of winning a probate case. Shortly thereafter he decided to take on the jury-planting system in San Francisco. In that system, only those people the bosses of the city knew and wanted for the job would be selected for jury duty.

"The jury commissioner was an out and out gangster. He, his partners, and his boss had conducted the gambling ring in San Francisco. When I took him on he managed to have a grand jury indict me three times for various felonies. I beat them all, and, eventually, I beat him and that planting system."

Those two events in the beginning of his practice set the tone for Hallinan's professional life; he was then, and remains, a fighter for reform and a rich lawyer—eventually, a self-made millionaire. In the fifty-plus years since he started practicing he has covered so much territory that it has made a book in itself, *A Lion in Court*.

His most famous case, and one that changed his own life radically was the Harry Bridges case in 1949. Harry Bridges was the controversial dock worker organizer who formed the International Longshoremen's and Warehousemen's Union. For his efforts on behalf of the labor movement he was rewarded, by the government, with a long period of harassment which culminated in this case. Bridges was being tried, along with two of his co-workers for conspiring to defraud the government of citizenship for himself. The government claimed that, when Bridges had applied for citizenship in the early forties, he had lied by saying that he had never been a Communist and that his co-workers, who had signed his citizenship application, had also knowingly lied.

The trial occurred as the witch hunt was going into full swing, shortly after the trial of the first Smith Act defendants in New York. Hallinan was cited for contempt on the second day of the trial and sentenced to six months. He successfully argued that the sentence be stayed until the completion of the trial.

The Bridges trial lasted five months at the end of which all of the defendants were found guilty and sentenced to the maximum terms. The Supreme Court did eventually overturn the convictions on the ground that the statute of limitations had expired at the time the indictments were returned. They did not, however, grant Hallinan's writ on his contempt conviction so he served six months, March through August of 1952, in the federal penitentiary at McNeil Island, Washington.

It was an unfortunate time for him to be incarcerated since he had previously been nominated as the Progressive party's candidate for president. His family campaigned for him but it was to no avail. The left in this country was so fragmented and frightened of the rising tide of McCarthyism that Vince made a poor showing and the party perished in that election.

Because of his candidacy, the government proceeded to harass him in whatever ways it could think of. At that period of history, it could think of quite a few. First he and six associates were indicted, in March 1953, for conspiracy to defraud the government, a charge that arose out of the transfer of a deed of trust. Because Hallinan had been in New York during the entire period when the conspiracy was supposed to have been in progress, the defendants won.

Three months later Hallinan and his wife, Vivian, were indicted for income tax evasion. After a trial in which much was made of their contributions to organizations that were on the attorney general's list, Ms. Hallinan was acquitted and Hallinan was convicted and sentenced to eighteen months which he began serving in January 1954, again on McNeil Island but this time in the prison and not the prison farm. Because of his conviction, efforts were made to disbar him, and the case went to the Supreme Court, which refused to disbar him but did suspend him from practice for a three-year period.

These experiences did not dampen his fighting spirit. When he was washed down the steps of the San Francisco City Hall on "Black Friday" of the 1960 House Un-American Activities Committee hearings, along with those of the young people demonstrating there, he filed suit against the police commissioner. The suit's basis was that the commissioner wasn't a resident of the city. The suit was successful and the commissioner was discharged, although he was later appointed city manager.

Of his six sons, two—Terry and Patrick—are also lawyers and ones with the same spirit. After Terry passed the bar examination the state bar refused to admit him on the grounds that he had been involved in all kinds of civil rights disturbances. They took the case to the Supreme Court, which required the state bar to admit him. On another occasion Vince defended Terry, who was charged with assault of a policeman.

"He had appeared as attorney for a group sitting in at San Francisco State during the demonstrations there and had tried to stop a policeman from excessively beating two young women. They hit him on the head and inflicted a wound that required sixteen stitches and then charged him with assault. We stood trial in front of a bastard judge who wouldn't tell the jury that Terry had the right to stop the cop from using unnecessary force, so the case was retried in front of another judge and we won an easy acquittal. Then we brought suit against the city for damages."

Vince's case load is light now. He only takes free cases that have a particular significance. Both Terry and Patrick now practice in the same office with him.

In 1972 he ran for judge of Department II of the Superior Court of San Francisco. Although he fought a good race under the slogan of "Humanize the Courts," he was defeated by the incumbent.

Vince has been a member of the National Lawyers Guild since it began.

"The younger people in the Guild are much more revolutionary than the older ones, and they are right to a large extent. The notion that you can effect changes through the courts is pretty much washed out. The courts are simply instruments of the status quo, extensions of the cop's club, and anyone who thinks he is going to get relief from them is kidding himself.

"I'm a socialist, surely. I think this whole system has to be kicked out. So I like the younger lawyers with their law commune ideas because that is approaching law practice in the socialist countries. The capitalist system is not the answer to the problems that confront mankind. Personally, I am extremely pessimistic about man's fate, and I don't think there are any real answers, but I do think that the unjust distribution of wealth must, and can, be corrected. I think that a good number of people in the United States are beginning to see that, and want to overthrow the capitalistic system. I don't necessarily mean armed or violent revolution, just revolutionary change. The revolution we have to watch out for now is a right-wing one. Nixon is a fool being run by madmen. The repression we are into now is the worst one we've had in this century. Many more people now are at least potentially involved.

"Basically, I believe in the perfectibility of man, but I'm still pessimistic. I think man is evolving and will eventually get rid of poverty, disease, illness, wars, racism, discrimination. And just about the time he arrives there the world will swing into the tail of a poisonous comet and wipe out the whole tragic farce in one fell swoop. Man is the victim of a malign destiny. It isn't his show. Its God's, whoever he is."

Another firm composed of fighters who have won their stripes in a series of legal battles, albeit not as long a series as Vincent Hallinan's, is that of Garry, Dreyfus, McTernan & Brotsky. Because of his role as chief defense counsel of the Black Panther party, Garry will be discussed in section III.

Benjamin Dreyfus, born in 1910, is a native of San Francisco. He went to Stanford University, then tried to make his living in business for four years before deciding to become a lawyer. He then attended Stanford Law School, and, because of the politics of that time—the 1934 Upton Sinclair campaign and the workings of the National Labor Relations Board (NLRB)—decided to be a lawyer for the oppressed.

"I began practicing here in 1939, joined the Guild as soon as I was admitted to practice, and started working as a lawyer for people who were getting kicked around."

He continued practicing on his own until he formed a partnership with Frank McTernan in 1945. Around that time he also served as executive secretary of the San Francisco Guild chapter. From 1960 until 1962 he served as president of the Guild.

The man he originally joined in partnership, Francis McTernan, was an Amherst College and Columbia Law School graduate who had begun his legal career as an attorney for the NLRB in Washington. Almost immediately after he joined that organization he was sent to California to investigate charges that the Associated Farmers were engaging in unfair labor practices against workers who were trying to organize. He found that they were but could not prove it.

When a budget drive spearheaded by the Chamber of Commerce resulted in his being let go from the NLRB, McTernan came to San Francisco and worked with a commercial law firm for a year and a half before going into the navy.

After the war he joined with Dreyfus in partnership, then, in 1948, ran for Congress on the Independent Progressive party ticket. He withdrew at the end of the campaign to throw his support to the liberal Democrat who was running. McTernan served as president of the San Francisco Guild chapter from 1958 through 1960.

In 1957 McTernan and Dreyfus joined with two lawyers they had known through the Guild, Charles Garry and his partner, Julius Keller, to form the nucleus of the present nine-man firm. Shortly after the firm began, Julius Keller died.

Allan Brotsky, one of the newer members of the firm, although he is an old-time friend of its nuclear members, was born in Detroit and raised there and in Denver. He went for a year to the University of Colorado, then finished college at UCLA.

"At the University of Colorado I was exposed to socialism for the first time and it blew my mind. It was almost a revelation to find out that that kind of an alternative existed. Then in Los Angeles I was involved in political activity and in the struggle to organize migratory workers, and it was at that point that I decided to be a lawyer for the people. I went to Columbia Law and organized a group there that became a Guild chapter. After graduating I spent six months in a labor law firm that mainly represented the CIO unions in the New York area. When the war came, I went into the army as a signal corpsman.

"After that, I worked for the United Electrical Workers in New York for a while, then came out here and joined the leading CIO labor law firm where I remained for seven years. Almost as soon as I joined that firm, the CIO expelled the left unions and the witch hunt began. We took on the legal battles of the expelled unions and grand jury attacks on the radical movement and attempts to tie people in with espionage rings.

"In 1955 a number of us left that firm to start our own firm, doing the same kinds of things plus immigration cases of people the government was trying to deport on the basis of the McCarran Act. We were also involved in the cases of doctors and dentists who were being drafted into the army as privates because of faceless informers making charges against them or their friends or relatives. The movement then was at its lowest ebb. I continued my Guild membership but the Guild was very quiet. There were discussions about whether it was worthwhile to have it continue after the attorney general proposed to place it on his subversive list with no notice or hearing. The Guild brought a lawsuit in D.C. and, after many years of stalling, the attorney general admitted he was wrong and dropped his efforts to declare the Guild subversive.

"But the damage had been done. The Guild was fighting for its life. A lot of people had been scared and resigned. It took a while before the Guild got back on its feet.

"After a few years with that firm I went on my own doing labor, civil rights, and defense criminal work. In 1967, ten years after this firm had been organized, I joined it. This firm has supported itself by general practice, mainly personal injury work which is the most lucrative, but in the last three and a half years I think we have done more movement work than any other office in the country. When we started doing so much movement work, especially when we took on the Panther work, we were lucky because we had good roots in the community from before, so people would still come to us. If that hadn't happened, I don't think the firm would have survived.

"Aside from those of us with our names in the firm name, there are five other lawyers in the office—James Herndon, Donald L. A. Kerson, Robert S. Marder, David E. Pesonen, and William F. Schuler—and seven other workers. We have a team here where everybody does whatever they are best qualified to do. None of our staff feel that they are oppressed. The idea of a lawyer answering the phones, et cetera, doesn't make sense to any of us. The lawyers have their level of income and, in the years when we reach that, we share the profits beyond that. That doesn't happen too often because we usually have financial problems although, so far, we have managed to survive."

Their case load, like the Center for Constitutional Rights, reads like a *Who's Who* of movement cases, although with more of a West Coast and more of a Black Panther party orientation. They've been involved in Bobby Seale's trials, Huey Newton's trials, David Hilliard's trials, the Los Siete case, the Oakland Seven, the Angela Davis case, other shootout cases, and the whole gamut of draft cases.

"I wouldn't say," said Brotsky, "that our views on the Panthers are uniform, but the thing that unites us is the belief that the Panthers are an important part of the movement, particularly the movement for Black liberation. Charles is personally more involved because, except for Los Siete and Oakland Seven, he's been doing nothing but Panther work for the past four years. But we're all deeply committed by conviction. Charlie has been made a star by the press and the movement rank and file by the publicity he has received from his Panther work, but he's not a star in the office and he doesn't conceive of himself as such, nor do we. He's just the part of the team that has gotten the most publicity because he has been in court and on the front line so much.

"To some extent, the courts are being reformed every day. Whether these reforms mean anything, I don't know. I don't think our society, as presently constituted, can ever have justice for Black people, for the poor or the young or revolutionary movement people because the society is a class society and that can never give justice to all members of the opposing classes who are trying to liberate themselves.

"But I think it is important to struggle for all of the rights and safeguards we now have in the courts so that the right to struggle and organize will be preserved. It's a hell of a lot harder to have a movement in a fascist state than it is in a conservative, democratic state. I'm optimistic. I think the people of the world are going to win their battle to make the world a humane, comradely, humanistic place for all people."

Garry, Dreyfus, McTernan & Brotsky is not the only San Francisco firm with a *Who's Who* case load of movement cases, nor with a media star in its midst. The other firm sharing this dubious honor does, in fact, go the Garry firm two better since one of its two partners and two of its associates are media stars of the radical law movement. The firm is that of Michael Kennedy and Joseph Rhine, and associated with the firm are Dennis Roberts and Michael Tigar. They are housed in a big red house with a largely red and black interior in which Mike Kennedy feels very much at home, partly because he is an Aries surrounded by Arien colors, and partly because it was decorated by his wife, Eleanore, who is an interior designer.

Kennedy was born in Spokane and raised there and in Seattle until he was ten when his family moved to Corcoran, California, the San Joaquin Valley town where *Grapes of Wrath* was filmed. From there he went to Berkeley, majored in economics, joined a fraternity, and quit after eighteen months because it had a white clause. He also during this time became friends with the Hallinans, Peter Franck, and Arjay Lenske. After graduating from Berkeley, he went to Hastings Law School in San Francisco.

"Being a lawyer seemed to me to be the slickest capitalistic rip-off and professional position one could get, and it seemed I could placate my conscience, to the extent that I had a conscience, by occasionally doing things with the law that one couldn't do in other professions. I had wanted to be a lawyer for a long time, to make a lot of money, get an elite position, and protect the hell out of it for the rest of my life.

"But the more I got into the law, the more I realized what a morass it was, that the poor and people of color were treated differently, and that it really hadn't changed that much from feudalistic times in England."

In law school he first met Joe Rhine, the son of union organizers who were active in the labor movement from the thirties through the fifties. Because of his parents' profession Joe had moved around a lot, attending high school in Indianapolis, Philadelphia, and Arvada, Colorado, before doing his undergraduate work at the University of Colorado and then going on to Hastings.

After meeting Rhine, Kennedy got involved in trying to make the law school employment people hire people from minorities and was washed down the city hall steps on Black Friday. While at Berkeley, Kennedy had received a ROTC commission, with a deferment to go to law school so he could go into the judge advocates corps when he finished.

"Because of my relationship with Joe and other left-wing people the Counter Intelligence Corps and the FBI started to investigate me along about my second year of law school. It pissed me off from the civil liberties viewpoint, and I refused to cooperate with them. Eventually they gave me my commission back, although I didn't want it. I graduated from law school in 1962 and was admitted to the California bar at the beginning of the next year. I went to work for a firm that did personal injury and negligence trial work because I wanted to be a trial lawyer. Then in the fall I was called to active duty. I fought with myself about going but went to Fort Benning, Georgia, for training. The army was not all bad because that is where I met Eleanore. In 1964 I went to Fort Knox, Kentucky, as an infantry company commander. I never went with the judge advocates corps because they wanted me in for three years. Talk about Vietnam was just beginning at this time, and I was relieved of my command four times for giving talks to my company about what was happening there, and I went AWOL a few times. In 1965 they gave me an early out, and I returned to San Francisco and went back to the same firm.

"I saw Joe, the Hallinans, and Peter again, and decided that the legal work I was doing wasn't important enough. The person who needed legal help then the most was Cesar Chavez, so we all began doing parttime work for him. Then Joe and I helped write the incorporation papers for San Francisco Neighborhood Legal Assistance Foundation [SFNLAF], an OEO program for the city. The senior partner in the firm where I was working was becoming president of the state bar at the time and he and the bar wanted SFNLAF to be under the control of the Legal Aid Society which they totally controlled. He and I publicly fought about it. After that the firm told me that they owned more of my time than they were getting and said that if I had so much free time to do work like that I could take on more cases. I ended up breaking my neck with two hundred and fifty personal injury cases, and then they offered me a partnership. I said that I didn't know whether I wanted it and asked for a leave of absence. I took the leave, got stoned out of my mind, and ended up a month later in New York City, still stoned. This was in the summer of 1967.

"I met Leonard Boudin, and he offered me a job as staff counsel with the National Emergency Civil Liberties Committee (NECLC). I took it. While I was there I met and worked with just about every East Coast left lawyer. While I was in the army I had had experience with military law because every time I was relieved of command they'd put me on courts martial so, while

with the NECLC, I began to use this knowledge. I met Andy
Stapp, who was organizing the American Serviceman's Union,
and began to defend people who were refusing to go to Vietnam.
I ended up as house counsel for the Union, and I was also doing
a lot of draft work. I defended Andy Stapp, the Fort Hood
Forty-three—the forty-three Black GIs who refused to go on riot
duty at the 1968 Democratic convention in Chicago—Gypsey
Peterson, editor of Fatigue Press and Founder of the Oleo Strut
Coffee House out of Fort Hood, Texas. I also taught a course in
military law at the Guild office in New York City.

"I was mostly into the civil liberties trip but the more I saw of
it the more I knew that it was bullshit. I understood what Mar-
cuse was talking about when he said free speech is irrelevant
when you're starving to death and totally disenfranchised. I
began fighting for the NECLC to take on cases of alleged bomb-
ers, conspirators, and murderers on the grounds that these, too,
were civil liberties cases because the people involved in them had
never gotten into the position where they could exercise First
Amendment rights. This drew us into the Buffalo Nine case, the
New Haven alleged conspiracy to bomb case in 1968, and defending SDS in the Iowa State conspiracy trial in 1969. In that
year I also taught lay advocacy through mock trials to several
hundred students at CCNY in New York City. They were part of
a mass bust during a GI sanctuary in the college chapel.

"Then Eleanore and I were asked to go to Sweden by the
American Deserters' Committee to talk to the deserters and resisters there about the political climate here, and to represent an
American marine who had deserted in Vietnam. We went in January of 1969, then went to Puerto Rico where I taught military
and draft law in San Juan to Puerto Rican lawyers and tried the
last draft case ever tried there, although one-third of the induct-
ees there refuse induction. I then taught a course at Rutgers Law
School in military law.

"When I got back to New York, I faced a heavy character
committee fight before I could be admitted to the bar. I had

passed the exam but the character committee was giving me a hard time for clearly political reasons although they used reasons like my sanity. From their standpoint, I was deranged and crazy. I was tired of the civil liberties stuff anyway and wanted to be independent. I had turned the corner from the civil liberties a long time before.

"I talked to Joe, who had remained in San Francisco, working with Neighborhood Legal Assistance, mainly on welfare rights cases and advising the Black community of the city on these rights. He had built up total neighborhood contact through teaching landlord-tenant law courses with the Berkeley Tenants Union, and done neighborhood law counseling within St. Francis Square. He had also coordinated the legal work for the San Francisco College mass busts with the Guild in 1968, and he is now working with them on the grand jury attacks in California and lecturing at the People's Law School. But, when we first talked he had quit practicing for a while because he was disgusted with the law so we said, 'Why don't we open a storefront office in San Francisco and work for ourselves?' Eleanore and I moved back, and we found this old house which Joe and I bought from a church for next to nothing. Eleanore decorated it with old junk we borrowed and bought and stole from different places and Joe and I started. Clients without money helped decorate the house as their fee.

"While I was in Puerto Rico, the Chicago Eight thing had broken and Rennie Davis called and asked us to represent him and we said yes at least as far as pretrial work. I went to Chicago once and got embroiled in that goddamned thing and ended up going to jail along with Dennis and Mike Tigar and Gerry Lefcourt because Hoffman didn't want to accept that we had only been working on the case in the pretrial stage.

"While there, I bumped into Charlie Garry again and he asked me to come into the Los Siete case with him. He said it was a little murder case that wouldn't take long. I called Joe, and he said it would be a good idea to do it because it would help us be meaningful to the community. We took the case on shortly after we started in June of 1969 and it ended up being an eighteen-month effort, four and one-half months in trial.

"Dennis joined us in September of 1970, and Mike in May of 1971. We have two fulltime and two parttime secretaries and six law students working out of here now. In the economic sense, we are a collective, although, now, the secretaries don't participate in the decision-making, although they do give feedback. Joe and I take out whatever we can in salaries. Some months, nothing; others, $1200 to $1500. We have agreed to spend half of our time on free work. Our fee-paying work includes personal injury, dope, criminal defense, and work on obscenity and pornography cases. In 1970, I was on Los Siete, and I also represented the GI Sanctuary group in Honolulu, and, along with Joe and Michael Standard, took over the appeal of Dr. Timothy Leary's conviction. We've been his attorneys since. So, that year, Joe made the money. In 1971, he was working on the Soledad case and Dennis was working on Angela Davis's case so the burden to make money was on me.

"In the fall, Eleanore and I went to Europe and Africa for six months. We did Leary's political asylum hearing in Switzerland, and then traveled extensively. As a firm we've decided that each person will try to take off at least six months every few years to keep them from being stifled by the law.

"Although I am a so-called 'star' laywer, I am opposed to the star system from a number of standpoints: it wastes resources and causes egomania and monetary rip-offs. I began arguing in early 1968 that that system couldn't work. At that time there were a half-dozen big names in left lawyering, and it was clear that those half-dozen couldn't meet the people's needs in any way and that their responsibility was to impart their information as best they could, and to demand that local resources be utilized when a big bust occurred. Some people out of the Center for Constitutional Rights—diSuvero, Lefcourt, Michael Standard, myself, and some others—started then to give assistance to young lawyers just out of law school.

"We felt that what was wrong with the star system was that when a star lawyer entered a case, you began to lose the importance of the politics of the case. For example, if a star who is powerful comes into a case he might be able to change the perspective of the organization under attack from an offensive political one to a defensive fund-raising one. Politics would begin to be made by the lawyers because the press would come to them and ask what was going on and they'd run down their line and nobody would go to the defendants and ask them what was going on. Stars are bullshit. You don't need them. Yet the system still exists.

"Given the cultural revolution we are in right now, and, in my opinion, it is that for whites rather than a political revolution, on all levels there is no great need for single, star-type leadership. This has been true in law for a very long time. Lawyers who become media freaks must understand their responsibilities and feed back the money they make into local lawyers. When the press knows you and runs to you it's all right to use that, to rip off the press and get out the right line when you can. But if you use it to change the political organization you're defending, you're dead wrong. Stars inevitably lose contact with the people, go off on an ego trip, and are no longer capable of making political decisions. The whole trip is deadass wrong. I guess the commune idea is the best way to control it.

"If radical lawyers are going to be able to rip off the spoils of their position and do nothing about fighting, then they are caught in the worst contradiction in the world. If you rip off the spoils but fight in the courtroom in the way you believe you could outside of the courtroom, then you're probably going to end up going to jail. I'm not into changing the courts and reforming them because I don't think that can happen. There can be no real change until there is a change in the power base.

"The courts are there to give the impression of equal justice for all, which they know is a lie, and to make sure nobody gets too much out of line. They do a fantastic job of keeping the lid on. But the courts are irrelevant when you consider the prisons which is where the revolution is in its most militant state. The courts won't be able to keep the lid on very long when people tear the prisons down and the courts realize they have no place to hide the people they don't like or don't understand. The courts can't deal with a dynamic situation. They are not decorous out of a gentlemanly tradition as they would like you to believe. They're that way because they know if they once allow anything other than obsequiousness and gentlemanly conduct, the whole damn system will explode because that is when you get at the truth. If you can make the courtroom mirror the horrors of the street, even in the slightest way, the whole damn thing will explode. That's what happened in Los Siete. We made that courtroom something akin to a street brawl on several occasions. That's what happened in Chicago, too. You have to make that courtroom laboratory as much like the outside as you can so the jury —and God knows that is the last hope of the legal system—can have a better idea of what is happening. That means as a lawyer you have to fight the judge, get put down, go to jail but, if you are going to struggle, it must be at that level."

Because of his efforts to make the courtroom reflect the street during the Los Siete trial, which did result in the acquittal of the defendants, Kennedy's and co-counsel Charles Garry's morals and fitness to practice were investigated by the California Bar Association upon the complaint of one of the Bay Area's more reactionary lawyers.

"I feel that all I can do now is beat them on a case by case basis on their own contradictions. That is all I can do as a lawyer. I think I'll be thrown out of the law within time, and I hope when that happens I'll have some other areas in which I'll operate. I'm optimistic. I think it is inevitable that we're going to kick their ass. Everything is on our side. It's just a matter of time."

While guardedly optimistic, Kennedy and Rhine's two younger associates are also confused at this time.

Dennis Roberts, a Brooklynite who grew up in the New Jersey suburbs, went to Rutgers University for three years before quitting to join the merchant marine. After doing that and working as a truck driver, he went back to school and graduated in 1961. He attended Boalt Hall at Berkeley, spending the summer after his second year working for C. B. King in Albany, Georgia. After he finished law school, he went back to the South to work for two years. He then joined the Center for Constitutional Rights where he remained for three years largely working on affirmative litigation.

In 1968 he received a Reginald Heber Smith fellowship to work with the Alameda County Legal Aid program.

"It was horrible there. Theoretically we had a project designed to sue the police for brutality cases, but then others in the project got interested in suing in federal courts around the area of police abuse. I'd done so much affirmative litigation before, I could hardly bring myself to do it anymore. I left and joined this firm. I'd known Mike in New York when he was with the NECLC and we had maintained a friendship. I wanted to develop expertise as a trial lawyer and this seemed a better place to do it than an OEO project.

"I do some court work on our fee-paying cases on pornography and they provide interesting, exciting, hotly fought criminal trials. We have a lot of political problems in the office because of this specialty though these cases do pay the bills here. My wife and I have had big fights over who's being exploited in the films. But if you start with the premise that you have to make a certain amount of money to survive, you can't only take those movement cases you want to take, although some of the law communes seem to be able to survive on less. I think part of it is that we're older, of a different era in a funny sort of way.

"I feel in the middle of a generational thing. In 1963 or 1966 or at the Law Center I was very much in the forefront of what was happening legally in the movement. But, in the last few years, people have moved so far so fast, that I don't find myself there anymore. It's personally disturbing. I see a lot of movement lawyers being left behind and I'm concerned that that doesn't happen to me, that I don't get caught in a certain way of looking at things and a certain life style. I have a tremendous amount of admiration for the people just out of law school who are working out of their own bedrooms doing good things we probably don't know about and just barely surviving.

"I relate to the court system in that, at this point of time, it's still the most useful place that I can be given my limitations and where my head is at right now. I still think it's very important for lawyers to be in the criminal courts defending movement people because it is another way to keep the people doing what I should be doing out on the streets.

"I've got a lot of conflict about what I should be doing and whether my role as a lawyer is a relevant one. But I'm not an organizer, I hate to speak publicly, and I do like trial work. So I guess that means I should be in the court right now, although I have a feeling that in a very short period of time that is not going to be very relevant anymore. I'm not sure what will happen, but I am sure that there are going to be some enormous limits placed on the role of a lawyer. I find it very hard to define myself politically right now. I'm going through a lot of changes."

So is Michael Tigar. He was born in Glendale, California, in the San Fernando Valley, was raised there and then went to Berkeley during the Slate period. Upon graduation he spent a year in Europe working for Pacifica Radio, the listener-sponsored radio chain. He returned to Boalt Hall about the time that the free speech movement was beginning. He was active enough in it to have an appointment to clerk for Supreme Court Justice William Brennan withdrawn. He went into practice in Washington, D.C., with Edward Bennett Williams's firm, doing a lot of ACLU, Center for Constitutional Rights, and SDS cases.

From 1968 through June of 1969 he was the editor of the *Se-*

lective Service Law Reporter. He then became a professor at the UCLA Law School where he remained until June of 1971 when he moved to San Francisco and became associated with the Kennedy and Rhine firm.

Mike was first thrust into the media spotlight, along with Dennis and Mike Kennedy, when he was arrested during the Chicago conspiracy trial. He was again put in the spotlight when the ACLU hired him to represent two of the defendants in the Seattle conspiracy trial in 1970. During that trial, which ended in a mistrial and contempt sentences against all of the defendants, Mike was maced in the courtroom when he attempted to break a full nelson one of the guards had on one of the defendants. Because of that trial at least one federal judge in Los Angeles refused to let Mike practice in front of him, although a court of appeals twice ruled that the judge was in the wrong.

"Since Berkeley I've been a movement person on and off. It's been very hard. In law school I was isolated because I had the notion that I wanted to get through and get high grades and that that was the best thing to do. In D.C. I thought it would be possible to practice law for a living and do other things on the side, that the firm would be a base. Then it quickly became apparent, although I don't regret having been there, that that was not so. So then I thought teaching would be the way to do it. But it turned out that was just an institutional cage. It turns out that the way to be is just to be, and not to be for somebody else—to start by figuring out first how to live, not as some kind of exigent thing but as a first principle, and then to work from there. The important thing is to be free and to feel free, to be a human being really committed to dealing with the society that really prevents most people from being human beings, which fucks them over from the time that they are born. If you can do that, then you've really done something.

"What a lawyer is involved in is giving advice about how he thinks the system is going to work in particular ways toward particular people in given circumstances. Oftentimes, his predictions are going to be less valid than his clients'. A lawyer also has a ticket: he can file papers, defend people, go to court. In that sense there are a few functions that only a lawyer can perform. Some young lawyers now are into collective decision-making with their clients and that is good, except that it can lead to a kind of paralysis in which lawyers are unable to do their jobs.

"Take the pattern of a typical political trial in which some people chosen by the government are indicted and charged with a crime, and the purpose of the prosecution is to deter others than the defendants—and the defendants, too—from doing their politics, and to put away those whom the government has identified as leaders. Now if the decision-making is collective about the case it can very often lead to a situation in which the movement that is under attack promptly begins having meetings about the best way to deal with the attack and those who go to the meetings regard all decisions as necessarily collective ones to be argued, debated, and discussed endlessly before steps are taken to deal with the government's attack.

"What happens is that because trials are interesting, particularly to white liberals who are kind of raised in this notion of American constitutional principle, because there is a real enemy to fight, because it is easier to work on a trial than to organize, the collective decision-making process embodies the movement as a whole, with the result that the movement stops moving and becomes a defense committee to defend the former movement and the government has achieved exactly what it wanted. Good organizing can be done around trials, but it's a mistake to assume that a trial is a place where people do their politics to the exclusion of all other places where they might be doing them.

"The courtroom is the man's forum, and it imposes certain limitations. It's not the place you'd choose to fight if you were choosing, and you didn't choose it. There are times when being highly political in the courtroom is disadvantageous in terms of trying to reach the jury. The jury is the twelve people you're trying to organize in a courtroom, whereas you'd never choose the people who end up on those juries as your constituency if you were into doing politics seriously in the community.

"I look at the court system with total skepticism. Not a chance that it can be reformed. We're at a time now when the ideology of bourgeois liberalism is, in many cases, contrary to the interests of the American ruling class. If you really enforce the First and Fourth Amendments, people get away with a lot. They get to organize.

"There are some good judges, ones who work not with power relationships but with abstract legal principles, who believe in change and want to do something about it. Law should be separate from the commanders of power. But we're at a point now where that idea of law and judges is under tremendous attack by what you could call the ruling class so I don't have any faith in the court system.

"At this point too, the movement for change is fragmented, distorted, and under attack. The job of the movement now is not to debate how we are going to have a revolution—which is what is necessary to get change—but to identify those forces in society whose interests are contrary to those of the ruling class and to join with them and work with them. The important thing for Americans to know about now is that the kind of society you get after you have a revolution is the kind you deserve. If you deal honestly with one another, in a comradely way, not suspiciously or viciously, you stand a much better chance when the revolution is over.

"I'm not optimistic about the movement here now, nor about the future of the country. I think we may well be in a situation where this country, as the leading imperialist power, simply can't be liberated from within, and that we may face a fascist period. A lot of third world countries will have to get liberated from American imperialism before the metropolitan countries get weak enough that something can be done. If you take the majority of people in America you're speaking of people who are the beneficiaries of American imperialism in a quite real sense. It's hard to know where you'd get a revolutionary coalition. It's like a race between the repression coming on and the movement taking off.

"Of course, it is also possible that the economy can't take its internal contradictions and the whole Keynesian theory will come apart. That would then determine what happens. It could cause a moving away from complacency and the forging of another New Deal alliance. That has to exist for the movement to exist because the necessary condition of a revolutionary movement is the existence of a large liberal movement which protects and legitimizes it.

"If I sound confused, it's because I really am. I just can't at this moment figure out where the movement is going and what it is to be. I feel best trying to figure it out issue by issue, trying to struggle toward some answers. I lack confidence in all of the answers that other people seem to have found."

While he is searching for answers and working with Kennedy and Rhine, Tigar is also working at the Center for the Study of Democratic Institutions, and doing some writing.

J. Tony Serra is another radical San Francisco lawyer searching for some answers. Unlike most of the lawyers discussed thus far, however, he is looking more toward the counterculture than the movement. Serra is known, in popular jargon, as a "dope lawyer." A native San Franciscan, he attended public schools and then went to Stanford University in Palo Alto on a scholarship that started out being academic but was later transferred to athletic. He made his way through college boxing, playing football and baseball, and drinking beer. When he graduated in 1958 he went to Europe and stayed there for a year.

"When I got back I had no definite plans about what to do next so I went to law school. That was in the late fifties and I guess people who didn't know what to do with themselves went to law school. In college I went around with the athletes and eight or ten of us ended up there."

Once in Boalt Hall, the Law School of the University of California in Berkeley, he decided to aim for criminal practice.

"I could never conceive of myself doing civil practice because I'm not oriented toward business or money problems. This was in the late fifties and early sixties and there wasn't, as there is now, the dual phenomenon of revolutionary-oriented students and psychedelically oriented students. There was just a straight world. But there were criminals and I guess I was satisfied at that time to represent straight criminals."

After he got out of Boalt, Serra took a job for a year with the district attorney's office to get experience with jury trials and juries.

"I took that job since I knew it would let me go against high-caliber defense attorneys, and in that one year I tried forty jury trials and countless nonjury trials. Now I would consider anyone who chooses to go with the d.a.'s office, even pragmatically for experience, to be guilty of an immoral act in light of what is happening. But then it wasn't so heavy because you were dealing with the traditional sorts of crimes against persons and property. I did those traditional crimes and I wasn't gravely immoral and I was as liberal as I could be.

"Now you don't have just that. The great bulk of criminal cases today consists of victimless crimes—narcotics violations, demonstration cases, political cases. These things don't belong in the criminal courts. They're sociological problems and should be dealt with in that way."

After that year with the district attorney, Tony opened his own practice in San Francisco specializing in criminal law.

"I was out of a kind of athletic, college, beer-drinking environment which produces the competitive instinct in people so as to perpetuate the society which is more or less predicated on competition and capitalism. I was married then to a woman who was also becoming a lawyer and I was making my role in that society by defending the criminals—indigent criminals or criminals with money. I was never really interested in money. I was just interested in getting into court and getting people out of jail."

After he was in practice for a short time, he and his native city were hit by the strongest phenomenon since the earthquake of 1906. The psychedelic age arrived and San Francisco became the center of its culture. Throngs of people flocked to the city in search of a new utopia. Often they were met by officials of the city who in no way approved of the means they were using to obtain this end.

"There was this widespread use of all forms of drugs and, of course, it completely modified my lifestyle since I didn't choose to remain a spectator. I chose to participate in all of those experiences as did everyone else with any creative imagination or curiosity. So my lifestyle, values, and practice have modified quite a bit in the period between then and now."

Today Tony Serra is known as one of the city's best counter-culture lawyers.

"At present I live communally with a lot of people—I guess you could best describe them as quasi-artistic musicians—and we share things; it's a nonmaterialistic way of life. I think all the things I own are worth around five hundred dollars.

"And I represent chiefly long-haired people who are active in whatever you want to call the cultural ramifications of the hip subculture or who are involved in the dissemination of drugs. I have many personal friends who are highly intelligent, educated, sophisticated people who do sell drugs as a parttime thing to survive and pursue art activities or activities that actually benefit our society. Then, the other level of peers or friends I represent are those who are actively involved in revolutionary activity. The two are coextensive here in the Bay Area. You've got long-haired people, hip subculture people involved in revolutionary acts, and then you've got those committed to the earlier view of the sixties which was the peace/love/brotherhood attitude.

"As an attorney and as a person living here you're always involved in both of those perspectives. You don't find that they conflict too much. Oh, I guess they do theoretically or conceptually, but while you're living it, it flows pretty evenly.

"So, in the last five or six years I've come out of a straight criminal defense position to what I guess you'd call a subculture lawyer with both an hallucinogenic and a revolutionary orientation. I practiced alone until 1971, then I went into partnership with Steve Perelson who is excellent in draft work, which I don't do. A little later Dale Metcalf joined us. Dale and I mainly do state court crimes, and Steve does the federal. His main emphasis is on draft work although he does a lot of our heavy dope smuggling cases. He's keeping a lot of people away from Vietnam and out of the service, which we see as a real social contribution.

"We don't work on any kind of monetary consideration. We just do what we can and if people have money we might take a little and if they don't we don't care. We just have to be sure the office pays for itself, but beyond that we live very humbly and consider ourselves privileged just to be able to help."

Their offices are in an old, charming warehouse section of San Francisco close to North Beach. They are on the third floor of a large walk-up building in a spacious, partially paneled office replete with wall-to-wall carpeting, head paraphernalia, antiques, and wall hangings.

"There are five attorneys working out of this office so it's not as expensive as it looks. Steve, Dale, and I work together and just share space with the others. It doesn't cost much that way.

"I handle hundreds of cases. The percentage of dope cases I have is in direct proportion to the percentage of dope cases there are in the criminal courts here—about 50 percent dope or dope-related. On dope cases I attempt to charge heavy international smugglers and heavy dealers cause they're making money. For the volume we do and for our reputation we probably charge less than most lawyers in the area. If we crack a grand a month it keeps the office going. I've only had one guy in five years go to the state penitentiary and that was his second offense while he was on probation for the first. I've had people do county jail time for heavy sales, but we, that is the judiciary and the legal community here in the Bay Area counties, with the exception of San Mateo county, have a more liberal attitude because things are changing so fast and dope is so prevalent.

"If you went into the houses of all the people around here and checked for dope, you'd probably find it in 75 percent of the houses of people under twenty-five. So now the police don't usually bother going after the possessors like they did in the early days of the Haight. Now all their energy is in going after the heavy dealers."

The other 50 percent of Tony's work falls about evenly into two categories. The first 25 percent is political cases, mainly coming out of Berkeley and San Francisco demonstrations. According to Doran Weinberg, head of the San Francisco Guild office, after a large political bust Tony will call the Guild office and tell them that he's willing to take ten or fifteen cases, a large number for an individual practitioner. Tony does all of these cases for no charge. The other 25 percent of his work is spent defending traditional criminals, those accused of crimes ranging from burglary to murder.

"I believe in doing this, too. I'm not so reform-oriented that I would discount these people. I work more or less from the premise that no one is guilty of anything. Either we're all guilty or we're all innocent. And no one should ever go to jail. There should be no concept of jail."

Tony also feels that the whole concept of the court system might be antiquated. "If you view radical people as an evolving social phenomenon, then the judiciary is one of the impediments to the flowering of that phenomenon."

However, he doesn't think that you can generalize about the people who compose the judicial system.

"Here in the Bay Area there are some fairly intelligent, liberated, humanistic types. There are a lot of judges I dig here who are trying to do as much as they can in their particular form just as I'm trying to do as much as I can in my form and a poet is trying to do as much as he can in his. I don't like to categorize or generalize because I think when you get down to it everyone is basically good. Everyone has the germ of striving, beauty, intelligence, but some people get involved in social forms that are hangovers from another era when social survival was predicated on different types of adaptive mechanisms.

Although he functions as an attorney, Tony possesses some rather harsh opinions on lawyers in general.

"I think lawyers, both civil and criminal, are cowards. The lawyer's position is a very chickenshit position since a lawyer is always getting off behind some other cat's act of courage, always playing mind fuck. It's always your client who is ultimately going to jail. Lawyers have always enjoyed all of the social benefits, prestige, wealth, and favor, and it's because they are highly tutored whore-pimp types. They stand behind other people's bravery and other people's martyrdoms. I particularly denounce that kind of attorney, and they exist in the radical world, too. It's so easy to be safe that way and take the glory and the credit and come out the semantic hero and go out to eat a big dinner when it's all over. While the cat there, he's for real, he's going to jail or taking his bumps. I don't believe in that.

"Lawyers should be out in front, getting arrested, going to jail, participating actively in the revolution, even as leaders if they have that kind of calling. They shouldn't be sucking off the side as they traditionally do. I think there is something wrong with everyone who becomes a lawyer. There's some paranoia, some cowardice, some lack of courage, or self-identification, some flaw in a person's constitution that makes him become a lawyer.

"At this particular point I'm doing a lawyer's job. If it gets heavier then I'll do a heavier thing. I consider myself a revolutionary. I'm not throwing bombs right now but there might come a time, and it might be in the seventies when you have to decide and throw bombs and I would do that.

"I don't now belong to any groups at all because I've never been concerned with organized types of mentalities, and I don't get along in that context. I relate to heavy movement people beautifully on an ideological level, but I don't on a personality level. They're uptight, tense, rigid—at least when I see them socially in their mythological role—and in the Bay Area there are just too many people who are open and loving and right now I'd prefer to associate my private life with those people."

Tony Serra has, however, taken some steps for upsetting the powers that currently are. Early in 1971 he announced his candidacy for mayor of San Francisco on the Platypus party platform. The Platypus party is devoted to "Renaissance Now!" and their major interest is in making San Francisco streets safe for dancing.

"This is the political dimension here in San Francisco, and I just found myself in a position to run because I'm qualified by having the establishment pedigree."

Although Tony only received a minute percentage of the vote, he does not feel that the whole thing should be taken lightly.

"We never thought there was a chance of winning. It was the mouse that roared. But what we were trying to do was to amplify a certain ideology so it really embraces hip subcultural values and political values. It was just one more voice getting up and saying the same old things, perhaps helping some of these things to be realized in five years or a decade rather than never.

"You know, political parties could say, 'None of our people are going to be drafted. We're going to provide real sanctuary here.' And if U.S. marshals came in they could have a confrontation that would have ramifications all over the world. It's unlikely that that would happen, but that was one of the values that we wanted to bring out: that war must end.

"Another thing we said was that the whole victimless crime area does not belong in the courts. The third large area we emphasized was the ecological one. If the cities don't convert into parks, then we won't have cities anymore. Most of them are dead now.

"Another thing we wanted to say is that you really don't have to pay taxes. They could be eliminated if war were eliminated.

Tax has always been the relationship between the captor and the captive, and we're still the captives both economically and sociologically.

"I think the early seventies will continue to be one further attempt at modifying the values and repressive features of American society by peaceful means, political means, voting, changing laws, demonstrations. I think with the vote being lowered to eighteen, a lot of people will focus on things like the Berkeley elections last year or our party and its platform. Alongside that you'll have revolutionary symbols—bombs, killings—but it won't really be strong. It won't reflect the majority of the people.

"But, if the early seventies don't succeed in changing things peacefully then, by the midseventies, there might be widespread terror and revolution and large acts of violence that reflect more than just a courageous minority.

"I guess I'm optimistic that the latter doesn't have to happen because I see so many good people in the Bay Area, people who are genuine about fulfilling the alternative lifestyle which doesn't depend on the establishment. And I think they are our greatest prospect for acquiring the social changes that we need to live humanly.

"They're not into bombing or revolution. They're just into saying 'I don't want anything to do with that way of life.' They're not into the game-playing that is going on in the political arena. They're just into going out very determinedly to live their own lives outside of the context of 'normal' society. It is selfish I guess, but if a lot of people do it, it's the way things will go.

"You can't do everything. You can't just attack without having some new way of life to offer. You can't just direct everything at destruction. They'll be more repression after a revolution than before. It's always been that way.

"But if you look at the Bay Area you can see both the vision and mobility of the political people and the lifestyle of these other people which is the political vision fulfilled. It's good always to dangle that vision fulfilled in front of you. You can't just blindly postulate a utopia. You've always got to experiment with a utopia, and that experimentation is going on here.

"You can't just hope that after the mechanism of oppression is destroyed, flowers are going to grow automatically. It doesn't happen that way. In a way it's more important to establish some kind of experimental, futuristic society than it is to destroy the old. And that is happening here and it charges me with optimism."

Because the Bay Area is the Bay Area, and because of the current ambiance that Serra mentioned, one would expect to find a host of innovative legal collectives there. While there are some, and while these are innovative, there are just not as many as one would imagine.

One firm in Berkeley—Franck, Hill, Stender, Hendon, Kelley, and Larson—did function collectively for a year as the Telegraph Avenue Collective. However, political differences and internal problems, not unlike those encountered by the New York Law Commune, caused innumerable changes in personnel, and, eventually, a complete disbanding of the project as such in the summer of 1971.

Some of the lawyers and workers who had left that collective earlier had done so to work on a project which, while not a collective, is very innovative. This, the Prison Law Project (PLP), began around the people in the Telegraph Avenue Collective who had been working on the Soledad Brothers case and other prison cases and problems. As they worked, they talked with a large number of prisoners about prison conditions in California. They also began to receive hundreds of letters each week from inmates. It soon became clear to them that a fulltime effort was needed to bring about change in the California prisons, to stimulate reform efforts by other groups, and to provide a model for prison reform work. The people working on the Prison Law Project attempted to get outside funding for their work. Beginning in April 1971 they received grants from several foundations and, after adding some people, became an entity separate from the Telegraph Avenue Collective.

The Project focuses on providing legal services, social services, public education, and community organizing around the conditions in California prisons. By September 1971, the members of the Project included five lawyers, six legal workers, including administrative, secretarial, press and public education, writing and research workers, and a number of cooperating attorneys who, though not on the staff of the Project, work closely with it.

Fay Stender, one of the Project's attorneys said, "Lawyers and community groups are working elsewhere to change the conditions in the prisons, but this is the first attempt to put together legal and sociological services in a mixed-media form.

"This project was formed out of necessity. We will be giving inmates a voice. They think now that they'll be murdered if they speak up about the prison conditions, but, even though they think that, it doesn't stop them from speaking up. There is no one that prisoners trust right now so an important function we perform is to show how prisoners are when they have found some people that they can trust. We feel that there is some first-rate political thinking going on right now in the prisons, but there is also an unbelievable amount of very serious oppression. For instance, a prison can torture a man for ten years, but then if he attacks a guard it is his fault, and not the fault of the conditions he has been forced to be in.

"Until we began, the prisons completely controlled the propaganda that came out about them. We hope that by having a group of lawyers and legal workers who have seen what the conditions really are we can counter that propaganda."

In this project, legal workers are considered as equally valuable members of the project, and do receive equal pay. However, although it was originally conceived of as a collective, it never operated as such. An executive committee, after consulting with the whole membership, makes the decisions.

"Speaking personally," said Stender, "I do not think that a process-oriented organization, such as a collective, turns out as much work product as a more traditionally organized operation. I believe in equal pay, which we have, but not in equal decision-making, not because of the status of the people, but because of the number of people and because of political differences. So many people today want to engage in dialectical process and decision-making instead of producing work. Those people should be in living communes and other organizations where they agree that the priority is the process. My own priority is prison work, and I don't think a collective gets out as much work. Others disagree with me."

A group that probably would disagree, at least in part, is the Community Law Firm (CLF) in San Francisco's Mission district. This collective, which began around the same time as the Telegraph Avenue one, is still functioning and has a good prognosis for the future because it is community-oriented within a defined community, and because its members hope to become part of a multiservice collective that would provide health care, legal care, social workers, translators, and cooperatives within the next few years. The firm began as the result of the work of two young lawyers—Paul Harris and Stan Zaks—who have been friends from junior high school on through their days at law school (Columbia for Zaks and Boalt for Harris) until the present. They also both spent summers working for Black civil rights lawyer C. B. King—Zaks in 1965 and Harris in 1968.

"We started discussing setting up a community law firm when we were both about a year into law school," Zaks said. "That was the height of the movement, and we were both enmeshed in it. We knew then that we were actually going to attempt this, a community law firm in the sense that we live in the community, set up our office there, and relate primarily, but not exclusively, to that community. Paul had a back operation, so it took him five years before he finished law school, but, while he was still in, about three years ago, we started meeting intensively with students from his class at Boalt, and we talked about the idea a lot. When people got out of law school, the geographical and financial questions became prime, and people started breaking off from the group. When Paul graduated, he took a one-year clerkship with a U.S. district court judge. In the meantime, I had worked as a Legal Services attorney and then spent a year with a Lawyers Guild general practice firm. In February 1970, I opened a small office in the Mission district with one parttime volunteer, and, then in September, Paul joined me and we moved to our present storefront office, across the street from Mission High School."

"We spent a lot of time trying to figure out what kind of community to relate to," Harris said, "and we had a lot of different criteria, such as our and our spouses' races, our special skills, the special needs of the community, our existing contacts with people in the community, the need for basic legal skills, the legal services, both private and institutional, that were already present, existing social services, police harassment, the potential for racial alliances, functioning political groups, and the level of political activity. We decided on the Mission district because it is a mixed Latino, white working-class, Native American, and hippie community. In setting up the collective, we then looked for legal workers and other lawyers who are from one or another of the groups represented in the community."

At the time of writing the firm had two legal workers, Bernadette Aguilar, who grew up in the Mission and had no previous legal training, and Rickey Jacobs, who had some legal-secretarial experience. They have also had ten to twelve law students who have worked in the office at various times. During the summers they have a fulltime, well-integrated staff of six students. High school students, funded by community groups, also work in the office, training to be community legal workers. They also have volunteers who come in to work on specific projects, including a handful of lawyers from traditional business firms who donate their time and their resources. After an excellent experience with Ronald Schiffman, an attorney who now has his own practice, the firm intends to try to continue to run a six-month apprentice program for new attorneys.

Although the two lawyers and two legal workers form the core of the office, the many other persons who relate to it make it possible for the CLF to do a large volume of work with high quality, and to serve as a model of the community law office idea to others.

"When I first came in here," Zaks said, "I was surprised how quickly I was able to build up trust with groups in the community. We had been hesitant about coming into a community we had not been part of before, but the first thing we found was that there was such a need to work with community groups that we were accepted right away and had more work in terms of our house counsel role than we could handle. And we found that the racial question was more in our minds than in the minds of the groups that we worked with."

The firm's work is separated into three categories: (1) house counsel for community groups, (2) criminal cases arising out of police brutality and harassment, and (3) general practice.

In their house counsel role, they have assisted Los Siete de La Raza with general legal problems and some criminal cases; La Raza Legal Defense Union, a community defense organization, with organizational, educational, and legal support; Mission People's Health Center, a free clinic, with problems in setting up and with legal complications that arise. The firm has also taken on some cases from other community groups, and has handled a lot of criminal cases, including some which they have been able to politicize. They have also worked with students from Mission High School, and with an insurgent labor group.

"The political consciousness in this area is rapidly growing so there is a need for movement attorneys. However, except for the Los Siete case, there has been no glamour in it yet, so it was hard for these groups to get other attorneys," said Harris.

"We're hoping that these community groups will continue to

grow and move so that they can dictate some of the changes that will be made in the community; for instance, stopping bad model city planning and police harassment. But, until they are strong enough to regulate their own community, we are going to have continual legal things going on. We've been turning down big cases—involvement in things like the Los Siete retrial and the Soledad case—because there are attorneys who will do those so we are trying to do these other things," Zaks said.

"Our main stress has been and will continue to be the house counsel role and the criminal cases that arise out of it. That accounts for 70 percent of our time. The other 30 percent we spend on regular cases which we make money on. Ninety percent of the people in those cases are community people that the groups we work for have brought to us, but they are paying cases," said Harris. "A lot of these cases have been personal injury, which is helpful in building up trust in the community, and many of the others have been draft cases. During our first six months of operation both of our wives were working, so we went without taking salary, but then salaries became necessary although, if we ever make enough money that it becomes an issue, we intend to limit them. We keep our overhead low, and have a makeshift library and furnishings given to us by community groups, and a monetarily successful Guild firm.

"While we are lawyers, we realize that the law works to maintain the status quo and to preserve the system. But we feel that we do have a bourgeois democracy at this time of history so that we can use the courts to get some victories. Until that democracy is past, we feel that if you have legal talent and can stand being a lawyer that it is one way to help the movement. We are either helping people who are changing things to stay out of trouble or creating certain conditions where organizing is allowed. We feel that that is all a lawyer can do. We don't put our trust in test cases and things of that sort because we know that the power is not in the Constitution, and that they take an inordinate amount of research and preparation. When a case like that comes up, we try to channel it to Legal Services, CRLA, or friends in the Reggie program.

"In our practice here, we have also found that many legal problems can be handled without extended paper work and often without court involvement, so we are developing our skills at informal pressure and negotiation. We've also recognized that our legal training has taught us to look only for legal solutions to power struggles. Having seen this, we have tried to overcome our tendencies to depoliticize issues, and we have tried to be aware of the political positions of the groups we work with and to avoid confusing these positions by the use of the legal process. We have also seen the tendency of people to depend on lawyers, and we fight that since we feel that lawyers should not lead their clients' organizing efforts. We also try to give the people some victories in court so they'll lose their fear of the established power and recognize their own power. However, we do try to avoid cases that might turn out to be 'liberal traps' or useless."

"We also realize," Zaks said, "that this whole thing of functioning as a radical lawyer is filled with contradictions. Lawyers are people who can manipulate the system. When you become radical, the system fights you. We have had to learn how to be able to survive and be able to go to the judge and insist on the rights of a client and at the same time know that it is an oppressive system, and that someday soon it is all going to come down."

"We feel," Harris said, "that, as radical lawyers, we should put our ultimate trust in the political power of the people, while remembering that we, as lawyers, have tools to help develop that power. We also feel that, as radical human beings, we should end the schizophrenia caused by our Communist ideals and our capitalist existence. That is why we have chosen the form of a community, collective law firm.

"We feel that the law is society's sophisticated means of restricting people and repressing revolution. But, as long as this society maintains its capitalist-democratic approach, we feel the lawyer has the power to free people and further the revolution. We feel that when the law is replaced by the hangman, there will be sufficient time to throw away the law books and pick up the appropriate tools."

Perhaps the most unique legal collective in the Bay Area is not a collective at all. It is a group composed of the lawyers, legal workers, and political people who center their work around the activities of the Bay Area Regional Office of the National Lawyer's Guild. These young people have taken the same Guild chapter that some of the older members had thought about abandoning less than a decade ago and, with their fresh ideas, have turned it into the most vital Guild chapter in the country, and one that definitely works in a collective way.

At the Guild's 1968 Santa Monica convention, a drive, spearheaded by the younger Guild members, to make the Guild a regional as well as national organization won. The mass defense office concept which was then only functioning in New York City spread, and regional offices were opened in San Francisco and Los Angeles. Later, offices were opened in Detroit, Chicago, Philadelphia, Washington, D.C., Seattle, Boston, Milwaukee, and Denver.

The Bay Area office did not open until the beginning of 1969, six months after the decision to open one had been made. That time was necessary to organize both people and ideas. When the office opened, the San Francisco State strike—which centered around the appointment of S. J. Hayakawa and the absence of ethnic studies at the school—was in full swing. The Guild office related totally to that strike and to the cases of the seven hundred-plus people who had been arrested as the result of the strike.

About four hundred and fifty of those cases were on unlawful assembly charges that came out of mass busts, but the other two hundred and fifty cases were on a variety of charges, and a good number of them were felonies. The office was inundated.

It took the people working there about six months before they could dig themselves out to the point where they could consider doing other work than that of mass defense. At that time, Peter Haberfeld, who had opened the office, left, and was replaced by Doron Weinberg, who along with Jennie Rhine, Sharon Gold, Janet Small, Susan Matross, and Carol Grossman, form the working core of the office. In addition, about fifteen other attorneys and legal workers consistently give significant time. General membership in the chapter numbers around four hundred.

"We decided after the San Francisco State cases that the case-to-case legal needs of the movement in the Bay Area were relatively secure and that the ongoing needs of the movement and the community were the things we should address ourselves to. We decided that we should concentrate on educating the community about the legal system, and educating lawyers about how they could best perform their own work in a nonoppressive manner. The first thing we did was concentrate on dissemination of information. We called a conference on high school law in December of 1969 as our first act of combining both external education and internal organizing. This was followed by a conference on landlord-tenant law in January of 1970, one on the handling of political, criminal trials in April and one on the omnibus crime bill in January 1971," said Weinberg.

"We also got into demonstrations for a while. We called the second demonstration of lawyers in the history of this country in October of 1969. The first one had been in New York City on May Day of that year. Our demonstration, in which both political and reform demands were made, was to be against the law as an instrument of repression. Then, the conspiracy trial began in Chicago and we decided to make the demonstration also against that. Four hundred lawyers and law students came, and out of that demonstration groups formed to talk about what radical lawyers should do. This was really the beginning of the radical law community here as it is now.

"We called another demonstration when the verdict for the

Chicago trial came in in February 1970, and three thousand people came to that one.

"And we expressed our opposition to the traditional conception of lawyership by passing out red armbands at the bar admission ceremony, and having people take their oath with clenched fist.

"We are now into a variety of things," Rhine continued. "Most political people in the Bay Area call here if they need a lawyer, so we have set up an on-call system. We have a lawyer on each side of the Bay on call twenty-four hours a day. We have enough lawyers participating so that each one is only on call one day each month. We respond to calls that way from thirty to forty movement groups in the area. We usually do these cases free.

"We also teach a lot about law to lay people. We have our own People's Law School, in connection with several other movement groups, where we give free courses on things like labor law, military law, street survival, women and the law, prison law, immigration law, consumer law, juvenile law, welfare law, landlord-tenant law, and legal research. That began in September 1971, and we hope to give series of classes three times a year. Prior to that time we had coordinated classes on the law at San Francisco State, *Venceremos* University, and the Berkeley Center for Participatory Education, and we still continue to do that."

"We also put out a lot of information for people. We distribute 'street sheets' on various subjects. These tell people how to deal with the law and the police in a wide variety of legal or harassment situations. We've also put out, through *Ramparts* magazine, a *People's Law Book*. And we bring out our paper, *Conspiracy*, each month.

"We also keep ourselves available for people to set up legal defense before demonstrations, and then we follow up afterward. We farm out the actual handling of the cases, probably two-thirds of it to Guild lawyers and one-third to lawyers who cooperate but are not members of the Guild."

"We've also helped set up legal-political collectives of people
who meet once a week to discuss the direction of our work and
their work and to politically educate themselves," Weinberg
added, "and we have a Guild women's caucus that also meets
weekly. Then we have our 'Gracious Living' series which is kind
of a lecture series where people around the Guild get together for
informal discussions of topics like labor law or legal workers or
the movement in the thirties. And the office is open every Friday
for lunch, and a lot of people come here to rap then."

The scope of these activities has caused some dissension within
the Guild chapter. Some older members of the Guild feel that the
Guild should be a legal organization with political overtones
rather than a political organization with legal overtones. With the
admission of legal workers to the Guild during the 1971 Boulder
convention, however, it appears that the younger members have
won their point and that the office's political activities will continue to expand.

Part of the reason that this regional office is so active is that
most of the people who form its core are together a great deal of
the time. While many of them have jobs outside of the Guild
office—several of them have or have had Reggies (Reginald
Heber Smith fellowships) that allow them wide latitude in doing
OEO work and other work—most of them live together in one of
two legal communal houses in Berkeley. Most of the lawyers in
this group also come from surprisingly similar backgrounds. They
were "red diaper" babies whose parents had been active in the
labor movement during the thirties and forties. They did well in
school but felt alienated from their school work. They were active in radical activities during the early sixties, and a good number of them went down South in the early civil rights period.
They decided to become lawyers because that seemed a good way
to keep active in the social arena, no matter what the state of the
movement was. They did well in law school, but found that experience even less meaningful than the rest of their education.
Many of them received fellowships of one sort or another and,

with the freedom that these fellowships gave, were able to use their time to integrate their legal knowledge and political beliefs.

They had been active in Guild chapters at their schools, and so when they all ended up in the same locality, they were drawn together around the workings of the Guild, found each other, and were able to develop their ideas even more. None of them have any faith in the court system. All of them have doubts about the validity of their roles as lawyers.

"I find that the house counsel role is the only lawyer role that is not alienating. A lot of lawyers, even movement ones, are people who will sell their services to anyone who asks. I don't conceive of myself that way. I'm not neutral. I have political goals, and I also have legal skills which is the same as having any other skill and using it politically. I'm an activist first and a lawyer second," said one of the attorneys connected with the office.

"When I was a Reggie I worked as much as I could with organizations to build political power by using legal skills. Unless lawyers and legal workers do this, a lot of what they do is counterproductive. I'd work with ten or twelve organizations at any given time, and I would be frustrated when I had to work on an individual case," said another.

"Aside from test case reform I think very little of Legal Services. It's a Band-Aid approach and of very little benefit. I used to have a hell of a time explaining to my clients that I'd done a good job for them when I got them a thirty-day delay before they were going to be evicted. The aim of the programs is cooption. Really there are very few radical lawyers in the program. Most people who are radical either are isolated or leave," commented a third.

"I feel that most lawyers who are radicals, whether they're into Legal Services or something else, are caught in the middle of tremendous contradictions, both personal and political. Everyone I know goes through periodic reassessments of the value of what they are doing. Everyone is always tempted to quit law and a lot do. I'm working in the midst of the legal system which I find is the antithesis of anything I find useful in human relationships. It is artificial and contrived, and it is loaded against anyone who wants to make changes. You're dealing with people who are racist and chauvinistic all of the time. The only thing that makes it worthwhile to me at all is that somewhere on the other side I'm developing relationships that are satisfying to me, personally, and I'm helping to tear the system down. I feel there is very little worth preserving. The way I relate to the court system is to try to figure out how to destroy it before it destroys me, which I'm not sure I'm winning on."

"That's how we feel personally, which is what tears us apart inside a lot. But the other side of the coin is that we don't have any choice. The movement is so caught up in the cutting edge of fascism, a good part of which is the legal system, that we have to deal with it. It's important to humanize oneself while doing it, to keep involved in nonlegal things and to watch what you're doing. I think more and more we'll be forced to be criminal lawyers. I don't know if civil law is still important at all.

"Some of us went on this legal trip to Cuba, and we found out a lot about lawyers there. Before 1959 some lawyers there were shot for defending some people, and lawyers were as crucial a part of that revolution as anything that happened, partly because Castro was a lawyer and partly because, when a system has reached the level of fascism that that one had, criminal defense is considered the key to some intermediary goals.

"It is important here now to distinguish between a lawyer who contributes his legal skills to the movement and a movement person who contributes the skill of being a lawyer. You can tell by dedication, by lifestyle, by whether a person gets outside of him- or herself. I never had a real sense of this before I went to Cuba. It's very difficult for us to be revolutionaries, living in the belly of the monster with all the pressures and temptations and escape mechanisms around us. For us to really believe so much in something outside of ourselves that we give our lives for it or whatever, well, sometimes I don't think any of us are revolutionary yet."

"Working in the court system is essential now. We go when we have to and that's going to be the way it is until we have enough strength growing out of the barrel of a gun, or wherever it's going to grow out of, to ignore that system. We don't have that strength now, and until we do the court system is going to be there."

"I think it is difficult to be revolutionary in any context in this country right now. The contradictions for lawyers are tremendous but I see an absolute political need for them. I'd hesitate to say that I'm a dedicated revolutionary ready to give up my life for the cause although that is what I'd like to be someday. I don't think many people are that now but I know a lot of lawyers who are trying. It's a very dynamic process. A lot of people are trying to do what they think is right which, in the long run, is going to have to turn them into revolutionaries because that is the only way to respond to this system."

"It's inevitable as you see more of the contradictions in life here. But I see validity in it not happening too quickly. I see a lot of people today who seem to have split from a middle-class family and become radical over the weekend. But then they're confronted by so many contradictions, by a volatile life that is difficult to survive in, that they are liable to end up in the mountains because they can't cope with what they see. That can happen to lawyers as well as anybody else."

Sometimes slowly, and sometimes more quickly than they would choose, the people around the Bay Area regional office of the Guild are learning, through experimentation, to cope with the many contradictions that they see in the system at large, the legal system, and the roles they happen to have to play in it. Their conclusions, their methods of coping, are very likely to point the way to the future of the people's law movement.

13

The South

Throughout the history of the United States, the South has been the outside part of the country, perhaps the true frontier. Even today it is still a largely agrarian, nonindustrial area, with a psychology and sociology to match.

To those who live outside of the South it is an area of stereotypes, largely negative. All of these somewhat stereotyped ideas came to the fore in the 1950s and 1960s when the country turned its attention to the South and liberal white missionaries marched there by the thousands to help get freedom and justice for their poor Black brothers and sisters.

In the beginning of the southern civil rights movement, this help from northerners was needed. Someone had to give southern Blacks the numbers and power necessary for them to begin breaking down the white power structure in the South. But, in the view of many southerners, northerners did not know when to pull out and let southern Blacks, and those southern whites who had become involved solve their own problems.

While this pulling out was not accomplished in many areas of social concern and policy, it was, to some extent, within the legal left. As has been noted, the southern civil rights movement gave much of the impetus to the people's law movement today. However, between the middle and final years of the sixties, most of the individuals and organizations who had been baptized into people's law in the South turned their efforts to the people's movements that were then developing in other parts of the country. While they still maintained their ties with the South, and while many organizations kept offices there, the direction of the southern legal movement was largely turned over to southern lawyers. The ACLU, the Center for Constitutional Rights, the Lawyer's Constitutional Defense Committee, LSCRRC, the Inc. Fund, all have representatives working in the South, either as administrators or cooperating attorneys, and most of these people are southerners either by birth or choice.

The Guild, however, while it does have members in the South, does not have a regional office there. In its stead is a strictly southern organization of radical lawyers called the Southern Legal Action Movement (SLAM).

Jack Drake, who is now with the firm of Drake, Knowles & Still in Tuscaloosa, Alabama, was one of the founders of the organization.

"In late 1968 and early 1969, Buddy Tieger, who works with the Haymarket Coffee House in Fort Bragg, North Carolina, and Alex Hurder, who had dropped out of law school and was working off his conscientious objector service, traveled through the South talking to law students and the few radical lawyers that existed about the need for some kind of organization, or at least the need to get together and talk. They had some very good response, and so then we had a meeting here in Tuscaloosa in the early spring of 1969 at which we did form.

"A lot of us who helped to form SLAM had been associated with the Southern Student Organizing Committee (SSOC) which was the white southern response to SNCC, and a lot of us had some strong southern nationalistic feelings which we still have, although we are more civilized about them than we used to be. We had a big summer institute in the summer of 1969 and about two hundred people came to that in North Carolina, and the organization really got off the ground after that."

SLAM now has about two hundred members and a mailing list of about twelve hundred. About half of the membership are lawyers, and the rest are legal workers, law students, and people interested in the legal problems of the South. According to its statement of purpose, the organization is "working to build ties among lawyers and other people working with the law who are fighting for human rights and human dignity; working to recruit from the southern bar attorneys who will commit themselves to preserve and strengthen movement groups and lawyers and aid them in their program; working to share knowledge in the fields of law which are crucial to the struggles of the people in the South in order to ensure a high level of competence among lawyers engaged in their defense; working to interpret the legal system to people who are subject to it, and to develop in nonlawyers an awareness of the legal principles that affect them."

SLAM brings out a bimonthly newspaper and sponsors at least two conferences for its members each year. Most importantly it provides a communications link for the movement-oriented lawyers in the South who are spread over a large geographical area.

"The Guild would find it very difficult to organize in the South now," Drake said, "because it is built around the chapter concept and their programs are keyed for that. We don't have any concentration of lawyers and legal workers in the South in any one place so it would be impossible to have a chapter except maybe in New Orleans and Atlanta. I would suspect that, if the Guild continues to be a viable, effective organization, eventually SLAM will wither away and the Guild will come into the South real strong with all of our help. Right now, although we are close to the Guild and do have a set number of people on their executive board, we feel that we have to have a separate organization because of the different conditions, the South's particular history and myths."

The location of SLAM's headquarters has changed each year

depending on the location of the staff person or people who are responsible for the newspaper and for organizing efforts. Following the 1971 summer conference where Cheryl Knowles was chosen as the staff person, the headquarters was moved from Atlanta, where Ginny Boult, the previous year's staff person lived, to Tuscaloosa where Cheryl lives and where, with a firm of three movement-oriented lawyers and one legal worker, there is the largest concentration of radical lawyers in the South. SLAM now has office space in the same large house that houses the Drake, Knowles & Still firm, on a tree-lined main street just a few blocks from the University of Alabama. Since there are relatively few movement law offices in the South it would not be fair to say that the Drake, Knowles & Still one is typical, but it is a viable model of how movement lawyers can survive in the South, and the personal and political histories of the three lawyers in the firm are, to some extent, representative.

Jack Drake was born in Gardendale, a suburb of Birmingham, and he lived there until he started college at the University of Alabama in Tuscaloosa in 1963. His father was a machinist, and his mother a secretary.

"In high school I was president of the student body, and I was active in campus and state politics until around 1966, but I wasn't ever active in the civil rights movement. I was scared because people were getting killed. When the Selma march was going on, I read about it and heard about it, but I was really too scared to go. I went to some meetings where people talked about going to it, but the kinds of white people who were involved in the civil rights movement at that time were really fucked-up people. I'm sure there were a lot of good people, both northerners and southerners involved in it, but it just happened that those confused ones were the ones I met. They were people who had some incredible mental problems. I remember going to one meeting and there was an obnoxious white guy from the Southern Christian Leadership Conference (SCLC) at it, and they told us there that SCLC wanted some white people to go to Selma and

get killed. They just told us that. Hell, I didn't want to go to
Selma and get killed. There were hardly any white southerners involved in the movement at that time. I think that they felt that
the northern whites who came had no appreciation for the South
and just hated it, and, consequently, hated them.

"I got involved in the antiwar movement around 1967, and, of
course, that was the time, too, that the drug culture was coming
South and getting strong and that had an effect on me, too. I was
in law school then, because at that time you could go after three
years of college, without a bachelor's degree, and I'd done that.
We didn't have any real big things going on here when I was still
in school. We had some marches and vigils where we would just
stand on the steps of the union building every Friday for fifteen
minutes and protest the war. We started out with about twenty
people doing that, and then it grew until sometimes we would
have as many as two hundred. But even something as mild as that
caused an incredible uproar back there in 1967 and 1968. I think
it was around that time, with the antiwar movement and the drug
culture, that southern whites began to come into what is generally
called the movement.

"When I finished law school in 1969, I had to have a job and
the Selma Project was looking for a lawyer. They wanted to hire
Ralph Knowles, but he was having draft problems and I wasn't,
and so they hired me."

The Selma Project was set up by the National Council of
Churches following the Selma March when the Council decided
that it wanted to have a person permanently located in the "Black
Belt" of the South to work with the poor people there. The person they chose to head the Project was Francis Walter, a white
Alabaman Episcopal priest, who began work, predominantly on
economic projects, around 1965. Since then, the Project has
grown to the point that it now employs Mr. Walter; a Black lay
advocate in Pickens County, Alabama; a Black man in Greene
County, Alabama, who generally advises the Greene County
government, which has been taken over by Blacks in the past

four years; a white woman who is working on setting up day care centers; and two lawyers, Drake and Knowles, who are on retainer to the Project. The Project is now funded by small foundations and individual contributions. The Project will handle the legal problems of any poor person, Black or white, who lives within the "Black Belt."

"I was working as house counsel for the Project," said Drake, "and then Ralph came in in the same role, and we decided to form a partnership and it became apparent that we would have to build our own practice. Now we are retained by them and handle many cases for them—about one hundred at any one time. Between that and our own practice we are probably handling three hundred cases overall now. We take every kind of case you can think of—criminal, affirmative litigation, a lot of work with the students here. There are certain counties where we take any case that arises for the Project, and, if their lay advocate brings in any kind of case, even a divorce, we take it because it makes him a better leader. We also take any cases that the GI and WAC organizers bring in from Fort McClellan and the Anniston area, and we also handle a lot of women's liberation litigation.

"If you're a movement lawyer in the South, you work with everybody. I consider the South to be South Carolina, Georgia, Alabama, Mississippi, Louisiana. Florida, Texas, and Tennessee ain't in the South, and I'm not sure North Carolina is either, or Atlanta. I consider the South to be those places that are more immune to northern financial control, and where the impact of a rising middle class is not that visible yet. There are maybe fifteen or twenty million people living in what I consider the South, and a lot of them are still in rural areas. Because of these factors, the kind of work we do is every kind you can do in the movement. Up North you wouldn't find that. Movement lawyers there are more specialized. We don't have that in the South because there are so few of us, and because people do get along better down here.

"I think people actually do get along better here. I think there is more of a history of racial integration for one thing. Not in any formal way. There always were prohibitions against Black people doing certain things like going in certain restaurants. But there always has been a lot of interaction between the races here, maybe integration is the wrong word. People knew each other and lived together. There weren't any ghettos. For example, the housing patterns are spotted in Birmingham, with Black enclaves throughout the city. I think there is just a history of a lot better relations among everybody. And the class situation is as stratified as it is in the North, but even here I think there is more interaction among the classes and not as much overt class discrimination.

"I think that is because the South is still a largely rural place and rural people can't afford to be mad at each other because they have to live with each other every day. While I think it was necessary that Black people achieved the kind of liberation they achieved through the southern civil rights movement, I think, looking back on it, that it was a complete mistake strategically in terms of the goals that were achieved. We work with poor whites now, and we ask them why they didn't support Black people when they were marching for the right to vote. One guy simply said, 'There wasn't anything in it for me.' I think it might have been different if Black people were marching for a minimum wage or health care. I understand that their problems were more immediate, that you can't talk about a minimum wage if you are unemployed and don't have the right to vote, but the civil rights movement never attempted to unify Blacks and whites and did a damn good job of polarizing them, and I think that is to be blamed on the people who were controlling the civil rights movement, all of whom lived in New York and knew nothing about the South. And they had this whole kind of medieval idea of 'if the peasants can just get to the king and explain how bad things are he'll straighten it out.' That's the liberal idea and it doesn't work. It didn't work in the civil rights movement.

"Occasionally now a northern lawyer calls and asks us to do something but not that many come South anymore except those from the Inc. Fund and I have nothing to do with them. I wouldn't even be in the same room with some of them. They are the kind of people who have made our work very difficult because there was, around the civil rights movement, a lot of ineffective and incompetent legal work done so there is still this residual feeling among lawyers and judges in the South that civil rights lawyers are not good lawyers. We have to disprove that all the time, and that impression was given largely by northern lawyers. They controlled the civil rights movement. There wasn't any question about who was running the show, at least in my mind. Of course, there were some fine lawyers who came down here from the North. Most of them were in the Guild. But the Inc. Fund, the Lawyers Constitutional Defense Committee, and some others had some really trashy lawyers. I think Kunstler and Kinoy did good work; in fact, I think Kinoy did some of the best thinking that was done, but he always had to contend with the red-baiting of Greenberg and other people who were fighting for the headlines. Arthur didn't give a damn for the headlines.

"There is resentment in the South about the people who came down here. I feel it probably stronger than anybody. I've actually run white people out of the South, and also kept some from coming here.

"I'm a member of the national executive board of the Guild now, filling one of the SLAM seats, but I remember one summer the Guild was going to have something called the Tom Paine School of Law, and they were going to send fourteen people through the South, seeing firsthand the problems of the South and all that. They sent out a pamphlet describing all of it and it was the most incredible racist, prejudiced, and chauvinistic thing I ever read. There was stuff in it about the intense need for people to stay together and warnings that if people violated the safety rules they would be sent home immediately. There was one thing that read 'There is a redneck behind every tree.' It was really terrible. I mean there are rednecks—they are poor white people, and we see the possibility of organizing them. In fact we're now working with the Gulfcoast Pulpwood Association which is an organization of Black and white woodcutters with five thousand members in Alabama and Mississippi, and the people in it are all struggling together against this intense economic exploitation, and they are losing their racism in the process. Things like that can happen in the South, but I don't think people who come here from the North understand that. I think it is easier to identify the sources of oppression in the South. You can go into a town like Tuscaloosa which was for many years a one-mill town, a paper mill, and it is easier for people to understand how that paper mill affects their lives in this town than it would be in some big industrial area.

"Because of the way that the South is I think it is probably easier for a radical lawyer to survive here because if you do a certain kind of work then everyone is going to come to you if his problem is that. I think it is easier on a day-to-day basis to serve a lot of people and maintain your own integrity. While it used to be difficult for a white lawyer serving Blacks, it isn't now because he or she can get support from the white community that is developing around politics. It is foolish for any white lawyer to think that the Black community is ever going to sustain or support him in any way, financially, emotionally, or otherwise. By and large I would like to see Black lawyers working with Black people here, but we're twenty-five years away from that so white lawyers will have to continue to do some of the work; but now, if they are selective about where they locate, they can get support from white southerners. For an operation like this I think a college town is best.

"A lot of people here won't speak to me because of the work I do but I won't speak to them either. I don't have any aspirations that would cause me to have conflicts with those people. I don't want to be rich, I don't want to go to the country club, and I don't care if people want to talk about me or anything. I never intend to be in a position where those people could hurt me.

"I've received threats down through the years, none lately. People are scared of lawyers, and you can exploit that. Policemen are scared of lawyers; everyone is really. Take policemen, they are less scared of lawyers on equal ground like in the street where force is at a premium, but those same guys have to come into the courtroom where the tables are reversed, and you can really be vicious and really humiliate them. We just completely humiliated a narcotics cop here one time because we knew he was running around with this girl who was a narc for him and he was sleeping with her and he was married. So we just asked him, in the courtroom, if he knew her and where he had seen her. If you ever do that to somebody or ever get a policeman fired, word gets around and people don't like to see you coming. Then they begin to be real nice to you. They used not even to let me in the jail when I first started practicing law. I had to force them, but, after a while, you make them kind of respect you.

"The way to survive in a town like this if you practice in the courts all the time, is to let people get to know you and like you. Then you can reach an understanding where everyone knows how you feel and think about certain things, so it's pleasanter for people to be nice to you and you can even get to the point where people begin to help you, particularly if you're a good lawyer. People then respect your work and, if you always do a good job, they like to see you come into their court because the quality of lawyers is not particularly good anywhere. If you take your work seriously and fight for what you believe in, they then begin to look at you in a different sort of way and you get along. It's all very superficial, but you can still be effective in the courts. Lawyers from the North could practice in the South if they stayed here but I'd much rather see people from the South take the responsibility of being radical lawyers here than have people from the North come down, and I think more people here are taking that responsibility. I have no use for lawyers who leave the South and go someplace else to practice law. They are traitors.

"The lifestyle questions that come up with radical lawyers in some places are not that important to me. I tend to think that winning is more important than functioning as a lawyer in a life-style that will allow me, in a long process over the next hundred years, if I live that long, to change some institutions. I'm interested in immediate results that allow people to gain power. So what if our courts begin to function in a superficially more humane way or a more sophisticated way; so what if they took the bench away from a judge and he sat down with the people and didn't wear a robe and nobody called him 'your honor'; so what if lawyers didn't sit where they are supposed to and didn't function in as much of an elitist, professionalist way as they do now, and people still went to jail and got shot down on the street? What changes things is power, and a lawyer has got to win in order to make movements stronger.

"Generally, I don't like the legal system. I'm not sure how I would change it. I think probably what we ought to do is do away with the legal system and have a whole new way of resolving problems. You don't resolve problems through an adversary process. An adversary process really becomes most destructive in a criminal situation when you're dealing with a person who needs to be helped and not to have someone fight for his life. And, if his lawyer doesn't fight as well as the other one, he loses. None of that makes any sense. The whole adversary process should be done away with and replaced by some sort of community council or something where people could resolve most of the problems that come up. Most of the problems that go to court shouldn't go to court at all. There should be some other way of handling them. Cuban courts, as I understand it, function in a pretty effective sort of way, sort of along the way that I think things should be done. But of course you have to build up a tremendous consciousness and a tremendous revolutionary spirit among all people before you can ever have something like that be effective because it functions on the desire of everybody to have the approval of their peers. And, if people don't agree on what people's goals and the goals of the country should be, it is never going to work.

"I don't consider myself a revolutionary, but I believe in radical solutions to our problems. I don't believe an armed struggle will ever happen. If it did and if it were successful, then it would be a solution to our problems because it would cause a shift of power, but it would not be a solution I would favor because it is so disruptive over the long run. It would destroy our whole society, and I don't think the whole thing needs to be destroyed. I think that is one problem radical movements have always had in this country, not being able to identify with what is good in the country. I think there are many things we need to be building on, especially about our past and the first American revolution. Of course, when you start talking about the South then you really are talking about a whole radical history that involves great people's movements that have been written out of the history books. Nobody even knows anything about them. And you have to build on that in the South if you are ever going to be successful.

"If you start with southern history after the Reconstruction movement everybody in Alabama was attempting to recover from the type of economic exploitation that was so visible during Reconstruction. And people were starving to death, and they formed all kinds of organizations that were very radical in one part, in the populist movement of the late 1880s and 1890s. During the industrialization thing, people were killed trying to form unions in Birmingham; steel mills had their own police forces that went around and beat the hell out of people and killed them. You had the great coal strike and the great steel strike in Birmingham where you had hundreds of thousands of people involved. But nobody knows anything about it, talks about it, or tries to build on that, or tries to build on the kind of populist sentiment that still exists in every southerner, except George Wallace, and he understands it completely and appeals to that sentiment in the class that still has it, the working class. That is why he is so successful. He talks about their problems, about their money problems, and the race issue is just a little icing on the cake that goes on to make sure that he wins. But people

really follow him because of what he has to say about their economic problems and about who runs the state. That is a whole
story in and of itself.

"But there is that radical tradition in every deep South state,
and it is true of the whole country too if you want to get into the
union movement and the history of the CIO. We just don't have
any literature coming out about all that, any ideology interpreting
all that, and people just kind of jump into Marxism without any
transition. And the people who need to buy it, the working people, don't.

"As far as repression, it is greater in the South as far as Black
people go. I think Black people get killed more easily by southern
white folks. But part of that is that the whole southern culture
places such a value on violence. Violence is a way of life. I don't
know why unless it was just that the South was an untamed territory and the wild West syndrome had much more of an effect on
the South than it did on Arizona. People don't shoot each other
down in the streets in Arizona but in Anniston, Alabama, people
kill each other every day for nothing. It has the highest per capita
murder rate for any city in the United States. People just shoot.
But I think that can be overcome if people ever decide to overcome it.

"I'm optimistic about the future of the South because of the
possibility of getting whites and Blacks together on economic
issues and the possibility of seizing power quickly. The race
issue exists but it's not insurmountable, and people here really
can forget about race if they have other, more immediate problems. But the liberal kind of solutions to problems forces people
to respond in racist ways. The whole federal court thing about
closing down community schools was an example. You had both
Blacks and whites demanding that it not be done. Of course
they went ahead and did it anyway, so you had this tremendous
response from whites that appears to be racist although I'm
convinced it was not. And then you had a response that never

got any attention from Black people who wanted the same things that the whites did because 99 percent of the people in Alabama didn't want their kids bused to school. They wanted their school which was two miles down the road and which, in many instances, the people had paid for and built themselves, because there never really was enough money in the South to build public schools, and so the community used to get together, raise the money, and go build themselves a school. Then the school system and the state would pay to operate them. But those schools were closed and taken away from the people and the titles went back to the state. And I don't think that anybody who comes from a radical political perspective can say that that is right. But no one responded to that in a radical or even interpretative way.

"I'm much less optimistic about the future of the country than I am about the future of the South. I don't know if we'll ever be able to deal effectively with General Motors and the people who have the money and the power in this country. I think the South will lead the way for the rest of the country, mainly because the South is still small enough so that power can be taken over in entire areas in a very short time, like it was taken over in Greene County, just twenty miles down the road, by Blacks in just four years. You can't do that in the North."

Drake's original partner, Ralph Knowles, shares many of his views concerning the South, and the law. Knowles was born in Lumberton, North Carolina, and lived there and in several other places in North Carolina and Virginia for the first twelve years of his life.

"My father works for the Railroad Express Agency, so we moved around a lot. I went to five or six grammar schools. Finally we settled in Huntsville, Alabama, and I lived there until I came to the university here. I majored in political science, then went right on to law school. Upon graduating from that in 1969, I went to Falkville, Alabama—a small, poor white town—and taught for nine months to evade the draft. I came back in June 1970 and set up practice with Jack. We worked out of the office of the Selma Project until June of 1971.

"We decided to open a separate office instead on continuing to work out of the Selma Project for a lot of reasons. One, it is very clear that the Selma Project won't last forever, that it won't be able to sustain itself financially forever. Two, in private practice we can make the money to try to suppprt ourselves. We feel that any lawyers on the left should be able to do that and not be a drain. Three, if you're operating for a nonprofit organization out of their office and taking fee-paying cases at the same time, you get into problems with the bar. We also wanted to expand our practice and we are doing that and also doing essentially the same work with the Selma Project. We cover five or six counties in Alabama for them and also do a little work in Mississippi. We work with people connected with the Project, not for the Project itself.

"It costs us about $60,000 a year to operate. The Selma Project pays the equivalent of my and Jack's salaries and expenses, and we get the rest from fee-paying cases and work we do for the southern ACLU office. Most of the movement cases we take we consider Selma Project cases, even if they aren't, and we do those for free. For fees we do divorces cheaper than others would do them, personal injury cases, drug and draft cases, and a hodge-podge of other stuff, but not much commercial work.

"Our major objective is to be able to sustain ourselves and not be a drain on other parts of the movement, and to sustain ourselves with cases that are at least politically neutral, that aren't politically bad—those we won't do—and then to be able to spend a good deal of our time working on free stuff. We're in an unusual situation. We have a lot of help. We have a good financial base right now, but we're not going to have that forever, and we think it is important that we make it. It is important to ourselves at least, and I think we can.

"We keep up our connections with legal groups down here. I'm pretty active in SLAM, and a member of the Guild and the ACLU. We had four LSCRRC interns working here in the summer of 1971. We also get along with the bar association here and with the judges in Tuscaloosa. Not to say they all like us, but as far as a working association, we know them and they know us cause we've been here. That affects how you try cases.

"I am a regional chauvinist which may be unfair to people in other parts of the country because I haven't lived in other parts of the country. But I think all the old garbage about people in the South being good people with, in many ways, radical sorts of instincts is true. I don't think people from the North or West or other parts of the country understand people in the South, or the South. Some of my chauvinistic feeling comes from a real sense of frustration with people from other parts of the country trying to come into the South and do things. There was a time when that was necessary in the sixties but that time is long since over. People in the South are working on their problems and, in the main, I think we're ahead of other people in human relations, in getting along with each other, in understanding poor people's problems and understanding who controls the country and how the country is run. We don't like big government, and we don't like big business because we have seen what it has done, and, in many ways, it has done bad things. People here have seen what it has done to them on integration, which they didn't like. Integration is good, fine, but that same kind of power can be used in other ways and that is bad. They know what big business has done to the South, and, largely, northern business, and they are striking out at it and I think that is good. I think the South is going to be where some really dramatic sorts of things will happen with poor people getting together.

"The Gulfcoast Pulpwood Association with which we work is interesting because they don't want to affiliate with any sort of trade union. They have the sense that once they affiliate with an established union, even though they get paid more, they lose control of what they are doing, and that is true. Even the politicians in Alabama are beginning to take real populist sorts of stands on issues again. Wallace has been very critical of industry, utilities, banks, and, in fact, has been taking actions against them. We just passed in the legislature the strongest air pollution bill in the country. Ecology is a pretty commonplace issue—nobody is against it, but the Chamber of Commerce wasn't for that bill. And they overcame that and have steadily been striking out at profits, utilities, and other public monopolies and putting more taxes on big landowners and farmers, so even within the established political channels there are some sorts of really dramatic things happening. They are little things but I think that is important.

"I think insofar as the racial situation is concerned, the South can lead the way. There is no question in my mind because there is really not the personal hostility from either Blacks or whites that I have seen in my brief travels in other parts of the country. I spent a week about three weeks ago in Choctaw County, Alabama. The Black people had had an economic boycott going on for about ten weeks, and rightfully so. It had been almost 100 percent effective and the white stores were about to crumble. They had also boycotted the schools, and there was no school going on and they'd been having marches every day. And in the middle of all that, the white people say 'nigger' and the whole bit, I talked to the white people and their instincts, their feelings, their motives were just as good as they could be. The Black people are going to have to keep kicking ass to change the power structure cause that is the way things are. People who are in power want to stay in power.

"But when it is over, people are still going to get along and they are going to get along as human beings. There's still going to be a shift in power, and there already have been real dramatic changes in meaningful ways in the South about social relationships. Nobody is upset about going in a restaurant with Black people anymore. That doesn't bother anybody and neither does having integrated schools. I think that even on the whole busing issue a lot of the white people are sincere when they say it is not the race issue anymore.

"I think the South has been kicked too long. The whole image of the South, which, admittedly, was projected mainly by southern politicians who played the perfect stereotyped role in the fifties and the sixties, led itself to be misunderstood. I don't think that people in other parts of the country, for a large part, have any conception that there are human beings in the South who live together and have ideas and thoughts just like they do. People look at the South more in general terms about what is going on. People say to me, 'My God, you mean you represent Black people and you drive around down there and you stay alive and don't get your office bombed and things?' That being said is a common occurrence. It isn't a thing that there are a few people who don't have an understanding, it is really that there is no understanding at all about what is going on in the South. I'm not an historian about the South, but I don't think people in other parts of the country have any real knowledge of the history of the South and the kinds of forces that have played a part. Slavery wasn't southern. It flourished here but that was for a lot of reasons.

"I think that I may be unfair to other parts of the country as people are unfair to the South, because human beings like to think that things are worse in other places; they like to have scapegoats. And the news media, in connection with the South at least until recently, has provided this. It is not that people have any ill motives. They honestly believe that that is the way that things are in the South and, as far as I know, the people who come down here, in main part, have had the best of intentions. They think that Black people are being treated terribly, which they are, and that they should be helped, which they should. But the stereotypes about the South are almost laughable and there is some resentment in myself when anybody comes from New York, and starts talking about George Wallace. You know, James Buckley is good enough."

Ed Still, the newest member of the firm, was born in Augusta and lived there and in Memphis until he was thirteen, when his family moved to Montgomery.

"I went to both undergraduate and law school at the university here, graduating from law school in 1971. I did research work for Ralph and Jack while I was in law school, but I had a ROTC commission hanging heavy over my head, so I didn't think much of the future. After I finished three semesters of law school I realized that I had become a conscientious objector. I worked through that and then wrote my family about it. My father said he didn't agree but that he thought I was sincere, although he would try to change my mind. Then I put in for a discharge, had a hearing, and they turned me down. Then I started thinking about what I would do. I made an agreement with Jack and Ralph that I would come here.

"I then sued the army in federal court for habeas and mandamus relief concerning my lack of CO status. In that suit we tried to establish the fact that an applicant should be able to review what has been said during a hearing because the officer who interviews someone in a hearing can lie. For instance, in my hearing the officers did not ask questions that got to the basis of my beliefs, but they wrote a recommendation disapproving my request for discharge.

"While that was still hanging, I took the bar and passed and started practicing here in September of 1971. Before and after, I was working on a case to prove that the Jefferson County jury system is unfair. On the day of my swearing in as a lawyer I had to go up and testify on that case. Other than that I haven't been in court much since I started. I've been working on a federal case, a statewide one, that charges that Black kids and poor kids are being charged fees to keep them out of school and asks that no schools charge or collect fees for anything that people need for their basic education."

Like Drake and Knowles, Still is also a regional chauvinist.

"I think the South is much better than the rest of the country. One thing I have against people from other places, especially

New York, is that they are condescending to Blacks and whites
both. They have this Albert Schweitzer attitude and they don't
understand the society down here. While I now view Blacks more
as equals, they have always been around me. Being from the
South I've lived in a segregated society, but never in a white society, which you have in other parts of the country. Perhaps the
South is a mixed English-African culture. Perhaps the South is a
Black society with white people in it. Everything is different in
the South. We were a conquered colony without a Marshall Plan
after the Civil War. Northern money came in but the profits were
always taken back to the North. There has always been an economic drain on the South. We've always been the stepchild of the
country, and we've always been poorer because we are an agricultural community, I think we were used by the North and the
West very much as the American colonies were used by
England."

Completing the Drake, Knowles, and Still firm are Pat Boyd, a
legal worker, and Cheryl Knowles, who is Ralph's sister and Ed's
wife and whose major work is on SLAM projects. Both women
also graduated from the University of Alabama, and both are involved in the women's movement.

"First," Boyd said, "we and about twenty other women,
friends from the campus and the community, were involved in a
consciousness-raising group. However, we had political differences and so we never did actions. Now we're in a smaller group
which we plan to be an action group. The women's movement is
beginning to take hold down here now. During SLAM's 1971
conference we had a seminar on legal workers and a women's
caucus. There aren't that many legal workers in the South now.
Most movement lawyers practice in firms of two or three so they
have one secretary and pretty much keep to the traditional division of labor. Ginny Boult, who is in Atlanta and was SLAM's
staff person up until September of 1971, now hopes to do some
organizing of potential legal workers to at least let them know
what is possible. At this point the only legal workers are in Dur-

ham, where there is one; in Tallahassee, working in the Legal Services program; here, and in Gainesville, where the only legal collective in the South exists. The firm in Durham was supposed to be a collective but it fell through, and there are two lawyers, Jim Keenan and Jerry Paul, there now practicing together with one legal worker."

The Gainesville Collective has all of the problems of the other collectives discussed, plus the additional problems that come from its location. The combination of all of these factors makes the collective a rather shaky proposition, although the people involved in it are very dedicated to their work, to the idea of collectives, and to the process of becoming such.

The idea for the collective began to germinate in the minds of some young people working with Florida Rural Legal Services (FRLS). Jane and Steve Johnson lived in Belle Glade, Florida, for a year and a half while he worked for the FRLS office there. Both Steve and Jane, who is now in law school, found the life there very isolated and difficult. They met Judye McCalman, who had been working as a secretary/organizer for FRLS in Pompano Beach, and found that she shared their feelings. The three of them had read about collectives and discussed them at SLAM meeting and Guild conferences. At one meeting they met some of the people from the Bar Sinister, and they began to seriously consider beginning a collective in the South.

They chose to locate it in Gainesville, the site of the University of Florida, which they all had attended. Probably because it houses the largest university in the state, Gainesville is the state's countercultural center. The university town has a population of 80,000 and a student population of 25,000. Blacks comprise about 15 to 20 percent of the general population, and less than 1 percent of the student population.

"We chose to locate here, because, from the information we had gotten from the underground paper, and, from what we remembered, we thought there was a good deal of movement activity going on. When we got here, we found that we were wrong.

At this point, there are no radical organizations except for women's liberation and gay liberation, some antiwar activity, and a Black Student Union which fell apart during the 1970-71 school year.

"There is a large counterculture here, a lot of longhairs. In the spring of 1971, there were a lot of co-ops, but there wasn't enough interest to keep them going, so, by the fall, nothing was happening. In the fall most students here are into football; in the winter, grades; in the spring they get restless. Maybe something will happen then."

The Johnsons left Belle Glade in March 1971. They contacted Clyde and Kay Ellis, whom they had known from law school, and asked them whether they would be interested in the collective idea. They were, and when Ellis got his CO discharge, he and Ms. Ellis, who still has a few quarters of law school to complete, joined the collective. In the meantime McCalman had joined them. Later, Vicki Ellis, who had met the Johnsons at organizational meetings for the People's Coalition and Poor People's March Against Repression Through Florida in March of 1971, came into the collective. Vicki Ellis had completed three years of college in California, and is taking courses at the University while she is working. With the exception of McCalman, who is from Tennessee, and Vicki Ellis, all the other members of the collective have spent most of their lives in Florida.

"When we began, we were housed in two rooms of Steve and Jane's house. In September of 1971 we moved into our offices. All of us together in the house for a few weeks was just impossible. Now we have six office rooms which we spent around two weeks decorating. Everyone planned his or her own office, and we all chipped in on the work."

Their offices are located on Main Street, between the university campus and the poor section of town. They have a second-floor walk-up located over a welding shop and next door to a pool room. The office is furnished in early radical—repainted, recycled desks, posters, etc.

"When we first started thinking of a collective, we wanted to assist the movement and to develop a new form of organization that was viable and would allow us to struggle against racism, sexism, imperialism, capitalism. We had a lot of dreams that haven't worked out but we have plenty more.

"We find that what happens usually depends more on happenstance than on plans. We do operate collectively in that all decisions are made at group meetings. Pay is subsistence and according to need. We want to do as much cheap or free political work as possible, but so far we have had to take what comes in the door.

"We did the Black Student Union cases, and we've done work for two tenant unions and gay liberation. We're house counsel for the Service Employees Union, which is mainly comprised of the janitors and maids on campus, and for the American Federation of Teachers, but no cases have come up yet. Those are really the only campus groups for whom we could be house counsel. We've also worked with the Micanopy Neighborhood Association, and the Justice of Blackness, two rural groups located nearby. We have had a personal injury case for a bus of Black kids who were hit by a truck, and one for the family of a Black woman who died because a white ambulance wouldn't take her to the hospital. We're also suing the state attorney in Gainesville because he beat up a longhair, and we're considering suing the city for appropriating $25,000 to the chamber of commerce to entertain visitors at a segregated country club.

"For fees we've handled drug, draft, military, and divorce work, and some work for hip capitalists. We don't know if there is enough work here to support us. We have some trouble getting countercultural cases now because the people in the counter-culture feel that we are too political. We're kind of an oddity here. It seems practically every day some downtown lawyer comes in to see what kind of creatures we are.

"The legal workers here are mostly learning. Two audit consti-tutional law courses at the law school and three are being taught legal research by a professor at the law school who is giving his time.

"We sit in on and discuss all the cases, whether we are legal workers or lawyers, because the goal is for everyone to learn how to do everything. We share the shit work as much as possible. We have problems getting the men to do their own typing, but Steve does all of the bookkeeping and Clyde is the janitor, and everyone answers the phones and cleans up in the kitchen. We confront male chauvinism and professionalism whenever we see it. One problem is male domination of the meetings because both of the men here are outspoken and talkative.

"We're thinking of getting into a sensitivity/encounter sort of thing, as a collective. We think it could be valuable because we have a political base to work from, and we think the results could be significant with political people whom you like and trust. The thing that ties us together now is the legal work, but we are serious political people and would like to explore the collective concept more.

"We're debating now whether we should be more activist. Some of us feel that collective development is as important as anything else, and others of us feel that more energy should be expended on external struggle. We have a lot of dreams—someday participating in a free law school, teaching adult education courses for legal workers and basic survival skills for everyone—but right now we are just trying to stay alive. If it keeps going like it has we have faith that things will keep coming through the door.

"We're still in the process of struggling for our identity as a collective, and finding out what we have in common as people. We feel strange sometimes calling ourselves a collective because we view that as the end result of a process, although we feel that calling ourselves that helps us get there. I don't see right now how we can make our future. It depends on what happens with us, and with the community that we want to serve."

III

SECOND
NATION
LAWYERS

14

The NAACP Legal Defense and Educational Fund, Inc.

The NAACP Legal Defense and Educational Fund, Inc. (Inc. Fund) is today one of the largest, wealthiest pro bono publico organizations in the country. Thirty attorneys work out of their large offices in the office building that towers above the New York Coliseum. They have five hundred cooperating attorneys located in thirty different states, with the largest number in the South. Their yearly budget exceeds $3.5 million. They administer the Herbert Lehman Education Fund which anticipates awarding three hundred scholarships—covering the complete cost of law school training—each year for the next five years to minority group students. Some of these students, after they finish law school, will enter the Inc. Fund's internship program for a year and then be subsidized for several more years as they set up their own practices in various areas, particularly in the South. They handle over six hundred cases each year dealing with race relations. They also sponsor a series of Lawyer Training Institutes and seminars on civil rights law each year.

Jack Greenberg, a Columbia Law School graduate who has been with the Fund since 1949, has been the director-counsel for over ten years succeeding Thurgood Marshall, now a

Supreme Court justice. When he began working with the Fund it was still housed in the same quarters as the NAACP although, since 1940, it had been a separate corporate entity.

"Because the NAACP advocated and opposed legislation and because we were tax-exempt, we had to be separate, but, being housed in the same quarters, it was difficult to keep the separation. As we continued to grow and get larger budgets, it became impossible to maintain the separateness so we moved into our own quarters in the early fifties.

"As we grew bigger it became more important for us to assert our independence and conduct our own program so we wouldn't be influenced by the NAACP telling us to file this and that. Even when the separation was formal and legal, it couldn't be fully meaningful because the NAACP was the only civil rights organization relating to Blacks which existed then, and we didn't generate cases ourselves. So, if the NAACP got involved with something, we got involved with it. And if they didn't, we didn't because there was usually nobody else generating cases.

"That began to change rapidly in the midfifties. When Martin Luther King developed the Montgomery bus boycott we began to represent him. Later we took cases from SNCC and CORE and scores of community organizations, and from a whole lot of individuals."

In recent years the efforts of the Inc. Fund have been directed predominantly at cases that affect education, employment, access to public accommodations and services, the administration of justice (police brutality, right to trial, changes of venue, jury suits, prison reform, capital punishment), voting, housing, and public land use. Some of these cases are Inc. Fund cases and some are National Office on the Rights of the Indigent (NORI) cases.

"NORI is the separate corporation we set up five years ago to handle poverty cases because we felt, and the country subsequently recognized, that a lot of the cases of Black people were also the cases of poor people. While it is a separate program we don't have a separate staff. Everyone does a bit of each. We differ from Legal Services programs in that we try to handle only those cases that will set precedents, although it is sometimes hard to identify which cases those are."

Although, in the twenty-some years Jack has been with the Inc. Fund this country has made more progress than it ever has before in racial relations and much of this change has come about through court decisions, he is only partially satisfied with the results so far.

"There's been definite progress, that's without a doubt. But it varies. I don't know whether the legal system can bring about adequate change alone. But there is no reason to believe that a radical change, which some people talk about, whatever that means, in the form of government and the principles of ownership of property will create a better legal system or superior rights for Black people. So, as things are, I think there can be changes and improvements, and there have been. Now with regard to rights which relate to race, just to take an area that everybody says is so simple that you're old-fashioned if you're concerned with it, a lot of people are saying that to abolish racial discrimination will not make a great deal of difference. Yet, in 1955 Washington, D.C., was a thoroughly segregated city. When we first began the school segregation cases, we had to stay in Black hotels. That is no longer the case and it's no longer the case because of a change in the law which came about as the result of a law suit called the Thompson's Restaurant case.

"In that instance the law led the social system at large. Then, in the case of the Civil Rights Act of 1964, the legal system followed the demands of King's demonstrations. Sometimes the law leads and other times it follows. However, a lot of the problems we face are not problems of the law as such, but of the socioeconomic system. If somebody is poor, ignorant, and disadvantaged, it's that much more difficult for any legal system, no matter how you conceive it, to afford him his full rights. You can call that a mixed social, legal, economic matter and no change in the rules of law as such is going to solve the whole problem.

"A law professor, now a judge, wrote an article I've quoted a number of times in which he said that the best thing a lawyer in a criminal case can tell his client to do is to wear a clean shirt to court. Now, that has nothing to do with the legal system, unless you want to abolish the jury system. Jurors often are going to be prejudiced against a guy in a dirty shirt, and they're going to like someone in a clean shirt, and you can do anything you want to the legal system and you're not going to change that, immediately anyway. That's a very insignificant aspect of how the law and social attitudes are all wound up together.

"If I were to look at the various areas in which we are working, like public accommodations, I would say there's been immense progress, but in something like school integration there's been much less. I think it's essential that schools be integrated and I think that the school integration movement has been one of the great contributing factors to a reappraisal of education generally. But I also think that integrating schools, by itself, while necessary, is not going to provide the education that everybody needs. Money is going to have to be put into schools and a whole variety of other things.

"As far as employment is concerned, I am optimistic about greater equality. I think the law has been rather successful in that area recently. But, again, it's not the law acting alone. It's the law and an activated social conscience which has been activated by a number of things, not excluding the ghetto riots.

"It's interesting, while we have been having trouble with the administration and actually opposing it in the school area, it has been supporting us in our employment program.

"On the question of the reform of the criminal law, which has been a matter of general concern, hardly limited to us or those who are concerned about the role of race in the administration of justice, there appears to be, partly as a result of the President's Crime Commission and partly as a result of Chief Justice Burger's interest in the administration of prisons and penal reform, a growing movement. I think litigation, including litigation by us, will play some significant part in all that. But certainly not the dominant part and it's not going to do it all by itself.

"I think that a lot of problems brought into court now, especially by poverty lawyers, really don't lend themselves to a solution through the courts, simply because, to a very great extent, they're questions of how much money there is and what the public attitudes on various issues of social policy are. The law can knock out this or that approach and it can make the administration of some things fairer. It can even make the administration of other things so inconvenient that you have to reassess your whole program and do something else. But there are limits. The law can knock out a racial restriction on housing and say you must integrate, but if there is no place to put the people the housing isn't going to be integrated."

Despite his view of the capacity of the legal system, Greenberg is convinced that one way to make it work more equitably is to increase the number of Black lawyers in the country. While there is 1 white lawyer for each 637 white Americans, there is only 1 Black lawyer for each 7000 Black Americans. In the South and Southwest, where 13,000,000 Black people live, there is 1 Black lawyer for every 37,000 Black citizens. The Inc. Fund's internship program is designed to correct this imbalance as quickly as possible.

"We developed the internship program here about seven or eight years ago in an effort to place lawyers in parts of the South where there is such a severe shortage, caused by many factors, some as fundamental as underlying economic conditions. You're not going to get a lawyer where there isn't a community with business to support him, and you're not going to get a lawyer unless you have people going to law school. So one of the things we've done is train people here for a year and then subsidize them and tie them into our network of cooperating attorneys. We, and our cooperating attorneys, now take twelve people in this program each year. By 1975 we hope to increase the number vastly, if we can raise the funds.

"We've had both Black and white interns. The white interns present difficult problems if you're talking about settling in the South. The social pressure under which a white lawyer in the South must live, if he or she is handling highly controversial things involving Black people, is very great. But we've had some who have stuck it out and been quite successful. The Black lawyer can fit into such a thing with greater ease. In fact, his opponents often admire him. Ours is really the only program of this kind, although some other groups, like the Lawyers' Committee for Civil Rights Under Law, now have programs of putting some recent Black law school graduates on retainer.

"Another thing is our scholarship program, which is getting more and more Black students going to southern law schools. In the 1971-72 school year we had 320 Black law students on scholarships. By 1975, we will have given 1500 complete scholarships to Black law students, although not all of them will be attending law school in the South. We also provide summer jobs for some of these students, either here or with our cooperating attorneys."

Aside from all of this, the Inc. Fund has also proven to be a training ground for its staff attorneys. After a few years of working here most of them go on to work with other organizations or with socially conscious law firms in a variety of communities.

Bill Robinson, who is currently on the staff, hopes someday to start his own community-oriented law firm.

"I grew up in an integrated community in Oberlin, Ohio. I decided to be a lawyer very early cause my old man had always wanted to be one and ended up being a hod carrier, a bricklayer's helper. I wasn't a serious student in high school and didn't really decide to go to college until my senior year. I spent my first year of college at Ohio Northern then transferred to Oberlin where I began to be aware as a person. I wasn't an activist but participated on an ad hoc basis in various causes. I graduated in 1963 and went to Columbia Law School on scholarship.

"Columbia, which is a training school for the Wall Street firms, is where I became an activist. Between the summers of 1963 and

1964, some law students, who had spent the summer of '63 working with the SNCC and CORE people doing voter registration and public accommodations work, had come back very excited about the opportunity of using what legal skills they had to directly assist people involved in human problems. They started the Law Student's Civil Rights Research Council [LSCRRC]. The guys impressed me with what they were about and how they were going about it so I joined.

"After my first year of school, I went to Mississippi and worked for the Council of Federated Organizations. The important work was what other people did for me, not what I did for other people. I really saw people who were suffering at the hands of some other people and at the use of doctrines. I saw the law in operation as I did not want to see it work. I saw people in Mississippi using the law to destroy some other people. It convinced me I wanted to make an effort to use the law in another way. When I got back to Columbia, I was faced with the question of what I should do. I decided I wanted to share the experience of that summer and continue my efforts while in law school on an organizational basis to have as big an impact as possible. So I and some others set up a local chapter of LSCRRC and worked on research projects with lawyers in New York and in the South.

"After my second year at law school, I was deeply involved in LSCRRC and I was designated southern coordinator, so the bulk of my summer was spent coordinating in New York, but I did spend a portion of it in the South. After I graduated from Columbia in 1966, I was elected executive director of LSCRRC. That job is virtually all administrative and fund-raising work.

"After I left the organization as executive director I kept up my contact with it. I'm on a committee to fund-raise and help with technical things. I'm very pleased with the effect I had with it, and vice versa, and I would like to see the organization continue and provide opportunities for other people to have similar experiences. It has developed as a model civil rights/civil liberties law student organization. It has not developed as a radical one. There are other organizations that serve the interests of radical law students in the same way as LSCRRC serves moderate ones, organizations like the Student Guild or the Black American Law Students' Association.

"LSCRRC started out as a missionary effort but that's where the movement was then: whites were going down South to save the niggers. The overwhelming majority of students who went South in the summer of 1964 were white. The overwhelming whiteness of LSCRRC at that time was due to the overwhelming whiteness of law school. There were five Blacks in my class and only three were involved in socially relevant things. Now, as law schools have more Black students, LSCRRC has more Black members. And I think an exceptionally large percentage of people in LSCRRC—30 or 40 percent—kept on being involved with social or movement things when they left law school.

"Toward the end of my term at LSCRRC, I had to decide what to do. I could have gone to one of several large, prestigious law firms which I thought about because one of my desires in going to law school was to live a much more comfortable life than I had previously. My family really wasn't poor; they were working-class. But I had a desire to raise my socioeconomic level. So, being honest, I had to consider those firms, but I ultimately rejected them.

"My final choice was between the Inc. Fund and a firm in Ohio close to Oberlin. I knew the community problems there. The firm was all white, fantastically successful, and wanted me to pursue political, civil rights things. They were nice white liberals and I thought the world of them but I wanted to pursue my interests a bit more aggressively and abrasively than they did. My real interest is in civil rights cases directly involving race, so I finally decided on the Inc. Fund and came here. In 1969 I became a specialist in employment discrimination, and I spend in excess of 90 percent of my time on that.

"All Inc. Fund cases must either directly concern race or contain legal principles that will directly involve Black people or affect statutes that will have a large impact on Black people. You may find us in Sixth Amendment, Fourteenth Amendment, First Amendment cases, and cases that don't involve the Constitution at all. The biggest component of cases, although not of man hours, is in school desegregation. Next is employment discrimination, then we ease out into a range of cases—criminal law, prison conditions, capital punishment, land use, use of zoning and other laws to control where Black people live. About an equal number of Black and white attorneys work here."

Cases where you won't often find the Inc. Fund are those involving radicals. The Fund has a list of guidelines which came out of the debate about the Davis case, defining when they will defend radicals. Basically, they will represent them if it appears that they are being persecuted because of race, and if the case isn't too publicly controversial.

"We have represented the most militant of all the groups in one aspect or another of their involvements with the law," Greenberg said. "We have represented the Panthers on the bail issue. We represented Angela Davis on the conditions under which she was held in prison. There have been those who have said, however, that we ought to represent radicals and militants no matter what they're charged with and what they did, or what the issues are. There has been a very considerable and vigorous disagreement over that here. But the resolution of that disagreement is that we will remain issue-oriented. For instance, we represented Bobby Seale in New Haven on the question of the conditions of his imprisonment but not in connection with the murder charge because no one has demonstrated to us that he was held on that murder charge because of race. We'll represent anyone if there is an issue in regard to the conditions of imprisonment or indeed anything else, or if it appears he is being persecuted because of his race, but we won't represent him just because he is Black and militant. Some of our staff lawyers disagree. Margaret Burnham for instance represented Angela Davis, but she was on a leave of absence and not being paid by us to do it, although she had a different view and would have liked to be representing her for the Inc. Fund."

"I don't know if I can say how the Inc. Fund relates to more militant Black groups," Robinson said. "We are lawyers and have a lawyer-client relationship rather than an institutional one, although it is institutional to the extent that there are some groups around who constantly look to us for representation at this point, and they can be pretty damn sure that they are going to get it. We've traditionally been the Southern Christian Leadership Conference's attorneys on civil rights matters, and there is also a range of local groups that looks to us for representation, like the Mobile Voters League. With other groups, we don't have an ongoing relationship but an ad hoc one. Some of us don't feel that we are representing the Panthers nearly enough, although we worked on the Seale contempt, filed amicus briefs on behalf of the Panther Twenty-one and various individual Panthers. I guess it is a matter of public record that we have had various in-house discussions of how we should go about deciding what controversial cases we should take when we're approached. The fact is, we're not approached frequently. Rather, more renowned radical lawyers are approached. Part of that is that people don't feel we would say yes because we don't have a track record of representing more radical Blacks.

"I don't plan on staying here forever but I'm happy here and making some contributions. I ultimately want to go into private practice in my own law firm and either be part of or build an institution that relates to the particular needs of a particular community and the people who are active in it. I don't want to spend the rest of my life relating to the nation of Black people and various communities on an ad hoc basis. I want to become part of one community. That may very well entail continuing my relationship with the Inc. Fund but as a cooperating attorney. Many of the cases an activist attorney wants to be involved in are impossible to litigate without some kind of institutional support either because of the time or money burden.

"There are notions around right now that a commune of people can do that without outside assistance and that may be. But I don't think really that the commune idea is realistic. I'd like to be in private practice on a permanent basis. For a limited period of time and a limited commitment, a commune might be an effective way to get representation for some people. But, for a permanent thing, I don't think much of the idea. As you begin to make other commitments in your life, to family and to creditors, you've got to have an agency which will do several things for you, one of which is make money. You've got to have it and a commune is radically against that.

"I'm not a socialist and I couldn't be. If all I was going to get was what I need, then, unless you define need to include what I describe as want, I couldn't work as hard. I work hard and put in long hours but that is because in large part when I put in those extra hours I'm making something for it—money, satisfaction, recognition among my peers. I think the world functions in large part on the basis of incentives. Now maybe some people can join a commune and put in long hours and know the commune is successful and thereby have the incentive to put the extra in.

"I don't believe you are going to get any Black lawyers in communes for a while. When you're talking about a Black guy going into the law, you are talking about a guy who went into it in part because he wanted to raise his socioeconomic level. If he's honest with himself, he's going to admit that the desire exists. I think most Black guys, and a large number of white guys, to the extent that they are being honest, will admit that.

"I think that other schemes of organization, besides the commune, might work. For instance, a public interest firm, or schemes where you can commit a certain portion of your time to public interest work might be viable. The problem there is that the people might sell out and, to the extent that you start taking corporate retainers, that really becomes a problem.

"I do see the southern civil rights activities as the beginning of large numbers of people's lawyers. I think it goes back to that

small group of brave lawyers, Black lawyers, who brought up unpopular cases and built up organizations—at least in the South—
that involved both Black and white lawyers from the North and
South. They gradually developed a view of the law that ultimately
resulted in there being people's lawyers. They litigated and won
the cases that supplied the precedents upon which we all rely
now. Out of this came the organizations that now give lawyers a
chance to be people's lawyers.

"I think that things have picked up so much from the southern
civil rights time that you are no longer going to get watershed
cases or cases with such great symbolic value. The crucial question now is whether or not the legal system will be able to provide a really fair trial to a range of dissidents, people who radically disagree with the system. That is the big challenge. If we
look at evidence now, it suggests that the law isn't doing a good
job.

"The court system is part of the political apparatus that is used
to govern a country and if you look at it otherwise, I think that
you are being naive. The use of that apparatus to confront politicians politically is essential.

"If you talk about political in the traditional sense, then I think
the most important political cases were the voting rights ones, because they involved transfer of power in a real sense, and they
gave power to people like Fannie Lou Hamer. All across the
South, people who previously had no power, no representation,
now have it. Awfully important, too, are cases that involve what
political groups can do, what political bodies can do.

"As far as political trials, there are two kinds. You may defend a person by saying that he did something but it isn't wrong,
or you may defend a person by saying that this is a political
trial and I'm not interested in whether he did it. I'm interested
in using this forum politically, in the same way that the prosecution is, and, along the way I am going to lock error in the record
so that you can't convict my client. If you get these two types of

political trials confused, then the quality of representation is going to be inadequate.

"I have a concept of the law being a set of rules which fairly and objectively governs the way we live vis a vis each other. Naturally, we have conflicts which have to be resolved. To the extent that the law of the United States is fair and objective, I believe in it. To the extent that it isn't, I don't, and seek to change it. You can say the same thing about any legal system. There is nothing sacrosanct about any of them.

"The court system, or the system itself, isn't the enemy of the people. However, they are run by people who have their own interests, which are frequently contrary to the interests of the people in various specific ways. If we took the control of the system out of the hands of the people who run it now, and put it in the hands of the theoretical good guys, it could work, although it would have to be modified. It needs some specific, identifiable changes so it would take into account some of the interests of the people, and of the community.

"Lawyers aren't really the people who should make the decision how the law or the legal system should be changed. Lawyers are technicians. If they are good, they are creative technicians who have a larger view of how the law can be of service to society, and by that I mean all of society. If the original lawmakers of this country had been creative technicians instead of white, propertied males concerned with building their own interests into the law, many of our current legal problems would not exist."

15

The National Conference of Black Lawyers

The National Conference of Black Lawyers (NCBL) is a relatively young organization of activist Black lawyers. It is the first such organization in the history of the U.S., and it has a bold, innovative attitude toward the legal and social problems of Black people. Haywood Burns is national director of the NCBL.

"There have been activist Black lawyers since there have been Black lawyers, but there have not been enough for them to group together until this last decade. In the early period of this country, Black people were not allowed to become lawyers. Whether or not they could be was a matter of state law, and it varied from state to state, but it wasn't a common thing until the late nineteenth century. The 1840s were the first time you saw Blacks in the courtroom as lawyers, but, in most states, it was much later. There were one or two prominent Black lawyers in the middle of the 1800s—Dr. John Rock of Massachusetts, who was both a doctor and lawyer, was one—but, for the most part, at that time you didn't see Blacks at the bar at all.

"Even when Black people started becoming lawyers they were not embraced by the legal community. Until well into the twentieth century Black lawyers were excluded from the American Bar Association [ABA]. That, of course, was one of the reasons for the formation of the National Bar Association [NBA] which has been in existence for over forty years, trying to serve the needs of the Black bar at a time when the organized white bar would have little or nothing to do with Black lawyers.

"The NBA was a traditional bar association with a program geared toward the problems of Black practitioners. When the Guild, which was an activist bar association, formed, a fair number of Black lawyers joined, but I think at that time most Black lawyers who were active in organized bar activities chose the NBA.

"The idea that there was a need for an activist Black bar group had been around for some time. Finally, about twelve lawyers got together in Capahosic, Virginia, in December of 1968. Some of them were very young activist lawyers and some were middle-aged and some were old activist lawyers but the one thing they had in common was that they wanted to use their skills in the service of the community. Among those present were Derrick Bell, now a law professor at Harvard; Samuel Jackson, manager of the community development section of HUD; Floyd McKissick, former national director of CORE; A. J. Cooper, then president of BALSA and now practicing in Mobile; Frank Reeves, from the Howard Law School faculty; Robert Carter, a lawyer from New York City; and Tim Jenkins of Washington, D.C. At that meeting they thrashed out the ideas of what needed to be done and, then, for the next few months, they organized a national meeting of Black lawyers and law students. That meeting took place over the Memorial Day weekend of 1969 in Chicago. It was out of that meeting that the NCBL was formed. The Black American Law Students Association [BALSA] formed a little while before, and members came to the Chicago meeting and decided to affiliate with us so that BALSA and the NCBL might exist under one umbrella."

The purposes clause of the NCBL constitution states that the organization was formed to: "(1) Seek out and eradicate the roots and causes of racism. (2) Vigorously defend black people from those who consciously or otherwise deny them basic human and legal rights. (3) Assist the black community in eliminating the root causes of poverty and powerlessness. (4) Make use of legal tools and legal discipline for the advancement of economic, political, educational, and social institutions for black people."

"For the first few months," said Burns, "this organization was run by a steering committee and run pretty much on an ad hoc basis. It soon became apparent that, for the organization to take off and accomplish things, a more permanent set-up was needed. At that point, the board approached me and asked me to resign my position as staff attorney for the NAACP Legal Defense Fund, Inc. [Inc. Fund] and become the first, fulltime national director of the organization. I decided that it was important to do that, and I took the position and set up an office here in this lovely old brownstone on West 120th Street which is an excellent example of what the architecture used to be like in Harlem before landlords started splitting up buildings and letting them go on in a state of disrepair.

"We now have in our ranks somewhere in the neighborhood of twenty-five hundred Black lawyers and law students. It's critical to note the latter because the number of Black law students today is far greater than it has ever been at any time in this country's history, and I would expect that, in the next three or four years, the number of Black lawyers in the United States is going to increase by 100 percent, so that it's significant that we have so many Black law students who are affiliating with us because I think that augurs well for the strength and growth of the organization.

"Now our greatest strength is in the Northeast in terms of numbers. We have members all over the country, but you could say that it is that old eastern establishment all over again, not by desire. But the Washington-New York-Boston corridor tends to have the greatest number of people who are active, and the strongest chapters in the country are there. But I think that is changing. We're gaining a lot of activity in the South and on the West Coast now, and we hope to see more activity in the Midwest soon.

"There are four fulltime people in the national office now. James S. Carroll, Robert Simpson, and I are staff attorneys, and Alfreda Bouyer is our secretary. But, from another perspective, we have literally hundreds of people in that everyone who is a member is supposed to work for the organization. So that, in a way analogous to the Inc. Fund or the ACLU, we have cooperating attorneys around the country. Depending on how you look at it, I administer either a very large or a very small staff.

"People can call here with a potential case and we refer it to our local people or sometimes we'll hear of a case and contact the people involved. Some of the cases that come to our attention are cases where people can afford to pay so we then operate as a lawyer referral service, but, in general, most of our cases are pro bono and most of the lawyers do not get paid for doing them.

"In general, we get involved in all kinds of litigation, affirmative suits on community issues as well as defense of unpopular clients. We also monitor governmental activity that affects the Black community, including judicial appointments and the work of all branches of the government. Then we also give service to the Black bar through lawyer referrals, job placements, continuing legal education, watching for discrimination at the bar, and checking out law school admissions and curricular reforms."

Since the NCBL was formed its activities have included: challenging in federal court the binding and gagging of Bobby Seale during the Chicago conspiracy trial; winning the dismissal of charges against thirteen Black Cornell University students charged in the 1969 occupation of the school's Willard Straight Hall; challenging the ruling of the New York State Supreme Court justice who discontinued the pretrial hearings in the New York Panther Twenty-one trial; challenging the constitutionality of a transit fare increase in a metropolitan area without a hearing; winning the release from federal prison for a Michigan civil

rights activist who had been wrongly convicted of a draft violation and sentenced to five years; helping to initiate a task force
to study minority group law practice in the South; operating a
lawyer referral and placement service; engaging in a program of
public education on Blacks and the law. The NCBL has also
been involved in the monitoring and investigation of the Attica
prison revolt, the investigation into the death of George Jackson,
the Angela Davis case, and the H. Rap Brown matter.

"While we have no formal association with any other legal association except BALSA, we have had de facto associations with
the Guild, the ACLU, the Center for Constitutional Rights,
LSCRRC, the Inc. Fund, and SLAM. From time to time we have
certain cases where we see a common interest with another organization and we work with them then."

Haywood Burns, who is thirty-one, came to the NCBL with a
background impressive from legal, academic, and activist view-
points.

"I'm from Peekskill, New York. My family is from the South
—Virginia—and I was the first one to graduate from college. I
decided to be a lawyer when I was about seven. Someone told me
that there weren't any Black cowboys, and so I decided that
being a lawyer was the next best thing. I also talked a lot so people told me I'd make a good lawyer. Those were very irrational
reasons but then, as I grew older I detected some very good rational reasons for being a lawyer. I began to think of the law as a
very useful tool for social change and decided that that would be
a thing I would like to do."

Haywood went to Harvard College from which he graduated
with honors in history. He had a scholarship and also worked. He
then spent a year as the Lionel deJersey Harvard Scholar at
Cambridge University in England. When he returned he went to
Yale Law School, graduating in 1966.

"Throughout this time I had a background of activism. In my
teen-age years I was active in the NAACP in Peekskill, which
was the only organized vehicle for activism in those days al-

though, by current standards, that is pretty mild. I got involved in the sit-in movement quite early, almost as soon as it began in the North.

"I did go South with the Council of Federated Organizations in Mississippi, the summer of 1964. When I was at Yale, I was an officer in a local chapter of CORE and I guess you could call me an activist for that. The mayor's office said so in a public address in New Haven, and that made me know that my three years in law school weren't wasted."

After he graduated from Law School, Burns spent a short time with the firm of Paul, Weiss, Rifkind, Wharton and Garrison in New York, leaving there to clerk for U.S. District Judge Constance B. Motley, who is Black, a woman, and has a reputation for being one of the most humanitarian judges in the country.

"I think she is a fantastically kind judge. We had a great experience together because it was my first year out of law school, and her first year on the bench, so that we were doing everything for the first time and it made things very hard, but also very exciting. I think she is a terrific judge and it was a good experience for me. After I left her I went to work for the Inc. Fund where she had been for almost twenty years, and I stayed there until I opened this office in January of 1970.

"I had decided, I guess from age seven, that I didn't want to use the law for private gains but rather as a tool for social change. My first thought upon leaving law school in terms of job placement was that I wanted to have some exposure to private practice to see how it operated so I did go to a large, commercial albeit liberal firm, but then the thing opened up with Judge Motley and I took a leave of absence and never went back.

"The function of the law schools over the years has been to provide the kind of lawyer who will serve the basic drives of the society—the drives of material acquisition, self-aggrandizement —and the law schools continue to do that with some modifications.

"I think the southern civil rights movement pricked the conscience of a lot of lawyers. And the Legal Services program made it possible for people to do poverty law and still eat. One provided the mental climate and the other provided the base for the proliferation of socially concerned lawyers. Before these things happened, if you wanted to do that kind of law there were not that many organizations available to do it within, and so it was hard.

"It may be too early to tell, but I think we're past the peak period of this drive for social relevance in terms of careers. I think the law firms are finding it easier to recruit people with increased starting salaries and the opportunity to do some pro bono work which gives young lawyers the opportunity to rationalize and be co-opted in a sense. I think a lot of the zeal and spirit that existed before the movement was fragmented has been dissipated. That spirit was very infectious in the midsixties before things began to break down in the movement.

"I think today money is a real consideration. I know with many students, especially Black students with families, they have thousands of dollars worth of debts to repay when they finish with law school. So, even if they intend to do something relevant, they often get hooked on the money. I know that Black law students are having an awful time just getting through these days because of the lack of financial assistance. There are more scholarships now but there are more students too.

"You will find many more activist Black lawyers and young white lawyers today because they are affected by the social climate around them but often they, especially the Black ones, can't afford to take on the cases of third world militants. By 'afford' I don't mean damaging their practices by being tainted with a political case, although that might be true, too. What I mean is afford from the financial point of view. The problem of Black radicals being represented by white lawyers is something we're all conscious of and sensitive about, but I think in many cases Black lawyers are not available to represent these clients. Sometimes that's due to a failure of communication but, beyond that, is the very considerable practical aspect of this problem. And that is that because of the marginal role most Black lawyers have been forced into, they can't afford to take on a major, political case. This is improving. The NCBL, for instance, did arrange for the defense lawyers for Angela Davis's trial, and I think that may prove to be the most important case of our era.

"In general, we are interested in increasing the number of Black law firms because one of the problems of the Black lawyer is that so many are solo practitioners, and that is a highly inefficient way to practice law. While we have discussed the commune idea, we're more interested now in setting up firms.

"Overall, there is an increased number of Black lawyers, and a similar increase in Black judges, but I'm not sure if it is enough to make a difference when balanced against the repressive measures coming on the scene. I really don't believe, in the last analysis, that you are going to get the kind of redress necessary for change in this country through the courts. We are in a situation now where we don't have the overt racism of the past, but, on the other hand, there is a lot of covert and institutional racism that still exists in the system. The legal system can't bring about change unless we're getting comparable change in the social system.

"There are some remedial or reformist changes I would like to see in the courts. I'd like more Black judges on the bench since quite often they have sensitivity or understanding of cases that white judges don't have, and they aren't polluted with racism in the same way. I'd like to see jury selection procedures changed so that legions of Black people don't have their lives tampered with by middle-aged, middle-class white people, and this is something that is capable of achievement. I think we need to look again at the whole range of victimless crimes and make some changes there. These are all things capable of achievement short of a massive upheaval.

"The courtroom is a classroom whether you want it to be or not. The question is which lesson people learn. I think the court system is going to undergo considerable stress in the near future, and I think there will be enough in the way of upheaval to call for some minor reforms. Whether there will be enough, I don't know. I think that the stresses will have to do not only with defendants who refuse to play the traditional role of silent defendants while seeing themselves victimized, but also with technical things like jury selection and the length of imprisonment before trials.

"The legal system is already cracking down on lawyers, and I think it will be increasingly difficult to be a vigorous advocate in the courtroom. The number of contempt citations and such have increased greatly, and that can't but have a chilling effect on the zeal with which you defend your client even if you consciously reject any fear.

"The law can change society, but I don't think things will flow in that direction because in a democratic system you need a majority of the people to make the laws that change society, and I don't think it is in the interests of the majority of people in this country, as they perceive their interest, to change the laws. One of the most significant things about this country is that for the first time, probably in the history of the world, you have a vast majority of people who are middle-class or better. The bottom is very very narrow in this society. What happens now in the courts is the systematic victimization of a whole lot of people, many of whom are at the bottom. There's a wide divergence of opinion about the court system in the Black community but, in general, I'd have to say there is skepticism and, in some quarters, downright rejection of it.

"I think that the courts have (1) the potential to help people; and (2) when you reach the limitations of their help, because that potential is limited, courts are still useful for insulating people so that these people can be about the business that they have to be about, organizing or whatever. In that sense courts still have a very positive role to play.

"I am also of the belief that we can use the court system

against itself in some ways. We can use the tools of the legal system to deal with some of the problems that have been created by the legal system. I think there is enough elasticity right now in the system to raise questions and to try to get precedents established which will create some structural changes in the law. To be specific, I mean raising questions about bail, capital punishment, the indigent, and taking these questions through the courts to the highest court, the Supreme Court, to get some kind of precedent established which will then filter down and have meaning in people's lives.

"But, at the same time, that rather optimistic view is tempered by the realization that the amount of structural change we are going to get through this process is not really great. At least I don't think it is really great because I think in many ways the law reflects the society, and there's no reason to expect that the courts, or any other institution in American society, are going to transcend the basic nature of the society. They are going to reflect it, and so I think there is a very limited potential for using the law. I think that major change will only come about in the law when it comes about in the society, and I'm afraid the change we're in for now is a wave of repression. It is not coming. It is here."

16

Sheila Okpaku and the Community Law Office

The Community Law Office (CLO), with branches in East and Central Harlem in New York City, is an example of what Legal Aid or Legal Services programs could be if they were not so overworked, if the communities they served had more control over them, and if they were not dependent on the financial assistance of the government, with its accompanying restrictions.

Getting money from foundations, law firms, and government agencies that don't attach strings, the CLO has been operating since 1968 giving residents of New York's Harlem and East Harlem the kind of legal representation that has heretofore been limited to rich, usually corporate, clients. This, instead of the spotty help of most Legal Aid programs or the often mass production representation of Legal Services programs.

CLO, which is the first office of its kind in the country, has been able to do this through a unique set of circumstances. It came into existence at the height of the "fashionable to help the poor" legal period when young attorneys were hesitating to go into lucrative corporate practices because they were having pangs of conscience about all of those poor people they felt they should be helping. Corporate firms, in order to help boost their sagging recruitments, were offering attorney novitiates company time in which they could do pro bono publico work, thus salving their consciences while filling their pockets *and* keeping the cogs of the corporate law machinery working smoothly.

Most of this time wasn't utilized in very effective ways. Existing civil liberties and civil rights organizations did not want, for the most part, to take the time or trouble to train people who'd only help a few hours each month. Public interest firms, where they did exist, felt about the same way. Those young lawyers who ventured unguided into ghettos or community groups with a radical tinge got scared mighty fast and scurried back to their corporate cubicles.

CLO, apparently, was the only organization that found a positive way to channel this raw conscience energy when it was at its peak. The effectiveness with which it did so is borne out by the fact that CLO still exists, and still functions effectively, long after that initial peak has passed, at a time when corporate law firms no longer have to dangle pro bono bait in front of the faces of their potential employees. Now, when socially conscious young lawyers decide, for the most part in law school, that they'll devote their full time to Legal Services, public interest firms, legal collectives or house counsel roles to organizations, CLO still has enough volunteer help to handle over thirty-five hundred varied legal problems of ghetto residents each year.

The director of the Community Law Office in 1971 was Sheila Rush Okpaku, thirty-one years old and born and raised in Buffalo, New York. Her father is deputy city clerk of Buffalo, and a small businessman, and her mother is a social worker.

"I attended Chatham College in Pittsburgh, an all-woman school, and finished first in my class. While I was there I was active in tutorials and rent strikes. I decided to go to law school when I was a junior and went to the Washington semester program where I took courses at American University and saw the practical aspects of the government. I decided that I was interested in government but I didn't want a doctorate in political science so I saw law school as a place where I could get a flexible degree. I didn't intend to practice then.

Okpaku went to Harvard Law School where she was the only Black woman in a class of about four hundred. When she graduated in 1964, she was the first or second Black woman ever to graduate from there. There were only four or five Blacks in the school when she started, and about seven when she graduated. Okpaku didn't like it very much, since it seemed very white and very isolated.

"While I was there, the Black students at Harvard started the Association of African and Afro-American Students which was a predecessor of the black student unions that began later. The Association brought together Blacks from all of the different schools, and also brought out a magazine, *The Harvard Journal of Negro Affairs*, on which I worked. The magazine still comes out.

"I felt then that the Harvard Law courses were irrelevant to my main concerns, since I had been interested in civil rights since my college days, and that they were different from anything I had previously encountered in my life. I had to overcome a lack of familiarity with the terms used in the courses. I felt then that the courses were unrelated to Blacks, but I found out later I was wrong. I now find that you need to know what Harvard is so good at teaching, and that the courses are relevant to things like Black capitalism and the setting up of community cooperatives. Since I left Harvard the struggle has changed from a civil rights one to an economic one, and you need to know the rules of the establishment to help the Black community now. I went back and spoke at Harvard last year and I told the Black law students that they need to know about incorporation, negotiations, job training, and that they need to know it well since they are dealing with good lawyers on the other side.

"After I left Harvard I went to work for the Inc. Fund and I stayed there for three years. At that time I was married to another lawyer who was also working there. I worked mainly on school desegregation and housing matters. I also worked on the first successful challenge to an urban renewal plan that would have affected many of the poor, Black residents of Pulaski, Tennessee. I started souring on the Fund when I became disillusioned with test cases, and their effect on poor and Black people. I felt the Fund had had a real effect on the school desegregation cases but had become less effective since then. The event that really triggered my disenchantment was when the Fund refused to take Julian Bond's case when he was refused his seat on the Georgia legislature. They said that it wasn't a civil rights matter, but I felt that this showed their timidity. Since I've left, the Fund has lost many Black lawyers and now has a distinct majority of whites on the staff. The Fund is very rich and extravagant. The director earns $65,000 a year, which is what he would get if he were a partner in a Wall Street firm.

"I became so disillusioned that I left and went to work as counsel for the Architects Renewal Committee here in Harlem. I felt then that the problem of Black people was one of powerlessness and that the Committee was trying to do something about it. They were challenging city agencies for the right of community people to participate in the planning of their own communities, and we won that right. We also published manuals for community groups and gave legal advice to the community. It was an ombudsman organization which also took the lead in planning work. I wrote all of their reports when I was there, but I didn't do that much legal work. In the summer of 1968, Stephen L. Kass, who had been in my class at Harvard, asked me if I'd be interested in joining CLO which had formed in July of that year. I began working here as an associate director in September."

Although CLO did not come into formal existence as the first autonomous, volunteer, poverty law program in the country until 1968, the seeds of the organization were sown sometime before that.

The idea of CLO began in 1966 when an Episcopal priest, James Lodwick, came in contact with a group of Black and Puerto Rican people who were in the midst of a landlord-tenant dispute. Rev. Lodwick, who was working at the church of St. Edward the Martyr on East 109th Street, contacted Stephen Kass, a friend of his who was working as a corporate lawyer, and asked him to assist the group since they seemed unable to receive the assistance they needed through the established legal channels. Stephen worked with that group and then began working on establishing a weekly free legal clinic at St. Edward's which was manned by volunteer lawyers from downtown Wall Street firms. At about the same time Kandis Vengris, a lawyer who was working for the East Harlem Protestant Parish, started a similar clinic.

The idea behind both of these clinics was to bring the skills of interested Wall Street and corporate lawyers—who number over six thousand in Manhattan—to the East Harlem community, which is composed of 80 percent nonwhites and where 71 percent of the population earns under $5000 a year. Stephen Kass brought together twenty such lawyers, and they began to discuss the need for establishing continuing legal services for East Harlem. The clinics and discussions continued through the fall of 1967 when the participating lawyers began to feel the need for a permanent organization, since many of them were unfamiliar with the community and with the specific types of law that the community needed.

One of the problems in any such operation, of course, is the cultural gap between an usually upper-middle-class lawyer and a poor client. Until the lawyer learns to loosen up, he is usually distrusted by the individual or group he is aiding. He is also often personally apprehensive, for a variety of reasons, about his role, and, sometimes, about his personal safety.

As the interested lawyers began to work toward a permanent organization, they found that they were having difficulty getting financial and moral support from firms and foundations because the Legal Aid Society and the Bar Association had not yet approved of their plan. Those two organizations seemed to be wary of community control of such a program. In March 1968 a compromise was reached in which CLO became a special program under the umbrella of Legal Aid. It was agreed that CLO would be independent, with its own board of trustees, and that it would raise and spend its own funds. However, in seeking support, CLO had to make it clear that supporting it was not a substitute for supporting Legal Aid, its funds had to be channeled through Legal Aid, Legal Aid had to see its yearly budget, three members of the Legal Aid board had the right to attend all CLO trustee meetings, and Legal Aid had the right to terminate the program. This was a compromise that could have proved deadly, as it has with many programs Legal Aid's bureaucracy controls. Luckily, up until now, it hasn't.

After this agreement was reached CLO got $215,000 from firms and foundations for an experimental two-year program. Their first office was formally opened in June 1968. Robert McGuire was chosen as the first director, administering a staff of four, and fifty volunteer lawyers.

The typical CLO volunteer was a young associate of a large law firm, upper-middle-class, and usually a graduate of one of the "better" law schools. In an evaluation later done by the Russell Sage Foundation, it was determined that 85 percent of the participating lawyers volunteered because they felt a sense of moral or professional obligation to help the poor, and they felt that their fulltime practice lacked social significance. It was arranged that each volunteer would come in one afternoon every four to six weeks and that his or her CLO work would take up 15 percent of his or her billable time. If a volunteer could not come to the office for his scheduled time, it was his responsibility to find a substitute. In the first year of CLO's operation volunteers handled about 58 percent of the cases. They now handle over 90 percent. As the program progressed, some volunteers began to specialize in areas that interested them. The staff attorneys supervise and guide the volunteers, do some representation, and also ease the volunteers into the community.

After the first year of the program, Robert McGuire left and Stephen Kass took over as director, a position he retained until July 1971 when he returned to his old firm and Okpaku, who had directed the Central Park North office since January, took over. The staff now consists of ten lawyers—seven Black, two white, and one Puerto Rican—and three hundred attorneys from sixty firms and twenty corporate law departments. The board of directors consists of ten lawyers, eleven East Harlem residents, five Central Harlem residents, and Okpaku.

The two offices get their clients by word of mouth and through the efforts of their two community liaison people who keep up very good relationships with community groups. In the first two years of the program's operation, CLO handled about four thousand cases. That number is now up to thirty-five hundred cases per year, ranging from loitering and divorce to felony charges. To qualify for assistance, an individual client must be a resident of Harlem and cannot earn more than $4000 per year, plus $1000 for each additional dependent. There are no residential or financial requirements for groups if they are working on something that will benefit a low income community.

CLO will handle both civil and criminal cases for individuals and will do group representation for community groups, nonprofit organizations, and new business ventures in normal business law transactions, when the participants do not have the money to retain a lawyer. CLO also provides accounting, notarizing, translation, and typing services, and referrals to other legal agencies for those who don't qualify for CLO aid. It also refers to other social services those whose problems are not legal ones.

"We do everything," Mrs. Okpaku said. "We don't turn away anyone who qualifies. When I first started here, CLO did not do much criminal work, but I wanted to do that so I worked on it,

with another attorney, for a year, and I also did domestic relations cases so that we could train the volunteer lawyers to handle
those sorts of cases. The staff is now divided into four people
who spend their time doing criminal work, trying some cases but
largely preparing practice materials and supervising the volunteers who are interested in criminal work, and five people who
specialize in civil matters. Most of the staff attorneys handle some
cases to keep up their skills, and then spend the rest of their time
in supervisory work. We do screen all of the people who come in
with criminal cases, and we do turn some away—for instance we
wouldn't help a drug pusher who was not also a drug user. We try
to handle those cases where we feel that competent private counsel can make a difference.

"The key to the success of any volunteer program such as
CLO is in the administration of it. We publish our docket and
dispositions of cases each week, volunteers do a status report on
all of their cases whenever they come up here, and we bring out a
newsletter that informs all participants and interested parties of
what we are doing and of materials that could be of use to them.
We also have periodic meetings with the volunteers, and we conduct seminars for them on specific subjects.

"We differ from Legal Services in that we are a separate program privately funded except for a Housing and Urban Development Model Cities grant which we received in 1971 to supple-
ment the initial funding. We have a different manpower source,
and, because we aren't government-funded, we don't have to follow OEO guidelines so we can take criminal cases and cases for
group and community development. Our lawyers can have a
manageable case load so they don't get overworked, and we
can handle cases in a rather traditional way. We use para-
professionals in the East Harlem office to draw up divorce papers
—although they must consult a lawyer if there is any question—
but that is the only expedited method we use. We prefer that our
clients have an initial contact with a lawyer, rather than with a
para-professional, because we feel that it is important for the

community to deal with professionals. We've found that most clients want to talk to a person with training and expertise in the law.

"An interesting thing we have found is that the community people here can detect a phony. They know if you know your stuff, and one of the reasons for our success is that our lawyers impress the community with their expertise. When they get a case they are systematic and thorough, they leave no stone unturned, and they usually get good results.

"Unlike some other legal organizations we will represent any-one who comes to us with a valid proposal. My politics are irrelevant to what I am doing. I think that most Black lawyers will help Black people even if these people espouse an ideology with which they don't agree. There is racial identification between a Black lawyer and a Black client, and most of these lawyers feel that their clients deserve good representation because, as members of a minority, they have been oppressed. If that is an ideology, that is my ideology.

"I think that a lawyer should try to change the legal system where he can and should work within it when he has no other choice. That is if he wants to be a lawyer. Many, of course, just turn away from it altogether.

"It seemed that the real gung-ho young volunteers, the ones who pressured their firms into letting them work here, came here in 1969 and 1970. Then, in late 1971, we launched a major recruitment effort, and found that we could still get enthusiastic young lawyers who were better informed about the poverty law area than the ones we started out with. They told us that they had done poverty law work in clinical programs while they were in law school, and they seem to have a lot of savvy. We did lose some of our best people from that initial group because they decided to leave Wall Street to do pro bono work fulltime.

"However, to compensate for that loss of younger lawyers we did get and are still getting older, senior associates, and even partners coming in to help us if we have a case that we feel they are especially equipped to handle. We couldn't get that commitment at first, but now some firms are coming around and deciding that a set percentage of firm time should be used representing the poor. When we started we had no liaison partners—ones we could call if we needed manpower or had a problem—now we have forty. I think that this shows a change in the attitude of the legal profession toward representing the poor.

"Sometimes we encounter conflicts of interest—a person working on the eviction case of a poor client by a real estate company which his firm represents, for example—but that is easy enough to solve. We assign the case to a lawyer from another firm. But, ideologically, we have no such problems. Both the rich and the poor want the best legal representation that they can get. Most poor people's legal needs are bread and butter needs, and that is what Wall Street firms are all about—fulfilling those needs for rich clients.

"I think that one of the reasons this mixture of people works is because of the friendliness of the staff here, which is predominantly composed of minority people. The volunteers know that even if they are not getting along with a client, they are at least getting a smile from a Black staff attorney. We are very selective about recruiting for the staff. We need people who can command the respect of the lawyers they are dealing with. The age range of the staff is from twenty-five to forty. It is a friendly, congenial staff but no closer than any other staff. I don't think that one should look for personal gratification in work relationships, and I do believe in a hierarchy for a program like ours. There has to be a director, a decision maker.

"We have an excellent staff which you must have for a program like this to work. The staff members realize that two-thirds of their time will be spent in the office, doing supervisory work. You can't have people who want to be in court all of the time.

"This is a pilot program and we have had inquiries from attorneys in about seven other cities who are interested in starting similar programs. I think this has worked. When I came in I was skeptical and just wanted to do criminal work, but now I have come around."

C. B. King, a Black Lawyer in the South

Chevenne Bowers ("C.B.") King, who is now a successful lawyer who made one unsuccessful try for the governorship of Georgia, was born during the pre-Depression years in Albany, Georgia, an urban area one hundred and seventy miles southeast of Atlanta.

"We were poor and, as evidence of the austerity of our meals during these years, I have to this day a psychological block which inhibits my knowingly eating mullet fish or collard greens, the staples of my daily diet when I was growing up. My mother tried to vary the taste of our staid menu by preparing and cooking the fish and greens along the bank of the Palmyra Creek one day a week. With the help of the GI Bill and parttime employment, I was graduated from Fisk University. Subsequently, I was admitted to law school, Case Western Reserve University. After graduating and passing the Ohio bar, I entertained some apprehensions about getting by the Georgia bar and about the discrimination there. I took the Georgia bar and, to my surprise, I passed and was admitted.

"I wanted very much to return to Albany because I felt that something could and ought to be done to improve those conditions, which were repugnant to my sense of fairness, that I had witnessed in growing up. As a child, though unaware of the rule of law, I intuitively felt that there was something wrong when white storekeepers in our neighborhood could, with the help of their friendly sheriff, put Black men in jail for not paying the white storekeeper's bill. I also remembered Black youngsters being arrested for not paying a street tax, that only seemed to apply to us. I saw the white man's 'now you see it, now you don't' law at work all the time that I was growing up. The constancy of its application and the conscionability of the ends to which it was put bore a direct relation to the color of the principals involved rather than the justice of the particular case.

"I came to Albany and started my practice on South Jackson Street in the back of a funeral home in 1954. I fixed the space to which I was assigned to look like a law office, but the funeral home was fittingly symbolic of the putrescent state of the law hereabouts. During those days I was the only Black lawyer southeast of Atlanta. However, now there are approximately thirty-seven Black lawyers in Georgia, and seven of us have practices outside of the Atlanta area.

"When I began my practice here in Albany, I took whatever work I could get, which usually meant Black people in trouble without funds to require the skills and empathy of the white establishment. My first criminal case was that of defending a Black teenager who had been shot by the police and then charged with resisting arrest. During that trial I raised constitutional questions as to the composition of the jury and posed questions relating to racial attitudes on the voir dire [questioning of prospective jurors by the defense and prosecution to ascertain their competence to serve as jurors on the particular case in question]. It was the first time, to my knowledge, anyone had ever done that in this community. Before I started practicing here, the courtroom had been quite generally like a country club with white judges and white lawyers all pleasantly agreed with each other regarding the 'happy' resolution of Black involvements. I did win my case.

"Leading up to the time of this trial, I had my first encounter with a local sheriff, who later bludgeoned me. Very early upon my return to Albany, one of his deputies, who is the present sheriff of this county, attempted to assign me a certain seat in the courtroom. This particular courtroom accommodated two jury boxes, one on the right (the one regularly used by the trial jury) and another one on the left of the judge's bench. It was a practice of lawyers to use the auxiliary jury box. So as I proceeded to wittingly exercise what had heretofore been the exclusive right and privilege of white lawyers, to sit and observe the law at work from close up, those that were in proximity to the seat I selected took flight to the far reaches of the courtroom in horror. The second day I again sat there and upon this occasion the sheriff came over and told me, 'Go sit with them other niggers.' I was numbed by my embarrassment and by the surrealism of pretended oblivion and snickering of lawyers and other court officers which, to my mind, reasserted my almost forgotten identity. This encounter abrasively reasserted an identity I was in the process of forgetting. I explained to the sheriff that, as an officer of the court, I had a right to use the jury box as did the others.

"At this time it was close to the time of the trial of my client, the boy who had been charged with resisting arrest whom I was yet to defend. I left my seat attempting to convince myself that in so leaving I was not yielding to the sheriff's threats but rather recognizing my duty and concern not to prejudice the case against my client. I walked out into the rotunda with the sheriff and protested this patent differential treatment. The sheriff said, 'We ain't had no trouble before you come here, we ain't going to have none now.' I walked to the outside of the courthouse in an effort to overcome a sort of drowning that is common to humans who have been stripped of a sense of self. Yes, I cried a bit as well. I justified my leaving, on command of the sheriff, upon concern for my yet untried criminal client.

"Following the trial I was brought face to face with my pledge to prevail as the equal of any man by sitting among and pitting my skills against my white antagonist, or, alternatively, facing the forced acknowledgment that I had indulged in self-deception by leaving the courtroom and addressing as the cause therefor the concern for my client, instead of the traditional Black fear of white authority. So the next day I returned to the courtroom and to the jury box from whence I had previously gone, somewhat unsure in my own mind as to whether my previous leaving was really responsive to my concern or submission to fear. Again the sheriff came and said, 'Goddamn it, nigger, I thought I told you to get back there with them other niggers. Do you want me to hurt you?' I looked into the face of the sheriff as dispassionately and as calmly as I could under the circumstances and said, 'Sheriff, that's what you will have to do, I'm staying here.' He then told me that he'd give me five minutes to move back to the area in the courtroom to which Blacks were relegated. The sheriff did in fact return some fifteen minutes later. The interim between the sheriff's last warning and his return to the courtroom represented moments of intractable nightmarish anxiety for me. I expected at any moment that he would return and there brutalize me in this forum of white justice. When he did return, instead of coming to where I was, he went to the judge's bench and in that instance I was sure that I had prevailed. Apparently the judge did not encourage the sheriff to forcibly remove me from my seat.

"Six years later I was trying to get into the county jail to see a white SNCC client of mine who had been beaten by some white thugs who were cellmates of his. This sheriff, by whom I had previously been verbally abused, came into his outer office and interrupted a conversation I was then engaged in with one of his deputies. He told me to get out of his office and wait in the hall. He left, and in a moment came back and said, 'You goddamn Black sonofabitch, you still here?' Whereupon he struck me on the forehead with a walking cane, which broke under the force of his blow. He used the remnant of the cane to strike me on the back of my neck as I ran, bleeding, into the hallway.

"Over the years that I've practiced in south Georgia, I have had many similar experiences (absent physical violence) with sheriffs all over rural Georgia. In the early civil rights struggle, an Early County, Georgia, sheriff had a client of mine from Bayonne, New Jersey, in jail. He had been arrested, arraigned, plea of guilty accepted to murder and rape charges, and sentenced to die in the electric chair, all within forty-eight hours. When visiting my client, I inquired casually of the sheriff whether he was sure he had the right man. His response was, 'Damn right.' The more I went to the jail to see the man, the more certain of my client's guilt the sheriff became. Subsequently, I obtained a federal writ of habeas corpus and went to the jail with it, and, as he read audibly the content of the writ, he was heard to say, 'I've been good to you niggers, trying to treat you like a lawyer, C.B. There is limits beyond which patience ain't no goddamn virtue. Now get out of here.' Despite him I was finally successful in obtaining a reversal of the sentence and the charges were ultimately dropped against my client.

"Virtually every aspect of the law, as it relates to my practice, concerns the civil rights and the civil liberties of those whose causes I represent. Tragically, my seventeen years of practice make me to know that the overriding reality of the Black experience in this country is the forced relevancy of race. I now recognize that branches of government—federal, state, and other inferior political subdivisions as well—deliberately promulgate the organic law, administer its benefit, and most generally interpret its meaning in a way most beneficial to those persons or classes that have the least melanin. Despite this the law has been a kind of therapy for me. It has served to quell, to some reasonable extent, feelings of aggression I had acquired in growing into manhood in the South. To that extent the law has been kind to me psychologically. I have a couch in my office which is little used. Hopefully, the law will continue to be therapeutic. Should it fail I shall then be forced to take refuge in my couch. Hopefully, it will suffice."

During the southern civil rights period in the 1960s, C. B. King was kept very busy. In 1961 he walked beside the late Dr. Martin Luther King, who is not a relation, in street demonstrations in

Albany that resulted in some violence and national headlines. He also represented Dr. King and conducted afternoon classes in welfare rights. During this whole period, his practice also provided a training ground for many people's lawyers, three of whom are discussed in this book: Stan Zaks, Paul Harris, and Dennis Roberts.

"Dennis was my first summer intern. I believe it was during 1961 that the National Lawyer's Guild convened an institute in Atlanta, Georgia, that had as its concern personal injury law, to aid in supplementing the income of southern civil rights attorneys. Ann Ginger, an attorney, now a director of the Meiklejohn Civil Liberties Library in Berkeley, at one of these conferences asked me if I wanted a law student to clerk during the summer. I entertained certain reservations as to whether this was the best idea. Would he be bright? White? Finally, I agreed and requested that she submit a list of names from which I would make a selection. Dennis's résumé said that he had been a steward in the merchant marine, a bellhop, and busboy so I thought he was Black. The rest of the résumés sounded like they were from real 'preppy' types or 'aliens.' So I accepted Dennis. I am inclined now to think that Dennis was quite conscious of what he was doing in the preparation of his résumé. He was with me the summer of 1963, and he was really superior in terms of his aptness of mind, his sensitivity, and his possession of basic instincts as to how the law should be used. He was of immeasurable assistance to me. Now that I have indulged Dennis in deserved adulation, perhaps I'll not be thought gross should I speak of his initial innocence. When all the youngsters who were involved in the movement were arrested and sent to the outlying county jails, Dennis and I made the rounds to see them. One of such jails was in Camilla. After Dennis and I had been admitted to the jail the sheriff said, speaking of Dennis, 'Lower than a goddamn dog helping that nigger C.B.' Responsive to which Dennis inquired, 'Is that for the record?' The sheriff said, 'You goddamn right. C.B. tell that goddamn white boy I'll rip his ass aloose.'

"My accepting Dennis and other interns, along with other lawyers similarly situated, was really the beginning of LSCRRC. Bill Higgs, a Harvard Law School graduate, was in Mississippi taking controversial cases for Blacks, in the early 1960s. He received, I'm told, substantial grants from Harvard alumni to defray the costs of maintaining Harvard Law students in Mississippi over the summer. Prior, however, to the initiation of Bill's Mississippi project, he was arrested on moral charges and given the option of leaving the state or being prosecuted. He left the state. So this platoon of Harvard Law School students was stranded and Bill appealed to lawyers in Georgia to absorb them. I accepted two of them, Elizabeth Holtzman and Frank Parker, the same summer that Dennis was here, and out of this absorption came LSCRRC.

"I still accept interns. I've had a minimum of two each summer since 1963. One summer there were six. In 1966 I got my first Black intern. In 1971 I was assigned a Black intern who was a native of Albany. It's coming around.

"I speculatively submit that I would hardly be suited, at this point, to practice in the North. I look at myself as a butcher, a cutting edge against the grain of accepted primitive southern courtroom conduct, that is, when examining witnesses, I bear little tolerance for old intolerances, like the use of the word 'nigger.' Many of my stratagems might not work in the North where things are more sophisticated, better oiled.

"Organizationally, I'm most closely connected with the Inc. Fund. I am one of its cooperating attorneys. I also belong to the National Conference of Black Lawyers, as well as to the Guild and ACLU."

After fifteen years of law practice in Albany, King made a foray into politics. "In late November of 1969 I received a call from Macon where five thousand people from the Black Coalition of the State of Georgia were meeting. The calling party indicated that I had been nominated, by them, to run for governor. Upon his urging I drove to Macon and, several hours later, acknowledged what I considered a great tribute. But I asked for two weeks to think about it. Andrew Young, among others, encouraged me to become involved and to accept the candidacy. Andy committed himself to raise the necessary funds. I agreed. Thereafter it developed that Julian Bond elected not to offer his candidacy for the congress of the United States, so Andy decided to run in his stead and those funds that he succeeded in raising were, of course, used for his own campaign."

It cost King quite a bit of his own money to carry on the campaign. He ran a distant third in the race for the Democratic gubernatorial nomination.

"I ran for governor because I felt then and I feel now that indispensable to the garnering of power by the powerless is unity, whether it be Blacks or even poor whites, or for that matter, any minority. That experience has made me a little bit more sensitive to what causes some people to become politically motivated. I, now, have no illusions regarding the significant number of political prostitutes that are generated in an election for political office. This experience, in retrospect, was good, despite the painful financial burden I bore. I would become involved, in the future, in politics only if I had sufficient finances to avoid the frustrations and anxieties that are experienced in terms of the things that you would like to do and can't do in mounting a serious campaign.

"Hopefully, this experience contributed something positive as well to the whole political spectrum of the state. Hopefully, it gave to the unconscious a political consciousness of the need for cohesion. Jimmy Carter, the candidate who won the election for governor of this state, said to me since assuming the status of governor, that my involvement in the campaign had profound effect on his consciousness of the responsibility of the office of governor to all of Georgia's people. My own reflection on the worth of that statement is that it is minuscule, particularly if we are to judge his deeds rather than his declarations."

After the campaign King went back to his practice in his modern brick and glass building which stands in the middle of the city's major Black community.

"About six years ago my brother, who was in the real estate and insurance business, and I built this building with two wings, one for each of our offices. I had decided it was time to get out of the funeral home not, however, because the symbolism of the dead and the law was any less valid. My brother died in 1969 and his widow asked me to serve as president of the insurance and real estate businesses, so it looks like I'm doing both law and insurance. Actually, my relation to the other businesses is in name only. The legal business keeps me busy enough.

"The number of Black lawyers is improving. In 1971 another Black Lawyer, who graduated from Case Western Reserve Law School, came here to practice with me. He turned down the offer of one of the biggest firms in Cleveland to come back to the South. I feel that law schools should solicit Black students who evidence a commitment to practice in the South, even if the solicitation is done out of feelings of guilt. I find many times that though people can be, and are, motivated out of guilt feelings the end results of such motivations are often good. I think that to some extent this observation is borne out by the number of white lawyers one sees today representing third world people and doing a good job. I know some of the younger Black lawyers resent white involvement but I don't know if their resentment can be justified on the basis of nonapplication of legal skills.

"I don't think that our jurisprudential system is very effective in achieving the ideals of justice. It has problems in form as well as substance and I don't know what can be done about them. I'm not very optimistic about the courts as a conscionable regulator of controversy between the sovereign and men, and men and men. I've been disenchanted with what the system has done and will do for some, while doing nothing for others. I remember during the early phases of the movement here many grass-roots people possessed feelings of great exhilaration, that the action and deeds of government, through its court system, would, at last, cause the Constitution to complement the majesty of its rhetoric. They felt that the federal government was now going to exert its awesome power in such a way that the primeval covenant would be fulfilled: freedom and justice for all. The people who came here to help did a lot of paperwork. They reported instances of major official brutality to the attorney general's office or to the four resident FBI agents in Albany and, occasionally, to their regional head in Atlanta. Nothing really happened. As the months progressed there was ultimately a trial of the sheriff of Baker County in one such case. A white storekeeper who had his store in a Black neighborhood was one of the jurors and he voted for the acquittal of the sheriff. Following the verdict Blacks, whose business he exclusively relied upon, boycotted his store. He complained that his civil rights were being violated and instantly *eighty* FBI agents were sent to Albany in response to his complaint. At a later movement meeting at which the latter situation was discussed, a very old woman got up and said, "Well now I done found out that even the federal government ain't nothing but a white man.'

"I have seen some indication on the part of young whites in high school and college that shows a variance with the attitudes of their forbears. But is this sufficient to stem the tide? I think something has to be done, in a more organized and deliberate way, or the whole thing goes down the drain. Though I am impressed with some of what I see from the young white lawyers, I wonder if the attitudes of Paul, Dennis, Stan, and the others is still current in law schools today. There was hope in the sixties but any number of negative factors on the part of the government —like Kent State, Jackson State, and now Angela Davis and Attica—has created disenchantment. The memory of these events plagues the young dreams of this country with despair and displaces hope with cynicism.

"The South is but a microcosm of what happens all over this country. Really, the face of America is essentially one."

18

Charles Garry, Chief Defense Counsel, the Black Panther Party

Charles Garry, the chief defense counsel of the Black Panther party, was born in Bridgewater, Massachusetts, in 1909 to Armenian parents who had immigrated there thirteen years previously after one of the many Armenian massacres. His father, Hagop Garabedian, worked for a brother who owned a coke and coal business until Hagop led a workers' strike and was kicked out of his brother's business and home. He then worked in a shoe factory until he saved enough money to move his family to Selma, California, where he had purchased a ten-acre cling peach farm.

"The joker he bought it from didn't tell him that it would be two years before he got a crop, so he got a bike and would travel eight or nine miles every day to work for other farmers for seventy-five cents a day. I remember that first Christmas, when I was about five, we didn't have a bite of food in the house, literally.

"Eventually the farm did well enough that we were able to trade it for forty acres. When I started school, I had to learn English because only Armenian was spoken at home. I learned pretty quickly, and I also learned how to handle my dukes. It became a ritual. Every day I would have to fight someone for calling me a 'goddamned Armenian.' That was my first lesson in prejudice.

"The Depression had hit rural areas before the crash of 1929 and I had had to go to work in the canneries. Near the end of my second year of high school, my younger sister died and my parents were so badly broken up that they didn't bother to harvest the crop. We went into bankruptcy and had to return to Massachusetts, and that ended my formal schooling for a while.

"I worked in the auto industry there for a while but then I got lead poisoning so I learned tailoring and went to Boston where I worked in a dry cleaning plant in Malden. I also did some writing, and sold two stories to a magazine that existed then called the *Boston American.* In 1926 I returned to Selma and worked in the canneries for a few months until I had enough money to send for my parents and two brothers who were very unhappy in Massachusetts.

"Then I came to San Francisco and worked in a tailor shop for a while, and then went back to Selma and finished up high school in one year. I had planned to go to Stanford and had invested some money so I could, but the stock crash came and wiped out those plans in 1929. I kept working; at one point I was the fastest can stacker in the state of California. Then I got married and my wife and I opened a small dry cleaning business on a shoestring. In 1934 I started to study law nights at the San Francisco Law School. That year too, as a member of the Dry Cleaners and Dyers Union, I became active in the labor movement, including the 1934 general strike. Also, that year most of our shop and the room where we lived behind it was turned over to the gubernatorial campaign of Upton Sinclair.

"I started practicing law in 1938, mainly representing unions that were trying to break away from the AFL to form the CIO. My clients then were looked upon with the same animosity as my clients now are. These rebel unions weren't considered quite respectable, and neither was I. I was beaten up a couple of times in those days by goon squads.

"When I had to go into the army, I went in as a buck private in infantry."

Just before going into the service, Garry had headed a delegation of ministers and others who visited Sacramento and persuaded the governor, Culbert Olson, to veto a bill that would have outlawed the Communist party. Perhaps because of this or because of his earlier involvement with the labor movement, Garry was interrogated by a major and a colonel from the Army's G-2 intelligence section in Washington, D.C., for two days while he was serving as an instructor at Camp Fannin in Tyler, Texas. After that he was sent from camp to camp.

"Finally I raised hell and they sent me overseas where I served as an infantry scout in Italy. I was discharged in 1945 and returned to San Francisco and my practice.

"In 1948 I ran for Congress because a political demand was made on me to run. I was a World War II vet and the country was hell-bent in a cold war, and World War III was in the offing, so I ran to expose that as best I could, along with Henry Wallace. Then in 1949, I ran in a three-way race to fill a congressional vacancy along with Jack Shelly who won and later became the mayor of San Francisco."

In the 1950s, Garry served as president of the San Francisco chapter of the Guild.

"I was up to my ears then in all kinds of civil rights work and loyalty battles. I probably handled several hundred loyalty cases. So they called me a radical and they called me a red and I remember that two of my brothers had their security questioned because of me, and they are not the least bit involved in politics at all.

"But I wasn't hurt by it all. As a matter of fact I went right on through the repression fighting back strongly. You see what I love about the Panthers today as compared to some of the liberals of the fifties is that the Panthers are not scared or frightened, and they don't go underground in their activity. But the people in the fifties were frightened, scared shitless, because they did not have a total commitment to their own goals. They were afraid of being poor; they were afraid of going to jail. I was called before HUAC in 1957, and I told them to go to hell and kiss my ass."

Garry formed a partnership with Julius Keller in 1957 and then they joined with Benjamin Dreyfus and Frank McTernan to form the core of their present firm. For fee-paying cases, Garry became an expert in forensic medicine, but he always interspersed political work with this fee-generating work. (During this time, he brought between $150,000 and $200,000 per year into the firm.) Beginning with the Wesley Robert Wells case, that of a Black man in Folsom Prison who was sentenced to die for throwing a cuspidor at a guard while serving a life sentence, he has been involved in over fifty cases of people facing the death penalty.

It was because of events that occurred on October 28, 1967, that Garry's life and career changed though not radically, since he has always been a socialist who felt that he was a part of the class struggle. On that date Huey Newton, the minister of defense of the Black Panther Party for Self-Defense, an Oakland-based group thet tried to control police brutality, educate people in the Black community, and institute programs that would help the community, was arrested and charged with murder of one police officer and assault upon another police officer.

"I was in Los Angeles at the time and I heard about the incident over the air, and I just felt that I was going to be defending Huey Newton when I heard about what had happened. I knew that was going to happen. When I got home at noon that day or the following one a Black friend called and said that I must defend Huey, that I couldn't allow anything to happen to him. Then several other friends and a few lawyers called and said the same thing.

"When I went to meet Huey I knew that I was the one who should defend him. I was just fascinated with him. Here he was lying in bed with a trachea tube through his nose and police officers all around threatening him, and he wasn't afraid. And he decided, right then and there, that I should defend him. It was after he made this decision that all of the second guessing began, not with the Panthers but with my partners and white liberals who thought there should be a Black lawyer in there. All that 'a, b, c' thinking started that you have to have a Black lawyer for a Black and a woman lawyer for a woman and all of this horseshit instead of recognizing the fact that you are involved in a revolutionary situation and that a person who can pick up the cudgel and go to work is the person you get. Finally Eldridge and Huey and the others said, 'Listen, Garry, we make the decision who we want to defend Huey Newton'—that was it."

After he agreed to take on the case, Garry began to read and prepare himself for it. He felt that he did not have the necessary knowledge at that time to properly defend a Black person from a ghetto. Huey began to educate him politically about the situation in the Black community and the evolution and philosophy of the Black Panther party. Garry has said that it wasn't until two days before Huey took the witness stand that they actually discussed the details of the case.

In September of that year Huey was acquitted of murder but convicted of manslaughter although that conviction was overturned because the judge had incorrectly instructed the jury. Huey went to trial for the same incident twice more in 1971. The second trial resulted in a hung jury and, in the third trial, the jury was also hung. The charges against Newton were then dismissed.

In the time that elapsed between his first meeting Huey and the first trial, Garry became *the* Panther lawyer. It was even reported that the San Francisco police chief would directly call him whenever a Panther was arrested in the area. Newton; Bobby Seale, the chairman of the party; and David Hilliard, the chief of staff, referred to him as their chief defense counsel, among other accolades, and he has defended all three of these men, along with other Panthers, since his association with the organization began.

"I would characterize my association with the Panthers as very close and intimate. It is not what is commonly accepted as an attorney-client relationship. They consider me as a brother and I consider them as brothers and sisters.

"To me they are where the labor movement was thirty years ago. They relate to the struggle, whereas the labor leaders of today do not. I think that the best thing they have done is form their organization. The second best thing they have done is to be able to take on the oppressor without any compromise, without mincing words about it. Their whole beliefs, in socialism, Marxism, democratic apportionment of wealth, and the courage and the dignity they have given to people both within and without the Black community are all part of that, and it has been contagious. In other words, they have played the role of the vanguard. Now, their other programs like breakfast for children and medical coverage aren't going to solve or change the situation, but they are part of an educational process, and they do feed and educate and care for the needy so that they can respond to the revolutionary change as they must, and, in the meantime, they survive.

"The jailing and repression by the government can't change this. It's immaterial whether there are few Panthers or not. The Black Panther party was never intended to be a mass organization. It's a vanguard organization that relates to the needs of the community and of the people. They don't need large numbers. They have a common terminology, 'You may jail a revolutionary but you can't jail the revolution.' Putting Panthers in jail won't stop them. Huey was in prison thirty-four months and that didn't stop him.

"The government was able to buy off certain top labor unions to the point where they go along with them in most areas, but they are not going to be able to do that to the Black community. We still have one person out of seven going to bed hungry every single night here in America. We have twelve and a half million people on relief who are living impoverishedly and not getting the needs they demand. This is where change will come from, from the lumpen area in the Black community and brown, and red and white, from the sixty million Americans who do not have the good things in life that the other hundred and forty million allegedly do have.

"The only time that you can get these hundred and forty million excited is when you take away their livelihood. You see, I lived through the first depression and I saw the associated charity wagon come into this white middle-class district of San Francisco and stop at nine out of ten homes and a lot of those people, when their dignity and means of livelihood were taken away, ended up being damn strong radicals. I think we are headed for some serious economic changes right now and that the same thing might happen again. If that happens what is so important is that there is a Black Panther party that has a direction and knows where it is going and is not going to be compromised but is willing to form coalitions with other groups.

"And the Panthers have patience, tremendous patience. If I were a Black man I'd probably have been killed forty years ago. I would not take many of the things that the Panthers take today. The way they get harassed and treated I would not have been able to take.

"I think America has a future only because the Panthers and others like them have a future. I think, because of them, fascism can be warded off, which doesn't mean that it isn't on its way here and doesn't mean that it won't win. But, with the Panthers, we have the tools to fight them with, the forces to fight them with. All we have to do is organize. The weakest link in the American movement is that the oppressed people are not unified in a political direction, that there is not a coalition about a common denominator. Well, the Panthers can provide that denominator and give America a future.

"As far as the courts go, the Panthers pointed out long ago that Black men and women don't get justice in the courts and that they haven't in three hundred years in this country. I agree. I don't see any more relevancy to the courts than I do to the universities. They are all part and parcel of the same thing. They just give the facade of legality to the robbery, in the economic sense, that goes on.

"But getting rid of the court system isn't the answer. The court system is only another arm of the oppressor, like the police. The average judge considers himself a human being, a person of compassion and, if you were to reveal to him that he is a pig and acted like a pig, he would be very unhappy because he doesn't see himself in that role. He has been brainwashed to see himself in a tradition that is four hundred years old and not related to the contemporary needs of our society.

"What you have to change is the system. Once we have the democratic apportionment of wealth I believe the ghettos will go, unemployment will go, the need for property claims will go. But, until the day comes that we can have a utopian anarchy—I consider that the highest form of society—there will have to be some regulations because you can't change people's minds and hearts overnight. We'll probably have to have courts but they will be people's courts where the judges have a sense of feeling and compassion.

"For now I believe the courtroom should be a place for a lawyer to represent a client as that client is. If she's a prostitute she should be represented as one, and you should explain to the jury what she is and why she is there. If your client is a revolutionary, a person who believes in immediate change and is being fucked over by the system for that belief, that ought to be presented to the court. You cannot represent a revolutionary today without bringing in their revolutionary spirit so that the jury, which is the conscience of the community, can understand it. You must bring struggle into the courtroom and bring it in in such a way that the jury understands.

"After all, the only reason you are there in the courtroom is because things weren't done out in the streets, and your client is there as an involuntary guest. The role of the lawyer is to see that the client gets out on the streets, but, while you're doing that, you have to expose the system that brought him there. If you can't do that you are not making your responsible contribution as an advocate for your client.

"Lawyers must attack the system by exposing injustice wherever they see it, which is three hundred and sixty-five days a year. The fact that Bobby Seale or Ericka Huggins or Huey or a few of the Panthers are getting heavy defenses doesn't change the fact that thousands of black people, brown people, red people, yellow people, and white people are being fucked over daily in the courtroom. This business of compromise pleading—they call it plea-bargaining—goes on day in and day out. A lawyer must expose this and refuse to go along with the compromises.

"The legal profession will try to crack down harder on lawyers who do this. I think if I'd been in Chicago for the conspiracy case I probably would have gotten a thousand years. As it is, now I've never even been reprimanded although the character committee is looking into my 'morals and fitness' as a result of the Los Siete case. But what the profession will do is disbar a few lawyers and put a few in jail—which is no worse than their clients' going there. But that could bring about the intimidation of the independence of the bar to a point where fascism will come about. That's how you create the police state. In that state, the first group of things to go is always the courts and the independence of lawyers.

"I'm working as a lawyer because somebody has to defend my clients. I didn't put them into the courtroom, society did, and I don't want them in jail, I want them out of there, so that they can do their thing on the streets. If I wasn't doing that I wouldn't handle any criminal case because I think it is a wasted effort. I guess I consider myself a person who believes in revolutionary change, a person who believes that when the law is tyranny, revolution is in order. But calling yourself a name doesn't make you such. You've got to judge people by their conduct, the way they work. I'd much rather be judged on what I'm doing than on the rhetoric I'm making."

19

D'Army Bailey, Berkeley City Councilman

D'Army Bailey, who was elected to the Berkeley city council in 1971, was born twenty-nine years before that in Memphis, Tennessee.

"I was named after my grandfather, and he, I understand, was named after a gypsy midwife in Mississippi. I grew up in Memphis in a poor and lower-middle-class Black economic and social scene. My father was a Pullman porter. My mother had been a maid, but then went to barber school, and later went to nursing school. There were only two kids in my family, me and my brother Walter, who is now a civil rights lawyer in Memphis.

"The community was substantially divorced from the white one, so we didn't feel the immediacy of whites except for the police, who were brutal.

"Walter, who is a year older, and I had a very close relationship. His friends were mine. He had intended to be a pro football player or a physical education teacher so his friends seemed rowdy in a kind of football sense. Mine were just rowdy. A lot of the people we grew up with are now hanging out on the streets of Memphis. The high school we went to was the largest Black high school in the middle South. Both there and in the community, you had to prove yourself to survive because there was a pecking order. Walter was a football player. I was viewed as a smooth brother. I wrote for the school paper, had a radio show, and was in a couple of social clubs which, for us, were vehicles to get together, party a lot, and have dances. There were no economic distinctions but there were image distinctions.

"Because of this image thing, some of the rougher people in school would challenge me and I'd have to fight them selectively. See, it wasn't enough to be smooth. You also had to prove yourself physically from time to time. I'd choose to fight the tougher ones in the school corridor because I knew someone would break it up sooner or later.

"I wasn't political at that time. The first politicizing for me came when I was thirteen or fourteen and the whole thing in Little Rock broke. I followed it closely but I still didn't connect it in terms of political involvement for me. Then there was the killing of Emmett Till, and that had an impact on me. Those two things began the process, but there wasn't really a civil rights movement at that time.

"But, even before I was politicized, I never did like to take any shit from white folks when I was growing up. I remember when I was fifteen and working in a hospital, I got fired because I had talked back to one of the white supervisors. I pursued the argument up to the board of directors of the hospital, but they refused to hear me. It was a good job but it wasn't that important to me except that I felt that I was getting fucked over by those people. But that was more a personal than political thing, although I knew that racism was involved. I kept working at night during high school, and I kept getting fired.

"Just as I was finishing high school there was some pressure from the NAACP for integrating downtown schools and I did work with them a little. Mainly because I dug any brother and sister who was taking on the power structure.

"Walter had gone to Southern University in Louisiana on a football scholarship the year before I graduated from high school in 1959. I decided to go there because he had. He was playing football and hooked up with the campus athletes. When I got there I was put in an honors group. I ran for freshman class president. Southern is the largest Black university in the South and there were sixteen hundred people in my class. My brother and his friends pushed me for the office and, about that time, there began to be this political thing in my head. I remember the day of the speeches before the election there had just been a slaughter in Johannesburg, so when I spoke I spoke about that and about how we, as Black students, had to relate to that. I won the election.

"After that, the university people had me pegged as one of the student leaders, which meant one of the people they could manipulate. I started writing for the paper, got elected as a delegate to the National Student Association [NSA] convention, where I had my first contact with whites politically. The next year, 1961, the civil rights demonstrations hit campus and closed the campus down for a while. I was peripherally involved. Seventeen got thrown out of school for them.

"In September, when I was a junior, they started again, and I intended to be peripherally involved again but the original leaders got thrown in jail and I was asked to help keep things moving. I did and we forced the university to close again. The university decided to expel the leadership so I and seventy-five to two hundred other students, nobody knows exactly, got thrown out in January of 1962. I was then a member of the Baton Rouge CORE and a member of the student advisory committee to SNCC, so about ten or twelve of us that got expelled stayed in the city, working out of crowded and funky hotel rooms until May doing voter registration and things like that.

"After that, I went to Clark University in Worcester, Massachusetts. They had one other Black student there, and I was supposed to be a Clark celebrity. I couldn't walk from one end of the campus to the other without all of these people wanting to talk to me about the South. After a couple of weeks I decided that, when they asked about the South, I'd tell them about the racism in the North, in the town of Worcester, and on campus. I alienated a lot of students then. They called me a trouble-maker. But by that time, I had gotten together with the radical students, about twenty of them, and then some of the Black townspeople came in and we formed the Worcester Student Movement for Civil Rights and picketed some department stores and things.

"Then we went in and took over the NAACP. Then we made attacks on the largest factory in town. The owner, Robert Stoddard, who also owned the local newspaper and television station and who gave a lot of money to Clark, was a member of the John Birch Society. The university administration began to get uptight. When I graduated from Clark, the editor of the student newspaper wrote an editorial saying that I was the worst thing that could have happened to the university.

"I went to Boston University Law School for a year and, while there, I helped to organize a chapter of LSCRRC. Then I went to Yale for the other two years of law school and I became one of the leaders of LSCRRC there. I'd go back to the South in the summers and do work there for LSCRRC or the Inc. Fund or other organizations. There were some of the worst people at Yale. I couldn't deal with them, so I only associated with a few people. When I graduated in 1967, I didn't know what I wanted to do except that I didn't want to practice law. Then I was elected the second Black director of LSCRRC, succeeding Bill Robinson. I directed that for over a year and also got involved in some other activities. After that, I came out to San Francisco and worked for the main office of the San Francisco Neighborhood Legal Assistance Foundation.

"At Legal Assistance it was a year of continual fighting and, after a while, I knew I was wasting my time. I was the only Black attorney in the main office. Most white people think Black people are dumb and that they can manipulate them and use them. That office had had pressure to have a Black attorney in there, and I was hired to be their token. I began to raise hell and tried to get them to be a community resource instead of an elitist, test case unit. I wanted them to hire Black people to get into the community, lawyers or nonlawyers, and help the community with whatever it was doing. I felt that the program wasn't destined to last long and the best thing to do would be to take the money and use it to create a revolutionary situation in the communities. So I had big fights with the office about that, about policy, about hiring more Blacks. I tried to organize the Black lawyers in other offices but most of them were family people who needed the jobs. I finally demanded that the director of the program resign. He did shortly afterward. So the board hired a shaky brother to take his place and his first order of business was to fire me.

"Me and my ally, a guy who had been run out of the Legal Services program in Houston because he was too radical, filed a suit in federal court charging the office with not following their own administrative policies. The nonprofessional employees demanded my reinstatement, and they finally took me back. After they did, I quit. I decided that I didn't want another job in another kind of legal thing. I was disgusted with the program, disgusted with the courts because they are so saturated with racism. I think that Legal Services is a serious co-opting factor. They are, internally, the epitome of the kinds of abuses of power that they fight externally. They are now mainly concerned with self-preservation, which wasn't the original intent. I was at the original conference, and it was decided there that Legal Services would set up some kind of revolutionary base in the community and then phase themselves out. But they became the preserve, mainly, of upwardly mobile Jewish lawyers who want to make a name for themselves at the expense of the poor. Self-preservation has become primary for them and helping poor people is secondary. There is enormous elitism in the programs. I was also chairman of the board of Berkeley Neighborhood Legal Services Program for a year but then they kicked me out as chairman although I'm still on the board.

"After I left the whole Legal Services thing, I wanted to get as far away from the law office as I could. I took off my suit and tie and hung out in Berkeley getting to meet some of the young brothers and sisters. I'd still take some cases helping out friends if I felt like it, working out of my house. I also was working on some cases with the National Committee Against Discrimination in Housing which operates out of New York City. Left over from the LSCRRC time I was still a program consultant to the Council on Legal Education Opportunity [CLEO] and a program advisor to the Field Foundation, on the executive committee of the San Francisco Lawyers Committee on Urban Affairs, and on the board of directors of the Council on Legal Education for Professional Responsibility [CLEPR]. In 1970, however, I was told that my services were no longer desired on the CLEPR board which is this ultra-establishment foundation in New York which gives money to law schools for the development of clinical legal education programs. They have a twenty-member board, and they selected me because I'd been with LSCRRC and was Black. There were only two other progressives on the board, Leslie Dunbar and Fred Graham. I'd go there and introduce a resolution calling for a national investigation of police actions against the Panthers and the others would get upset.

"When I started working here in Berkeley, I took time getting to know people. Ira Simmons and I had been looking at recent elections and seeing an almost total absence of issues being raised that dealt with the needs of Black or other third world people in the city. We talked about entering the next city election. Win, lose, or draw we knew that we could raise some issues which would force the real corruption and dereliction of the local government out into the open. Around November of that year we told some friends that we would be running for the city council. Thirty-three people, about eight or ten of whom were serious, were running for four seats. Ira and I were the only two Black candidates who were for community control of the police, which lost in the election. However, with the backing of the radical forces in the city, Ira and I and a third radical candidate, Ilona Hancock, won.

"I think the political philosophy of Black people needs to be a revolutionary one, one geared toward the interests, problems, and needs of Black people. There can be some Marxist-Leninist philosophy and some others mixed in. I don't like to be identified with a particular kind of ideology because it then pre-empts your flexibility both in terms of your own thinking and your operating with other people. I think that is a mistake the Panthers made in trying to impose a Marxist-Leninist ideology on the Black community. What you do is go out and relate to the community where it's at and try to build that to the point where it becomes revolutionary in its thinking. If the result is Marxism-Leninism that is all right. The main thing is how you revolutionize the system so that the oppression which now affects Black people is eliminated.

"Black people have a precarious existence in this country which at any moment can be translated into total subjugation by the police forces of this country. I think the idea of the system is to co-opt Black people and keep them oppressed and then to throw carrots onto the dungheap. Now, if that doesn't work—if Black people get hip to that kind of thing, which is what is happening—then they're just going to resort to all-out suppression.

"They are definitely ready to put us all into camps if it becomes necessary to preserve their power and their influence. That's why Black people must not only perceive the domestic situation, but also realize what the American power structure is doing all over the world, because once we know who our natural allies are—those the money-grubbing, power-crazed capitalists are stepping on all over the world—then we are stronger.

"I think some white radicals are serious revolutionaries, that is, ones who will go out and work effectively against the present order of things no matter what the possible personal risk may be. But I think every Black person *has* to be a revolutionary. How can you reform a system that is corrupted and controlled by the enemy?

"There may appear to be an inconsistency between that position and being on the Berkeley city council. But, if you're going to build toward a revolutionary movement, you can't do that unless you have some allies within the system who are going to give you information, funds, and help in the development of such a movement. In a position like the one I'm in, there can be co-option depending on how easily a person is co-opted. One of the reasons I keep moving is that if you get tied down into something then you are co-opted. That is why I only served a year as director of LSCRRC. I did the building I could and found out what I could in that year. If I had stayed longer it would have only been to reap personal benefit.

"I like to think of myself as a pragmatic person. I don't think that people are going to go out in the streets tomorrow and topple the government. I think we have to build and to remain able, free, and flexible enough to build. And we need a base—which gets into the question of why I got into this political thing. I did not because I think I can do anything as a city councilman—even if the council were not half-progressive and half-conservative, and therefore tied on almost every issue. If I had thought that, it wouldn't have been worth the people voting for me. Rather, I got into it because, in order to win, I had to create a strong movement in the community that supports the ideas that we are throwing out and those ideas are really based on what is most bothering the people that we are working with in the community. We're trying to pull these people together across class and economic lines which you've got to do because you can't build a revolutionary movement in the Black community until you break down the class barriers there. We're trying to do this now, not in the white community at this point but among the people who can be politicized. Then we can begin to build a strong movement; and the power comes not from my being on the city council but from that force in the community which was strong enough to put me on the city council in the face of all the reactionary opposition.

"So, when I want to do something, I don't try to do it on the city council with the votes that can be amassed there because I don't really think that that's where it is going to work. Rather, I try to do it with the power sources created in the community, and what the people are doing.

"I can do more here than I could as a lawyer because I think that the court system is a reactionary tool of the white power structure that is used by the commercial, industrial, and political interests in the country to exploit further the poor and Black people.

"I think law can still be practiced in the South because it hasn't come to the point of giving people the minimal rights allowed under the law yet. The fact is the rights are so minimal that once you reach the point of their maximum utilization, frustration sets in because people are still poor and oppressed. The legal system was constructed neither by nor for Black and poor people, and it has no legitimacy for us, and so the power structure has no right to demand that Black and poor people obey the power structure's law. Part of the revolutionary process must require reconstructing the laws to take account of the needs and interests of Black and poor people, and Blacks and poor people must help guide that reconstruction.

"I don't think that the legal system can survive as it is now structured. The people who run it, the judges, only know the interests of the power structure that put them in, and they know what their task is. I think the kind of legal system that can survive is a decentralized one at the most basic local level. Why should all the judges be lawyers or political hacks? You should have special people to deal with special problems. There should be community people to do the judging. But I think that the court system, however you structure it, becomes the handmaiden of whatever institution is in power. I think a lawyer, in particular circumstances, can be revolutionary if he refuses to abide by the rules that are set and instead comes forth with a set of rules that show his own outlook.

"I think a Black lawyer, to be effective, must understand the political and equitable bankruptcy of the legal system. To go into it a Black lawyer should have skepticism and a real awareness of how it exploits, and he must set his own rules because in this legal system his task is to understand and relate to and push the needs of Black people. Black communities should have Black lawyers and judges; Chicano, Chicano lawyers and judges, etcetera. What we've got to do now is break the grip of non-third world lawyers on the activities and affairs of the third world community, and that is going to be a struggle. I think a large number of the young third world lawyers coming up now are political, but they are not so political that they can't be co-opted unless there are immediate alternatives when they get out of law school—alternatives that don't exist that much now, when really there is only Legal Services or the Inc. Fund, neither of which is particularly political, or socially relevant.

"I'd like to get a group of eight or nine of the best young Black lawyers here in the Bay Area. It would be structured something like the Inc. Fund but with different priorities.

"I don't really like most of the white radical lawyers that I know. I think they're parasitic and breed on the problems of the oppressed without really being seriously committed to helping solve these problems. There is so much in-fighting, and the issues that they end up fighting about are issues which have nothing to do with representation of people and their interests. So many of them are egomaniacs and have subdued messianic complexes. And often the interests of their clients become secondary to their own interests in pushing a heavy sort of political trip. For instance, there were four Panther brothers here up on a murder rap and they were counting on help from certain prominent radical lawyers, but the minute more public kinds of cases broke, these prominent radical lawyers forgot about those cats who were up for their lives. You get a whole phalanx of radical lawyers to help on the Davis or Seale cases while other brothers and sisters on the streets with no legal help are getting run into jail. That has something to do with my feelings about radical lawyers.

"Also, they came up in an era in which they were the only lawyers willing to help in certain cases which were highly controversial, involving Black people particularly. But now that young Black lawyers are emerging they find a lot of resistance among these established radical lawyers in terms of their attempts to aid in the Black movement. For example, when the Panthers had a convention in Philadelphia in 1970, Hayward Burns and some NCBL lawyers went to offer their help. It was made clear to them by Garry and his people that *they* had the shit and they weren't going to give it up. And that is symptomatic of white radical lawyers.

"I think one device used to keep Blacks out is this whole commune thing. There ain't no sister or brother going to come out of law school and work for $80 or $100 a week. The device may be unwitting but that is the result, because the money is kept so low it almost demands that no Black lawyers come in. If you're serious about getting Black lawyers in, you are going to dig up the money to pay them. Some radical lawyers have told me that one of the ideas of paying the commune lawyers $100 a week is so they can become more closely identified with the people that they are working for. That's horseshit because they know if they ever really feel pinched they can shave and put on a suit and tie and get a job that will pay. And I know many who have done that and that is another reason I don't think that much of some radical lawyers. They go through all kinds of trips. One minute they are a radical lawyer and the next minute they are rethinking it and doing something altogether different.

"Another thing is that Black lawyers are becoming increasingly race conscious. The communes present a total kind of philosophy —salary, women's lib, etcetera—a lot of which is totally irrelevant to Black people. You have to understand where Black people and radical Black lawyers are at politically and understand that they are not going to be that psyched up about the equality of decision-making between lawyers and secretaries. So, if you structure a commune like that, you have to understand that it isn't going to be that attractive to Black lawyers.

"The only alternative is the creation of Black legal centers. I don't like the idea of having to pay Black lawyers more to do relevant work, but if you're serious about getting them you get them by whatever means necessary and then hope that they'll get politicized to the point where the money becomes irrelevant. But you do have to go out there and pull them in at first and that is not being done. Of course there is the answer of white radical lawyers that that is not their job, that it is the job of Black lawyers. But I think it is their job and the job of everybody involved in this movement and really talking about the empowerment of third world people.

"It may seem hard to prove to a white person that a radical is racist. So if I said that I think a good part of the [National Lawyers] Guild is racist it'd take a long time to develop that into a convincing argument. If you say that to someone who is Black, though, who has had experience with the Guild, many would agree. The Guild makes the same kind of assumptions that other racists make, and that is, in their relationships to Blacks, and this includes Black lawyers, they make the decisions and the Blacks take the cues. I found that that is very true in relation to many Guild lawyers. And they do use Blacks. They have their token Blacks that they put out front. Why should I have to deal with all of their hangups when I can either not go into any group at all or go into a group that is Black and not as potentially exploitive of the Black community?"

20

Jerome Cohen, Attorney, the United Farm Workers Organizing Committee

The San Joaquin Valley is even more barren and desolate-looking than a generation raised on *Grapes of Wrath* would imagine. The land, with its ironically fertile soil, stretches flatly, lacking dimension, and seems to meet what appears to be a one-dimensional sky. This land is the center of California's agribusiness, a business that accounts for 10 percent of the national gross cash receipts for farming, a business that grosses over $4 billion per year, a business in which 79 percent of the agricultural land is owned by 7 percent of the farms: in other words, a very big, very lucrative business that leads the nation in the production of forty crops ranging from honey to turkeys.

Most of the work in this valley and the other valleys where agriculture predominates is done by migrant farm workers, who, until recently, had average incomes that were just above $2000 per year. These workers lived in horrible conditions, had an occupational disease rate that was twice that of all other California industries combined, and had a generally low educational level. Sixty-seven percent of these workers are Chicano, 21 percent come from other ethnic minorities, and 12 percent are white.

Now, as the result of the efforts of

the United Farm Workers Organizing Committee (UFWOC), led by Cesar Chavez over the past decade, the lot of these workers has improved. Chavez began his organizing work in 1962 with a group called the National Farm Workers Association (NFWA). During his first grape strike in 1965, he saw clearly the influence that the growers had over rural courts, and how they used this influence to get injunctions against the striking workers. At that time he was dependent on the legal help he could get from outside groups and outside lawyers.

In these early days of organizing, another group, the Agricultural Workers Organizing Committee (AWOC), largely composed of Filipino workers and affiliated with the AFL-CIO, was working independently for the same goals. In 1966 the two groups merged to become the United Farm Workers Organizing Committee, which retained AWOC's AFL-CIO affiliation. After the merger UFWOC's legal staff consisted of one very overworked lawyer named Alex Hoffman.

Jerome "Jerry" Cohen, now the head lawyer of the Union's four-man legal staff, said, "Alex was basically a good guy but he didn't have the books and they didn't sit down and think through what they should have him do to help the Union. When I first came here there was basically nothing to work with."

Cohen, a Chicagoan whose childhood hero was Andy Pafko, center-fielder for the Chicago Cubs, and whose father was a navy doctor, moved around a lot during his early years.

"I went to high school in D.C., college at Amherst, and law school at Berkeley. I learned a lot in high school fighting the fraternities there. At Amherst we got together a bunch of independents, and we busted that goddamned fraternity system. I graduated from there in 1963. Law school was great. The first and second year at Berkeley there was the free speech movement, then the third year we couldn't figure out what to do to keep our sanity so we organized this thing, Citizens for Kennedy and Fulbright, because they had come out against the war. We got some friends from back East and we put out press releases and then we had this organization, or letterhead anyway, and I learned a lot about politics from it. It was as real an organization as the Democratic party I guess. When I graduated from law school in 1966 I could have worked with some people in Newark, or gone into private practice, or gone with CRLA. I chose the last.

"I made that choice because I was told that they were representing Cesar. I went to work in the McFarland office, which is about six miles from Delano and the first thing I found out after I got there was that there was a condition in the grant that they couldn't represent the Union and that they couldn't have an office in Delano. At that point CRLA was taking a lot of individual cases, but I thought that no matter how many of those you took you weren't really going to change anything. I felt you had to take certain cases directed at the people with the power and try to focus in on a few important issues, not take all of these individual cases. So we fought like hell within CRLA to change it, and we did change it. In the course of that Cesar asked me to come see him in Delano and he said, 'Look, do you want to help the Union?' and I said, 'Yeah.' He said, 'You can't help the Union working for a federal program. There are too many restrictions on you. No matter how good the program may be in comparison with other programs, it's not going to do it. Why don't you come to work for the Union?' I was really happy to do that. I only stayed at CRLA three months and then I came here.

"As I said, when I came here there was basically nothing, so Cesar and I thought about it a lot and decided one of the things we needed were the tools for me to function just like a lawyer. We got secretaries, books, filing cabinets, all of the tools of a lawyer. Then we made the decision that I wasn't going to be taking any of the individual problems of the farm workers. I was going to look at the needs of the Union as a union and I was going to take on only problems related to those needs. We knew immediately that that would mean defensive work because every time you strike in the valley the rural judges have all of the power and they enjoin you. So we knew we had to make it expensive for the growers to stop the workers from exercising their rights. We laid down these ground rules and Cesar was very good. He said, 'I don't know what you can do legally and, at this point, neither do you.' So he told me what the problems were and asked me to figure out what I could do. The first summer was a really good education.

"That was 1967, and in the Giumarra table grapes strike I lost my virginity on the whole business of injunctions. Here we had all kinds of violations heaped upon the workers: foremen driving trucks at them, workers getting beaten, people threatened and spit upon, and in law school I had learned that you can't come into equity to get relief unless you come into equity with clean hands. So I had all of these violations laid out, and I didn't think they could issue an injunction against us in court. But five minutes after the growers laid out their papers for a temporary restraining order, Judge Steel signed their order limiting us to three pickets at an entrance and one every fifty feet, and, they took away our bullhorns.

"So I went on a writ of prohibition to higher courts and got our bullhorns back and got the injunction modified a little bit, and we began to learn that there were certain things you could do under California law to really hurt the growers, like use the discovery process to obtain damaging admissions. You do everything you can: filing individual suits against employers, taking individual cases that help the strike.

"So I learned this and I learned how best to stop injunctions, how to raise every constitutional issue I could. And whenever they sued us, we countersued them and found out what they were doing wrong and then sued the hell out of them for that. When the workers had complaints, they would always come in with them and we'd listen to them and, when the workers were ready to move, we'd use them. And the workers would come in because they want to help the Union. They know that when they are on strike something that helps both them and the Union is better than something that just helps them. You can learn a lot from the workers.

"An issue we found out about from the workers that was really good and helpful was sanitation—we did a lot of suits on toilets until we got those bastards to put toilets in the fields. We also started countersuits every time they would hurt a worker. They eventually stopped because they didn't want to pay the costs. Then, as we began to learn more, we got a lot more sophisticated and we began to find out that they had certain ways of jacking the market around that are illegal, so we found out about the antitrust laws and sued them. They sued us for $75 million in an antitrust suit, so we countersued and raised their bluff by $30 million for a total of $105 million and that made it a lot of money they had to spend for lawyers, and the guys working for the Union aren't that interested in money or we wouldn't be here. We like the fight. So we weren't spending a lot of money and they were. We like to work long hours and we want to help Cesar and everybody else so we can really screw the growers that need it. So an hour of our time became another hour of time the growers would have to spend on legal help.

"And we found that in these extra hours we could find out a lot of information and a lot of things the growers were doing wrong. For example, we found that their use of pesticides made a beautiful issue. Down in Coachella in 1968, two women came in and said that they were nauseated and dizzy and didn't know what had happened. So I got them a doctor, told them to go to workmen's compensation and said that I didn't have the time to check it out then because we had a picket line going. Then the same women came up to Arvin and still were sick, so I thought I had better find out what they were spraying. I went to the agricultural commissioner's office and asked to see the records of spraying. You have to have a permit in California to use injurious or toxic materials, and you have to keep a record of how they are used. Two hours after I went in to Commissioner Moulet, instead of showing me the records, he went to the pesticide company and told them I wanted to see them. They got an injunction against his showing me the records. So we had this fantastic issue of what they were hiding.

"We got it out to the boycotters and took it to a hearing on a preliminary injunction. That is a beautiful example of how you can pinpoint an issue, get it out to the public, and educate the workers even if you can't win the suit."

As UFWOC has grown in numbers and political sophistication, so has its legal staff. There are now four lawyers on it: Cohen, Bill Carder, Frank Denison, and Steve Engelhardt, all between the ages of twenty-six and thirty-two. During the summers they are joined by some law students and some LSCRRC interns. The lawyers are based in Delano, Salinas, and Santa Maria, although they travel all over during the strikes.

They also utilize cooperating attorneys around the country, notably Pat Eames in New York City, Barbara Hellman in Chicago, and Al Radar in Los Angeles.

"We don't have a Chicano attorney yet, although the Union is 65 percent Chicano, because we haven't found a guy who wants to bust his ass enough to do the job, although I think there are some who are coming up," said Cohen. "Around here they're mature on the question of race. If you do the work, it doesn't matter who you are. You stay here and do the work."

The Union now has between two hundred and three hundred contracts with growers. They've organized 80 percent of the grape industry, and about 25 percent of the lettuce industry, and they have some contracts with tree fruit growers in the Fresno Valley. They also have nine service centers where workers can go for help with problems not related to the Union or working conditions—things like tax and welfare problems. Two of the centers are located outside of California, in Texas and Arizona, so they also have members there, although they don't ask these members to pay dues because they are not getting contract benefits.

With the exception of the time that they worked for Robert

Kennedy, the energies of the union workers were put into the grape boycott from 1967 until the contracts were signed in the summer of 1970. At the beginning of that strike, the workers were getting $1.10 per hour and wanted $1.20. By the time it was settled they ended up with $1.75 per hour.

"Right after that," Jerry said, "the Teamsters signed sweetheart contracts with the lettuce growers. A rough strike followed and we were started on the lettuce thing. People were shot. I was beaten up and had to be hospitalized. Our office in Hollister was dynamited. Out of that came the lettuce boycott, and we're doing the same things to them as we did with the grape growers only we're more sophisticated now. We knew from the grapes that as soon as the boycott began, the Defense Department would increase its purchases of lettuce by 800 or 900 percent and pay artificially high prices, so we immediately instituted a suit. We started to get the facts and sue on them. We sue a lot.

"The beauty of working with a movement is that whether you win or lose is sometimes entirely irrelevant, because there is not a defeat you can't turn into some kind of victory. If we had won on that original pesticide thing and gotten the records then we would have had them. But, even if we lose, there are a lot of people in this country that we can rely on. The movement is really based on that, that there are enough people who want to see justice done that they'll help us if we can get our case to them. They'll help us with economic power which is something that people aren't very sophisticated about using in the U.S. A lot of good people say, 'Well, we know the farm workers are out, but what can we do?' It's a very simple thing to tell them not to buy grapes or lettuce. The good thing about a boycott is that it's power and a good way of using power because you can get a lot of people involved. There are a lot of people around and all they have to know is how to help you.

"We also then get to present our case because they want to know why the workers are striking, and you begin to talk about pesticides and you begin to drive an issue home. The law is a very good way to raise that issue and to obtain information. So it doesn't matter if they say we can't see the records because then we go to the public and say that they won't show us the records. We say 'A' and 'B' are pesticides that they applied for, but they won't tell us how they used it. Then we ask them if they want to eat the grapes. And people know what is going on if they won't show you the records. We still haven't seen those records, but we've done a lot of work with pesticides since then, and we've put a lot of heat on the state: sued them about time limits on pesticides [when workers can go into a field after a pesticide is used] and poisons that should be banned.

"First they fight you saying that you're self-serving for the Union and that it is a sham suit, blah, blah, but then they change their regulations instead of fighting the suits.

"There are many kinds of specific subjects where you can use the law to focus issues. Sometimes you can even win a suit because you are so overwhelmingly right that even these prejudiced rural judges have to rule in your favor because there is no place else they can go. But, more often than not, you're going to lose. In California we're lucky now because the supreme court here is one of the few good courts in the country, so we have that check on arbitrary power below. For example, in Salinas when we started the lettuce strike every time we turned around we got enjoined. The Teamster sweetheart contracts raised wages about one-half cent a year for the next five years and gave no pesticide protection, no anything, so we went and struck, and the judge enjoined us saying it was a jurisdictional strike. Now that was outrageous because it meant that any grower could insulate himself from the legitimate union aspirations of his workers by signing a contract with somebody who didn't represent his workers. The law of jurisdictional strikes is designed to protect an employer with a legitimate contract who is being raided by a union that is trying to expand its jurisdiction. The law should protect the employer in that case, but the judge perverted the law. So we went into a boycott and another judge issued an injunction against that. Well, that was going too far because a boycott is a pure free speech issue.

"He issued an injunction preventing us from talking about the facts of the labor dispute. We violated that injunction deliberately and put up no factual defense. The judge threw Cesar in jail for contempt but the supreme court reversed the decision because we were right on the unconstitutionality of the order. We got a lot of publicity around that jailing, and that really helped the boycott. The damn fool judge played right into our hands even though Cesar didn't want to go to jail because in those twenty-one days he was in he could have done a lot of work. But he was not going to let that judge run over our rights. If we had obeyed that injunction other judges would have ordered the same thing.

"Every once in a while a higher court is going to vindicate your rights but, by and large, poor people don't have access to the higher courts, and they're in front of the lower ones day in and day out and they are not going to get justice there. The only way you're going to do it is to take what limited legal talent there is interested in doing these kinds of things and focus it on those issues that most directly benefit the Union, because the Union is the only independent source of power for the people in this valley. That is what we've been trying to do and that's what we are going to keep trying to do until we win because they aren't going to stop us. So we have found that one of the things you can do is use the courts as a vehicle and the law as a political tool to help you gain certain specific goals, and you can do that within every canon of ethics. You don't have to solicit because the workers come in and they want to sue. But you do have to be able to say no to suits that aren't going to help the Union. If you have an unorganized group of people you aren't going to be able to do that because people would be selfish and want you to represent them on their individual problems.

"We're really lucky here because it is one of the few places in the country where a lawyer can function in such a way. We don't have to deal with the internal strife there is in a lot of organizations of poor people around the country because we've got a goal that is definable. We know damn well who the enemy is, and we know we want contracts and that the workers have to organize themselves to wrench power from the growers and get some dignity in the process. So the fight is clear. We have the confidence of the people and they know that we're trying to help the Union. I haven't had one gripe in the time I've been working here.

"Besides using the courts we have found that sometimes there are friendly congressmen who will help, and that congressional hearings are good platforms to lay out some of the issues, like pesticides. There are organizers who get all of these facts and then we take all of them and call some friendly congressman and lay them all out and it can have a great effect. Then what you hope to do is get some right-wing bastard, like Senator Murphy, into a public fight.

"We knew we had a good issue with the pesticides, and we knew it was important because we wanted to make it a negotiating issue. We knew that suing in the courts wouldn't do any good, that it had to be a good issue when we went to the negotiating tables so we'd come out with a contract that had a specific pesticide clause in it, because we had certain goals about banning some pesticides and putting time limits on the others. Senator Mondale gave us a public hearing. Murphy attacked me personally and called me a liar. We let him hang it out, then found out that Safeway had done all the same tests we had on pesticides with the same results. So he had to retract, and we went to the negotiating tables and knew that the growers couldn't duck that issue.

"But the really important thing is enforcement. If you get an appellate decision and can't enforce it, it's no good. So we take public laws and make them into private laws by writing them into the contracts. Then, if the growers violate the contract, the workers can enforce it. We banned those pesticides and then got a workers' committee that the growers had to consult before they could use pesticides.

"The Union has grown fantastically in the last few years. In 1970 we increased in size by about 1000 percent and we're going to keep on growing so that the more workers that come under contract, the more workers we have to help enforce contract provisions. There are three million farm workers in the country, and we're going to keep on going until we have all of them.

"There are a lot of things that have to change in this country. There are a lot of things that have to change just here in this valley, but you have to start with some economic base for the workers. So they're now in charge of their own destiny as far as the work. They have contracts and they can enforce them so they don't have to rely on the courts. Writing a contract, negotiating it is the lawyer's function. It is important. But there are not that many lawyers in the country who have the opportunity to sit down with the workers and say, 'OK, what do you want,' and then translate that into legal language and then see it negotiated. In a way it is a really unique place for a lawyer to function. You can use the courts, you can use political figures who are helpful to you, then you can use collective bargaining as a vehicle for translating needs into certain kinds of law.

"We do public interest, consumer law if it's in the interest of the farm workers. For instance, the consumers were vindicated in the suit on pesticides. But we don't do that unless it is in the farm workers' interest because if you file an appellate suit and have a statute on the books, what is it going to mean? Who will enforce it?

"We feel that the work we are doing is militant in the true meaning of the word. You realize that the workers have to have the power themselves when you see them getting the shit kicked out of them by the growers. Now I don't feel that the free speech movement was radical. It was just about a basic civil liberties issue.

"One of Cesar's basic assumptions is that the workers started out with nothing and, despite the efforts of anybody to hem them in, they're just going to keep going, plowing like water down a hill. Within that general goal of getting the workers economic and political power, there's a lot you can do and Cesar gives us complete freedom to move. It's a pretty damn healthy atmosphere to work in, and everybody has an input, but the workers most of all.

"Again, as far as the law, we feel that if it were applied to the workers they would be a lot better off than they are, but the law is not enforced. It's not the judge's fault, it's the whole bureaucracy's: the cops, everybody else. To focus on the courts or any other agencies or to be like CRLA and fight with the other bureaucracies is not where it's at. The people with the power are the people with the dough and the property and, in this state, agribusiness is the biggest industry. So, in this state if you're talking about the people with interests adverse to the workers, you're talking about the growers. So, we find that the court system can be very useful in illustrating the problems, even if we lose the cases, because we have defined specific enough targets and specific enough goals that we can attain them.

"The reform of the court system isn't even a goal you can worry about right now. You've got to have political power to do that, so the people you're trying to help have to have power and, in order to have it, they've got to organize. So, if we do win enough fights, I think that the court system can be reformed. It's not any more immune to change than anything else in this country and it has all got to be changed.

"But, you can't chop down a redwood tree with your dick. What you have got to do is isolate the problems you can work on and change and, if you can change that one, then move on to the next one. I don't think there is any group in the country now that can change the things everyone—who is at least a liberal—hates. But there is progress being made on certain fronts and by people who have acknowledged the fact that there are limits on what they can do and who spend their lives trying to change specific conditions. If enough of that goes on, there can be change. But I couldn't do more work than I am now. If Cesar's ideas catch on, they are going to change rural America. It's too goddamned romantic to think of yourself as a revolutionary. You don't get any work done if you get caught up in the rhetoric game.

"We realize that we are lucky to have people around, not to be operating in a vacuum, sitting around in some city and wondering what is good for poor people. You don't have to be smart around here to figure out what people need because the people are always pressing on you. There is a constituency around, and they need help. And our goals are not so specific or limited that once we obtain them we'll destroy ourselves like the FSM did. Here winning the fight with the growers is just the beginning because then the ranch committees are organized and the workers begin to sense their own political power.

"We have a built-in mechanism whereby the organization keeps getting bigger and the workers keep getting stronger and they learn about their own power. It's a continuing, strong, cohesive group, almost a family really. I like it out here. There is no great self-conscious bullshitting about what we should or shouldn't be doing, just work."

21

Oscar Acosta and the Chicano Movement

Like their brothers and sisters who labor in the fields, Chicanos who live in urban areas have problems. Besides the normal problems common to all ghetto-dwellers, they, like other small ethnic groups in this country—Filipinos, Native Americans, Orientals, Puerto Ricans, to name a few—have an additional set of problems that come from their unique heritage, and the way in which they were absorbed into the United States.

In the case of people who call themselves Chicanos today, understanding the absorption process is essential to understanding their current philosophy. One night half of the Mexican nation went to sleep as Mexicans, and woke up the next day as citizens of the United States. Because of the U.S. invasion of Mexico during the Mexican-American War of 1848, Mexican officials agreed to cede half of what was then their nation to the United States. The residents of that area—now known as Atzlan to Chicanos and as Texas, New Mexico, Arizona, and Southern California to the U.S. government— came with the package. These newly nationalized U.S. citizens soon found that, when they entered America's melting pot, they, like any other group of people with a darker skin pigmentation, sank to the bottom.

It was not until the 1960s—the era when people who were black, brown, red, and yellow could dare to be proud of the fact in public—that they began to fight their way out of the abyss. There are now two locations in the Southwest where the radical Chicano movement has become a viable force: Colorado, where Chicano leader Rudolfo "Corky" Gonzalez has his Denver-based Crusade for Justice; and Southern California, where in "El Barrio" of East Los Angeles Chicano students, street people, and just plain people have all become Brown Berets, fighters for the idea of Chicano unity, identity, and land.

In 1968, when the militant Chicano movement in L.A. was just beginning to jell, Oscar Zeta Acosta, an attorney who had stopped practicing law, came to El Barrio to see what was happening. He stayed and became one of the few militant Chicano attorneys in the country. East Los Angeles in those years was a far cry from El Paso, Texas, where Acosta had been born in 1935.

"Because my family couldn't make a living during the Depression there, we moved to California so my parents could work as migrant field workers. We lived in Riverbank in the San Joaquin Valley. The towns there were all the same, built around the railroad tracks. On one side of them you had the Mexicans, on the other side you had the Oakies, and then farther out you had the Americans. Where I grew up the world was composed of that—Mexicans, Oakies, and middle-class Americans—and nothing else, no Jews, no Blacks.

"My father was a little different than the other people where we lived. He wanted me to compete more than anything else so he pushed me into competition with himself. When I was five he encouraged me to argue and fight with him, which is unusual in a Mexican family. I guess that is where I became as nasty as I am.

"When I got to high school I was not like the average Chicano who, in the forties, would either drop out or go quietly off to the side. I became involved in sports and music and was president of my class. I got a music scholarship to the University of Southern

California but I was going with this Anglo girl whose parents didn't like me because I was Mexican, so I decided to get out of the way by going into the Air Force band. We planned to get married when I came out. After a year of her visiting me and our hiding she split, and I was stuck in the service. I thought of going AWOL but changed my mind. That's when I started smoking grass and taking bennies. I was a jazz musician mainly.

"Within months after her splitting—which was the first big trauma in my life—I thought that maybe religion had the answer for me. I started going to the Catholic church pretty regularly and reading all kinds of religious literature. Then there was a guy in the band who started telling me about Baptists. I was stationed at Hamilton Air Force Base near San Francisco so he started taking me to his church in Petaluma which wasn't far away. Everybody at the church saw me as being really different. I was a Chicano, a musician, a Catholic, and a sinner. So all of the little chicks dug me and loved to hear me tell about all of my sins. This blew my mind and I started going to the church. Within a few months, I was converted. I saw Jesus coming down from a cloud one night. I got saved, really, Billy Graham-style. Being the fanatic I am, I became a preacher immediately. I became the head of the student or youth Baptist group, whichever it was, and, within a matter of four months after my conversion, I had converted my entire family with the exception of my brother.

"I was also holding noontime prayer meetings in the basement of the barracks of the band with about fifteen of the jazz musicians in attendance. It was unbelievable. It got so bad that the first sergeant asked me one day if I'd go easy on his Catholic boys. Being the idiot that I was, I said, 'They need God. You need God, too.' So, a few weeks later I was shipped out to Panama.

"Between the ages of eight and eighteen I hadn't spoken Spanish or hung around with the other Chicanos because, especially in high school, they stood off on the sidelines while I went ahead to do other things. Consequently when I got to Panama I couldn't speak Spanish at all, so I took a class in it along with the other guys and then I became a missionary. In the two years I was there I set up about five missions. I was still in the air force but my only duty was band rehearsal in the morning, and I had the rest of the time off.

"When I had about six months left to do, I realized I was going crazy, so I made a last, final study to see if what I was teaching was true. I made a study of the gospels and, on one side of the page I put the things I felt good about, and, on the other, the things I felt bad about, in comparing the life of Jesus. Within three months the bad side was about twenty times heavier than the good side, so I no longer believed in him. That caused the second big trauma in my life. Here I didn't believe in him, and I had one hundred people believing in me in my congregations. I had Indians, Panamanians, servicemen of all races. They looked on me as their pastor. So for three months I had to go on preaching and teaching shit that I didn't believe.

"That really affected my whole thing with the result that when I got out of the service I attempted suicide. Naturally I chickened out like everybody else, but I ended up with a psychiatrist. I started school at San Francisco State and I started writing. I was majoring in creative writing and mathematics and I dug both of them. I had one more semester to go to get my degree in math, but, by that time, I was halfway through a novel, so I dropped out to finish that and then intended to go back. I never did, because by that time it was 1960 and the Kennedy campaign, and I got involved in that. I hadn't had a political thought up until then. I decided I didn't want to be either a mathematician or a professional writer after that involvement, but I did finish the novel and submitted it to three publishers all of whom almost accepted it. They all said that I was great, earthy, poetic, the most brilliant unpublished writer in the world *but* I was writing about Chicanos at that time—it was a Romeo and Juliet story of Oakies and Chicanos in the valley—and that subject wasn't acceptable. So I decided I would write because that is what I am, a writer, but that I didn't want to have to write or to be a professional writer.

"Since I was interested in politics and Chicanos, I decided to go to law school, then work with Chavez and the farm workers and be a union organizer. So I did it, and got involved in the Black civil rights movement for the next four years in San Francisco but it wasn't really me. I told people that it wasn't just black and white, that there were Chicanos too, and they laughed at me, so I told them to go fuck themselves and they split. I graduated from San Francisco Law School, a night law school, in 1965. I was working at the *San Francisco Examiner* all of this time through college and law school as a copy boy, along with all of the political activity. When I got out, I took the bar exam and flunked it. It was the first time I had flunked an exam in my life, and it was the third major trauma so I ended up back with the psychiatrist. I studied for the bar again, and passed it a couple of months later.

"I became a Legal Aid lawyer in Oakland in a half-Black, half-Chicano section. I hated it with a passion. I'd wake up in the morning and throw up. All we'd do was sit there and listen to complaints. There were so many problems and we didn't do anything. We didn't have a direction, skills, or tools.

"After a year I became totally depressed. I couldn't do anything, so I said fuck it to everything and I told the psychiatrist to shove it and to stick the pills up his ass. I said I'd been with him on and off for ten years and that I was still as fucked up as when I began, just taking ten times as many pills. I took off and ended up in Aspen.

"I met some people who were pretty nice to me including Hunter Thompson, the writer, and I started dropping acid and staying stoned most of the time and doing all kinds of odd jobs— construction work and washing dishes—and, within about three months my head was clear. I felt like I knew who I was, what I was, and what I was supposed to do. I stayed there for about six months, and then I was on my way to Guatemala to smuggle guns to the revolutionaries down there and to write about them. I got stopped in Juarez, and thrown in jail. When I got out I called my brother who suggested that I go to Los Angeles. Well, I hated L.A. Being from up north I was subject to this old prejudice between Northern and Southern California, which was ridiculous. I asked my brother why I should go there and he said that he'd heard about a group called the Brown Berets and about a newspaper called *La Raza*. That was in January of 1968. I arrived here in L.A. in February intending to stay for a few months, write an article about it, and then get out.

"Then the high school walkouts occurred and I agreed to take a few misdemeanor cases. Two months later thirteen of the organizers of the walkouts were busted on sixteen counts of conspiracy, which could have resulted in forty-five years in prison for each of them. I agreed to take the case. It was my first major case, my first criminal case, and here I am three years later. This is it for me because I've gone though intensive changes in myself and my consciousness has developed about Chicanos, La Raza, revolution, and what we're going to do so it looks like I'm here to stay. This, East Los Angeles, is the capital of Aztlan because there are more of us here than anywhere else.

"To understand where I am, you have to understand how the Chicano movement has developed. In 1967 and 1968 young Chicano students, both in high school and college, began to identify as Mexican-Americans. The first issue was what to call themselves. They began to organize coffee houses and clubs but were mainly interested in the educational system. So, in March of 1968, they had massive high school walkouts from four of the Mexican-American high schools in East L.A. The result was numerous busts and that is when I became involved. Those walkouts were the first major activity by Chicanos as Chicanos in the history of this country. There had been labor groups, and political-type groups but there had never been any group organized to organize and politicize the community as Chicanos on broad-based issues. There are two million Chicanos here in Southern California. I think we're the largest ethnic minority in the Southwest, certainly here in Los Angeles we are. Statistically we're the lowest in education with an eighth grade education being the median, and we're the lowest in housing and jobs. We have the problems here in Los Angeles and the Southwest that the Blacks have throughout the country.

"But the history of the Southwest is totally different from the history of the rest of the country, which is something that most people don't understand, and they don't understand that this historical relationship is what causes the attitudes that exist here today. They tend to see us as immigrants, which is absolutely wrong. We were here before the white man got here. The American government took our country away from us in 1848, when the government of Mexico sold us out. They sold not only the land, but they basically sold us as slaves in the sense that our labor and our land were being expropriated. The governments never gave us a choice about whether or not to be American citizens. One night we were Mexican and the next day we were American. This historical relationship is the most important part of the present-day relationships but it's totally ignored or unknown or rejected by the Anglo society.

"In 1968, when we started making a movement toward attaining better education and schools, we wanted the literature to reflect our heritage and our culture. We started meeting with school boards and the city council and we began to know the enemy. At that point, I think that most of us believed we could integrate into the society and get a piece of the action since nobody denied that we had problems. But now, three years later, there have been few changes. Now there are two assemblymen in the California legislature, one congressman, and one member of the school board who are Chicanos, and that is it for a class that constitutes 13 percent of the population.

"In 1968, our first problem was that of identity. As time went on we no longer questioned that. We had chosen a name—Chi-

cano—whether we had Spanish or Indian blood, and we knew
that we existed alone. That is, we relate to Mexico but in a nos-
talgic way. We know that when the going gets rough, the Mexican government ain't going to do shit for us. And we know that
no other aspect of the broad movement is going to do shit for us.
They'll pay lip service, they'll condescend to us, but basically
they're just as paternalistic to us as the white racist pigs. For example, I've spoken at numerous rallies for the Panthers, for Angela Davis, and every time I get the same bullshit treatment. I'm
the last on the program with five minutes to speak and we get no
offers of any real unity or working together.

"I think that the Black movement has been co-opted. Three
years ago I used to know a lot of heavy Blacks. They're just not
around anymore. I'm talking about the Black Panthers. They're
just rhetoric, they're just sucking in that money. They talk heavy
as hell, but when it comes down to what they're fighting for I
don't think even they know, because they're integrating into the
society that they despise as fast as that society allows them to. I
made this decision during Corky's trial.

"Corky Gonzalez is head of the Crusade for Justice which is
based in Denver. He is also a poet, a street-fighter, a theorist, and
an organizer, and he is recognized by a lot of Chicanos as the
boss, the leader. Chavez is like a grandfather to the movement.
We respect him and love him and would help him anytime he
asked, but we don't feel that his progress, his ideology is Chicano
enough. Cesar used the white liberal quite a bit and, more than
anything, this offends the average Chicano. It is bad because they
take jobs that Chicanos should be taking and using them is the
easy way out. There were probably more competent white militants three years ago than there were available Chicanos, but we
feel that he should have trained his own people more, as we do
now.

"Corky was on trial here on a weapons charge arising out of
the August 29, 1970, police riot here, where three people, including Ruben Salazar, were killed by the police. Corky had been

trying to get away from the violence with his two children when the police busted him for a traffic violation, suspicion of robbery, and a concealed weapons charge. He was on a truck with a lot of people, and we never denied that somebody on it had a loaded pistol, but it wasn't Corky. He wouldn't dare carry a goddamn gun around with him. He's a leader. He doesn't have to carry a gun for the same goddamn reason that Nixon doesn't have to. But we didn't stress that point at the trial for fear of alarming the jury and perhaps inflaming the press and cops. Why should we give them an excuse to shoot at Corky like they did at Ruben when they thought that he was a leader.

"What I did stress in picking the jury was whether they would be prejudiced if Huey Newton testified for Corky. See, Huey had called and said he wanted to talk to me. I asked him if he'd come down and be a character witness for Corky. I thought it would be a great show of unity. Everybody said he would. Then, after I'd announced it all over town and picked a jury by hammering at that question, he wouldn't come or talk to me on the phone so I have nothing more to do with the Black movement. I'm talking about the professional revolutionaries, not the people. Corky was found guilty and got forty days.

"I think, in the past year or so, the Chicano movement has begun to solidify. After the August 29 thing there was the National Chicano Moratorium 'Nonviolent March for Justice' on January 31, 1971. It was against police brutality and repression and was nonviolent until the end when fighting broke out and the cops swarmed out of the police station with everything including twelve-gauge shotguns, firing buckshot balls straight into the crowd. After two hours one person was dead, thirty seriously injured, and there was about half a million dollars' worth of damage including seventy-eight burned police cars.

"Things have gotten heavier since then, and Chicano consciousness is spreading. Everybody in El Barrio is a Brown Beret. It's a concept, an idea. MECHA—*Movimiento Estudiante Chicano de Aztlan,* the Chicano student movement—is also growing.

Aztlan is the land we're sitting on now, the land where my forefathers lived hundreds of years ago before they migrated to the valley of Mexico. The Aztecs referred to the entire Southwest as Aztlan. Now the Chicano movement has no need for anyone else's ideas but our own. We have a way of life that we've learned from childhood. The concept of *la familia,* the respect for elders is not Sunday school bullshit with us. It's part of our culture. A Chicano can no more disrespect his mother than he can himself. Which means he can, but at great cost to himself. The concept of community—of La Raza—isn't a political term to us as I feel it is to Black and white radicals. The term 'brother' is a social term to us, one we learn before we learn about politics.

"We don't kid ourselves anymore. We know we're headed for a head-on collision with the rest of society. We're absolutely convinced of it and we're not being paranoid. We know that the main thing we want now is not better education or better jobs or better housing, because we know that they are not possible to achieve. It is not possible as the result of the history of human nature and the animal instinct against the races integrating in the liberal sense of the word.

"You can't be a class or a nation without land. Without it, it doesn't have any meaning. It's that simple. So we are beginning to see that what we're talking about is getting land and having our own government. Period. It is that clear-cut. As to what land, that is still in the future. We have to develop the consciousness of land as the principal issue just as three years ago we had to develop the consciousness of identity as the principal issue.

"The Black man came here as a slave. He is not of this land. He is so removed from his ancestry that he has nothing but the white society to identify with. We have history. We have culture. We had a land. We do feel solidarity with the American Indians because we are Indians. We have a total unification in ideology but no unification organizationally. I look upon them as my blood brothers. It is the Indian aspect of our ancestry that gives meaning to the term 'La Raza.' We are La Raza. Of course there is Spanish and European blood in us, but we don't always talk about it because it is not something that we are proud of. For me my native ancestry is crucial. This consciousness is beginning to develop now, symbolized in the word *'tierra'* [land]. We want our land back and this is what we are going to be fighting for.

"I don't think you're going to see too much more of demonstrations against education or things of that sort. I think that has petered itself out. A lot of kids have gotten into OEO projects and school projects as a result of the movement, so they've been in college for a few years now, and they are as hip to what's being taught in the colleges as the white radicals have been for some years now. They think it is a waste of time, that it takes away what little you have of your identity.

"A perfect example is the Mexican American Law Students Association, the National La Raza Law Students Association here in L.A. which I am pretty much associated with. The very first day they started school here on some OEO project I went in and spoke and told them 'Half of you will never be lawyers. Those of you that do are going to become so only because of your race. You got into these programs because you're Chicano. So you owe something to your Raza. Yet, I predict that in three years I'm going to be fighting 50 percent of you guys. You're going to be my enemies.' They laughed. But it is a fact. This past year I've been working on these major cases of importance to the Chicano not only organizationally but legally, and often I've been unable to get the assistance of the Chicano law students. My prophecy to them has come true except I was wrong in one respect. It is not 50 percent I'm fighting. It is about 75 percent. This is why I'm no longer pushing for more school programs, more handouts, more welfare. I think that will destroy the movement. They are attempting with those to do the same things they did to the Blacks.

"For example, the law students—when I subpoenaed all 109 Superior Court judges to prove that the grand jury system is racist in 1971—didn't want to be associated with it because they were afraid that it might affect their future, their careers. That was my third challenge to the grand jury system here. I was defending the Biltmore Six, six young Chicanos who were busted for allegedly trying to burn down the Biltmore Hotel one night in 1970 when Reagan was delivering a speech there. They were indicted by a grand jury, and I contended that all grand juries are racist since all grand jurors have to be recommended by Superior Court judges and that the whole thing reeks of 'subconscious, institutional racism.' I was trying to get the indictments quashed on that basis.

"To prove my contention, I examined all 109 Superior Court judges in Los Angeles, under oath, about their racism. After almost a year of work on this, the judge on that case, Arthur Alacron, who is Mexican-American, rejected the motion. The way it looks now, I think we're just about finished with that whole legal game.

"I'm the only Chicano lawyer here. By that I mean the only one that has taken a militant posture, to my knowledge, in the whole country. When I got here, I decided that if I was going to become anything legal I couldn't use the profession as it was. Lawyers are basically peddlers of flesh. They live off of other people's misery. Well, I couldn't do that. I made a decision that I would never charge a client a penny. As a matter of fact, I end up supporting some of my clients. I get money by begging, borrowing, and stealing. Sometimes I get a grant from some foundation like Ford. For a while I was under a Reggie program although all I was doing was political, criminal work, and they knew it. I don't even have an office. I'm in court practically every day.

"I relate to the court system first as a Chicano and only seldom as a lawyer in the traditional sense. I have no respect for the courts and I make it clear to them from the minute I walk in that I have no respect for the system, that I'm against it and would destroy it this second if I had the physical power to do it. The one thing I've learned to do is how to use criminal defense work as an organizing tool. That is my specialty. I organize in the courtroom. I take no case unless it is, or can become, a Chicano movement case. I turn it into a platform to espouse the Chicano point of view so that that affects the judge, the jury, the spectators. We organize each case, set up defense committees, student groups, and use the traditional methods of organizing.

"I don't have much contact with many of the other radical lawyers here. I think a lot of them are still finding themselves. Consequently they'll often chicken out of something at the last minute. I think it's chickenshit, reactionary, and that they're the enemies of the people. I like them, they're nice guys, but it's too late for these personal things. Too many of them aren't doing the work that has to be done.

"Now some of the Chicano law students are thinking of organizing a collective but I've disagreed, because I think it is looking to the future as any other lawyer would do. They are thinking in terms of money to make, cases to take. They're thinking of business. For me to think of the future is inconsistent with my thinking of the present. It is only the present that is important."

22

The Native American Rights Fund

Not surprisingly, the first group of people to be decimated by the white man's manifest destiny was the last group to be helped during the "fashionable to help the poor" era of the sixties. Long after Black and poor people had demanded power, Native Americans still lived in oblivion and squalor. The lucky ones were still on their reservations, while those less lucky were scattered throughout urban areas and robbed of everything—their tribal identity, their land, their self-respect.

The lot of the almost one million people who inhabited the United States before European settlers came here seeking freedom and equality has not been a happy one. From the start, tribes were robbed of their land and pushed into ever-decreasing reservations. Tribal religion and culture, now coming under close scrutiny by a generation of young people disgusted with the results of the dreams of their forebears, were ignored as the settlers pushed their boundaries 'from sea to shining sea.' By 1860, the tribal population of the country had decreased to about 300,000. At the end of thirty more years of wars against the Indians, it had decreased even more. Those tribal people who had survived were relegated to reservations or rancherias in the least desirable parts of this country where they were kept and largely forgotten until the 1950s.

When they were remembered at that point it was by a group of politicians who, totally ignorant of the tribal culture, had decided that Indians should be fully integrated into the American society. Zealously, these legislators pursued a policy of termination of reservations, thus forcing Indian people to leave their tribes and go out into a dominant culture which they did not understand and, in large part, did not care to emulate.

Today, there are about half a million Indians who survived all of this and still live on the two to three hundred reservations that exist in the country plus almost three hundred thousand living in other locations. No one knows exactly how many Indians live off of reservations, in large part because, until recently, urban Indians did not know of each other's existence, and, therefore, made no effort to band together. The poverty suffered by American Indians is the greatest of any small ethnic group in the country. The average Indian's income is $1500, 75 percent below the national average; the unemployment rate among Indians is nearly 40 percent, more than ten times the national average; the average life expectancy for Indians is sixty-four, while it is seventy-one for all other Americans; the infant mortality rate is 40 percent higher than the national average; housing and education for Indians is totally inadequate, as is health care.

Given all of this, plus the fact that Indian demands, when made, were not for things like power or money but rather for the right to live as Indians, it is not surprising that good liberals and smart politicians shied away from the Indian issue until they could no longer ignore it, simply because, at that point, Indians were one of the few unhelped minorities in the country, and one of the few left who did not reject the help of whites when it was offered.

With general help, of course, came legal help, and that proved to be something of use to tribal people. Indians, like all other second nation groups, have a long history here of being treated poorly in the courtroom. In addition to that, they have added legal problems because they are in a "trust" relationship with the United States government. This relationship, which is just beginning to be defined in any real way, means, most simply, that when the government took Indian lands away it promised, in return, to act in the best interests of the Indians forever. The Bureau of Indian Affairs (BIA), currently within the Department of the Interior, is the government agency charged with carrying out this mission. What has happened in the past is that the BIA has usually forgotten the best interests of Indians when they have come up against any stronger government agency, and no one has been there to reprimand them for their laxity.

Now, however, there is a growing number of lawyers working to develop a definitive body of law that will protect Indian people from their protectors. The Native American Rights Fund (NARF) is the first national program of legal aid to Indians, although Legal Services programs have been present on some reservations since the midsixties, under the auspices of OEO.

In an indirect way, the Native American Rights Fund is an offshoot of California Rural Legal Assistance (CRLA). Some lawyers in a rural office of CRLA discovered that, in their practice, they had to deal with the unique legal problems of Indians. To do so effectively, the Indian Services Division of CRLA was formed. In 1968 this branch of CRLA became a separate organization called California Indian Legal Services (CILS).

David H. Getches, a young alumnus of the Escondido office of CILS, is now directing attorney of NARF.

"NARF began as a special project of CILS, funded by the Ford Foundation for an eighteen-month period beginning in July 1970. We got the project because several people had been trying to get a national program started, and we kept criticizing the proposals. Because of our criticisms, Ford gave us the grant. At that time our assignment was to undertake a limited number of important cases on behalf of Indians throughout the country, and to consult with Indians and others in order to determine and define the need for a national program. We found, almost immediately, that such a program was needed. Indian law is a very specialized law because of the trust relationship, and there were very few competent lawyers practicing it. There were only about forty Indian lawyers in the country, and many of them were not in Indian practice. Other lawyers who took Indian cases often had a difficult time because of the cultural gap between them and their clients.

"We found that our problems were more diverse and complex than those faced by other Legal Services attorneys. The federal government hasn't lived up to the trust relationship in many cases, and the BIA time and again doesn't act in the best interests of Indians. For instance, the BIA is supposed to take care of Indian education. Most often they do so by taking Indian children thousands of miles from their homes and putting them in schools where they are beaten and manacled. They are also supposed to take care of public health. We found one instance where, after a flood in California, some Indians were given sanitary, all-electric homes to replace the ones they had lost. The problem was that there was no electricity within twenty-six miles.

"We also found, not to our surprise, that when Indians go to court they generally lose. Anytime there is a victory, it's a real surprise. The courts have made some excellent Indian law in little cases where there isn't much at stake, but when we try to apply that law to big cases that involve substantial land, water, hunting, or fishing rights, we have trouble.

"And those rights are terribly important because, in some tribes, hunting or fishing is the only link they have left with Indian culture. For instance, Pyramid Lake is the only asset the Pyramid Lake Paiute Indians in Nevada have. When we began we found that the Bureau of Reclamation had begun to divert the water from the Truckee River, the only source of the lake, into a watershed that feeds water to white farmers. As a result the water level of the lake is dropping and this is causing the death of some of the species of wildlife in the lake. The tribe depends on fishing for these dying species and on selling fishing licenses to survive.

So their very existence depends on that lake. We've been in litigation for some time now trying to save Pyramid Lake.

"That is another problem that we encountered. All of these cases on land and water rights take a long time to litigate. Sometimes, while the litigation goes on some irreplaceable natural resources are being lost.

"We've also found that some states don't even recognize the treaty rights Indians have been given, and make state laws that forbid Indians to hunt or fish. In the Northwest, this is a real problem. For instance, in the state of Washington, when sports and commercial fishing had grown to a lucrative point, the state did not recognize Indian fishing rights. It got to the point where sports fishers started vigilante groups against Indian fishers, and even shot Indians found fishing on their own reservations. Finally, the government instituted a suit against the state but it was not comprehensive. Tribal leaders and individual Indians requested our assistance and we moved into the case, making it much broader. Some points that have never been litigated before are included in this suit.

"We find that that is often the case: that we are litigating points that have never been raised before. One of our strategies is to develop a body of law so that the trust relationship is grounded in law, rather than in political whim which has often been the case in the past. We are also trying to define legally the power of state governments vis a vis Indian tribes, and the obligations of state governments to Indians and Indian land. We are also trying to set the boundaries of tribal sovereignty over tribal land. Tribes should have the power of regulating and protecting their land, water, and natural resources from infringement by others."

During the period of their original Ford grant, NARF moved their offices from California to Boulder, Colorado. Because they received grants from other foundations, and from individuals, they were also able to increase their attorney staff to eleven, including two lawyers in a Washington, D.C., office. Now four of their attorneys (John Echohawk, Pawnee; Yvonne Knight, Ponca; Thomas W. Fredericks, Mandan; and Douglas Nash, Nez Perce) are Indians, as is a majority of their office staff. NARF is governed by an eleven-member, all-Indian steering committee which establishes policies and priorities for NARF attorneys.

Generally the committee has concurred with the previous priorities set for the NARF, so NARF continues to work on the protection of Indian natural resources, treaty rights, tribal sovereignty, education, termination, culture, religion, and Indian rights. They've been involved in virtually every major case involving Indians since their inception—from the Pyramid Lake and Black Mesa cases to the case concerning the death of Raymond Yellow Thunder.

NARF also provides support and technical assistance to any OEO Legal Services program that needs help in solving the problems of its Indian clients.

In recognition of the work they have done, the Ford Foundation gave them a three-year grant for $1.2 million in November 1971. This is the largest grant that Ford has ever given in the Indian field.

In 1972 their library, the National Indian Law Library (NILL), was given a $119,000 grant from the Carnegie Corporation of New York so that it can be developed into a clearinghouse for American Indian legal materials and resources. The grant will enable the library to gather pleadings, briefs, and decisions from many sources. The collection will then be completely catalogued and indexed. Copies of documents will be provided to anyone who requests them, and a monthly newsletter is published to announce the library's holdings and recent developments in Indian law.

John Echohawk, a Pawnee, has been with NARF since its beginning. Echohawk was born in Albuquerque, New Mexico, and raised in Farmington, which is in the northwest corner of the state. Although he did not grow up on a reservation, his father was a land surveyor and, working with him, he spent a lot of time on nearby reservations. He was one of a few Indian students who attended the public schools in Farmington.

"I don't recall any problems because of being an Indian. I felt more of a tie to the white culture, and was an American boy, I guess. I went through college on a National Merit Scholarship provided for an Indian student by the Santa Fe Railroad. I spent my first year at the University of Oklahoma and then went to the University of New Mexico. I had decided to be a lawyer before I started college. I abstractly thought that it would be more flexible than engineering, and that it would allow me to work with people. I'd been president of the student body in high school, and I also thought the law would let me use my talents as a politician.

"When I graduated I tried to get into several law schools but I got no scholarship. Then I found out that the University of New Mexico was starting a special program to train Indian lawyers. They accepted me on the spot, and I was the first graduate of that program. At that time that was the only such program in the country, but now there are several others and there are a hundred Indian law students in them. That's good considering there were only four Indians who graduated from law school in 1970. I was president of the student bar association during my last year of school. I also chartered the American Indian Law Student Association, which now includes virtually all of the Indian students in law school.

"When I was younger and in the dominant system I felt that it would be good for Indians. Then, when I was in law school, I began to feel that as an Indian lawyer I could solve Indian problems in Indian ways, although I know that the problems have to be solved through the dominant system because that is the system that is imposed on Indians. Indians must learn how to use the system for themselves.

"When I came here, right out of law school, I was the first Indian lawyer to work for a Legal Services program. Other Indian lawyers were in practice or helping the BIA or helping Indians for free, usually on the side. I had no reservations about coming here. I knew there were restrictions but there was also a lot of leeway. I think we can use the courts to make the government live up to the trust relationship. If lawyers had been doing that before, Indians wouldn't have lost their land and treaty rights. Now, because Indians have a lot of resources left on reservations, we have to battle so that they can hold on to them or make the best use of them.

"I haven't seen great changes in anything in the time that I've been here. I've just seen a lot of rhetoric coming out of Washington about protecting Indian resources, and I don't know whether they will live up to it.

"I'm optimistic about the future of Indians. Maybe I haven't been around long enough to see how the system works, and maybe when I have, I'll get out of it. It is in kind of a mess now. That's why I like the business I'm in. I can work to allow Indians to be Indians instead of just people in the dominant society. If we're successful, Indians can have some leeway. They can take the best of both systems."

Yvonne Knight, one of the very few women Indian attorneys in the country, and a fiery public speaker easily able to bring her audiences to their feet, is a more recent addition to the NARF staff.

"I was born in the Pawnee Indian hospital in Ponca City, Oklahoma. My father is a Ponca. I grew up on the Ponca Reservation, which is technically an Indian Community. People own land although the land is in trust. There is a tribal council and tribally owned property. My father is a leader in the tribe—he's been on the tribal council several times, and he's now executive director of the Tribal Acceleration Program, and on the board of directors of the tribe's housing program.

"My family's Catholic and I was sent to a parochial school in town, not for religious reasons but because the community school

was a poor, de facto segregated school. Ninety-nine percent of
the kids were Ponca. The community was checkerboarded by
whites but the white kids went to the city school.

"I did go to public school from the tenth through the twelve
grades. It's a good high school because Ponca City is an oil-rich
town, housing the Continental Oil Company. We started an Indian Club in high school there that still exists, although
extra-curricular activities were difficult for us because we were
bused back to the community right after school. In high school
the Indian kids kept to themselves and kind of clung to each
other. I was in college-bound classes and I was about the only Indian in them, but I still associated only with Indians. It was scary
to get that far in school because of the high attrition rate among
Indians.

"When I was a senior my father brought me a Bureau of Indian Affairs (BIA) college application and I filled it out and was
accepted. At that time the BIA wanted Indian college students to
work at one of their Indian schools for their room and board at
college. I worked at Haskell Indian School in Lawrence, Kansas,
and commuted to the University of Kansas for two years, then I
moved on to campus for two years. I graduated with a degree in
English education in 1965. In high school I'd been encouraged to
be a teacher and since sociology and anthropology seemed to be
the only other fields open to me, I thought teaching would be
best.

"I wasn't sure I could teach so I decided to try myself out on
non-Indian kids rather than make guinea pigs out of my own
people in a Bureau school. I taught for two years in a white Kansas high school and I didn't like it. I couldn't teach and the
bureaucracy discouraged me.

"My cousin was going to the new University of New Mexico
Law School program. He wrote and told me it was good, so I de-
cided to give it a try. I went to the summer program in 1968 and
I met Indians from all over. For the first time I found out about

tribal courts and tribal sovereignty, which Oklahoma Indians didn't have. I wondered why we couldn't have the same thing.

"All of us there knew we were after the same thing—being able to do something for our Indian tribes and people—and this created a strong bond. I decided I wanted to do it through law because I felt I could reach more people and do more for Indian people in the law than I could in any other profession. We also felt that this law school program was temporary and that we had to get as many Indian people as we could through it while it still existed. When I started there were only fifty Indian law students in the country. Now there are at least a hundred.

"In 1970 we formed the American Indian Law Student Association [AILSA], and I was on the first board of directors. To form it we brought in Indian law students from all over the country, and it was formed solely by Indian people. We felt that this was really important because we felt that the law is and would be essential for Indian people. We felt that AILSA was insurance that we'd be in law school even if the government withdrew money from the Indian law program. When I was in the program OEO funded it, now the BIA does. In 1972 the BIA proposed taking out the funding, the summer program, and the central administration of the Indian program at the University of New Mexico law school. Also in that year we formed the American Indian Lawyers Association, the first Indian Bar Association.

"When I graduated I came right to NARF on a Reggie. Originally I wanted to go back to Oklahoma but I couldn't find a Legal Services program there that served Indians. I thought NARF would give me a chance to work on both Oklahoma Indian problems and national Indian affairs. At NARF I've been working on the problems of terminated tribes and on education. My first education case was in Oklahoma and concerned boys who'd been expelled from school because they'd grown their hair to participate in Indian activities. That case was won.

"I think the problems of the American Indian are very complex. I don't see law as an ultimate answer, but I think it can play a crucial role. The thing to me isn't winning one case but attacking a very complex problem from all sides—law being one.

"I think the law played a greater role and is more crucial for Indians than for any other minority. Treaties are laws because tribes are sovereign nations. The law can keep Indians together as a people.

"I think American Indians should have the option of being Indian or going into white society. I believe that if Indian people are destroyed as a people, as tribes, the nation is in real trouble because it has gone back on its own principle of allowing people to be what they are if they're not bothering others.

"Although it's hard to be optimistic about a country that's followed a policy of trying to exterminate Indian tribes, I think if ever there was a time for optimism this is it. Now we can be as optimistic as we ever could be.

"I don't think there's any doubt that there are two standards of justice in this country—one for the rich and one for the poor, and most Indians are poor. That's why Indian lawyers want to see more Indians become lawyers. Attorneys for the poor will have to take the lead, with interested white attorneys, in changing the double standard of justice in the country."

Conclusions

The people's law movement today is composed of lawyers, legal workers, and concerned citizens who have in common an interest in people above property or money, and a general dissatisfaction with the way the court system and the country are working. Aside from these two similarities, the people involved differ greatly in the degree of their interest in people, in the degree of their dissatisfaction, and in their proposals for correcting the wrongs that they see. They range from liberal to revolutionary, from ethnic nationalist to total integrationist, from male chauvinist to women's liberationist. Their ideas for correcting both the court system and the general system go from reformist patchwork to revolutionary overthrow. In short, the differences in the people's law movement parallel the differences in the general movement for social and political change.

Like the general movement, the people's law movement is now threatened by two things: external repression and internal fragmentation. The first problem is an obvious one and expected. Whenever large groups of people demand change in the society, the government of that society responds with fear, repression, and a pulling back to the status quo, preferably, the status quo of a hundred years ago.

In this last century the world in general, and this country in particular, seem to have experienced the greatest quantity of change that has been known in recorded history. The United States has gone from a largely agricultural psychology, sociology, and economy to the most developed technocracy in the world today.

Unfortunately, the human psyche has not been able to keep pace with the development of the machine. Consequently, we have become a global village with a horse and buggy mentality. We've become a computerized, technocratized, bureaucratized nation yearning for the good old days of the friendly country sheriff and judge saving us all from any threats to the order in the streets or the law in the courts. Having invented and developed all of the machines and other implements that have allowed us to reach this highly developed mechanical state, we now basically yearn to reject them. They've just proven to be too threatening to the old roles, the old values.

Since no one seems to know exactly where he does stand today —with minorities challenging the dominant white culture, women challenging the dominant male role, children challenging all adult authority, socialists challenging the dominant pseudocapitalistic economy, radicals challenging our image of democracy, small nations challenging our imperialistic role, and lawyers challenging the court system of which they are a part—it should be expected that the establishment would respond with a desire to return to the old days when roles were clearly defined and everyone stayed in his place. Such a desire does, of course, lead to repression of the people who are attempting to forge change.

Since the United States has long held dear the myth that we are a country ruled by laws and not by men, even though this myth has never been supported by fact, it is inevitable that, during decades of protest or challenge, the country would retreat into law as the foremost upholder of the status quo.

However, during this past decade, when just such protests,

challenges, and retreats were taking place they spread from the streets into the courtrooms in a way, and on a scale, that has never happened before. As lawyers challenged the country club atmosphere of the courtroom and the white skin and penis privilege that people needed to become members of that club, they blocked off the government's first line of retreat to the status quo. Blocking off anyone's retreat is always disconcerting and frustrating to the blockees, thus often causing them to lash out at the blockers with a fury that they might prefer not to reveal.

It is not surprising, therefore, that people's lawyers were arrested, or given contempt sentences, or hassled by the organized bar during the last decade. What is surprising is that they were not repressed more. As challenges to the court system and the legal structure of the country increase, even on a less flamboyant scale, than, for example, the challenge that came with the Chicago Seven conspiracy trial, it is likely that the negative reaction to these challenges by the government and the organized, traditional bar will increase.

The only benefit of increased repression of the people's law movement would be that it would probably rectify the internal fragmentation which stems from a wide variety of causes.

The lawyers identified with each section of the movement are basically different kinds of people, with differing philosophies, world views, solutions to injustices, and personalities.

Rights lawyers are the liberals of the movement. They serve amorphous constituencies—the Bill of Rights, the poor, the public interest. Their contact with the people, since many of their cases are on the appellate level, is limited. Consequently, they tend to be more intellectual, abstract, and independent of control by their clients than lawyers in the other two sections. Especially in the case of civil libertarians, they tend not to side with any one group. The ACLU might fight for the rights of the Black Panther and George Wallace in the same week, although this sort of activity has been modified somewhat by the infiltration of more activist attorneys into that and other civil libertarian organizations.

However, because of their history of having this viewpoint, other people's lawyers accuse them of having too much of a parochial, fence-sitting attitude at a time when others feel that there are obvious good, and bad, guys.

Rights lawyers also tend to believe that the system can be repaired, can work, if only good, concerned people, like themselves, were running it. They believe in the Constitution; they believe in democracy; many of them believe in a modified capitalistic economy. Other types of people's lawyers disagree with them down the line and accuse them of abstract wishy-washiness.

Radical lawyers range from the radicals to the revolutionaries of the movement. Since they do a lot of trial work, they are in closer touch with the general movement than are the rights lawyers, and they, therefore, go through the same struggles that the general movement does. There have been splits within this section of the people's law movement between the older lawyers and younger lawyers. For instance, older lawyers generally opposed opening the Guild to legal workers since they wanted it to remain a somewhat traditional bar association, while younger lawyers were generally in favor of their admission since they wanted the Guild to become a large-membership, political organization. There have also been splits between male and female lawyers, and male lawyers and female legal workers over the whole question of the women's movement. There was a point when the women felt, with good reason, that the men, while against oppression of ethnic groups at home and of third world people abroad, were practicing the same sort of oppression toward women both inside and outside the law office. The women also felt that the men were not sensitive enough to the problems women encountered from the generally sexist structure of the entire legal system—from law school to the courtroom.

Another split in this section of the movement came about between lawyers in traditional law firms who did little or nothing about professionalism, elitism, and sexism in the law office, and collectivists, who were attempting to struggle with these forms of oppression on a daily basis. People from traditional firms accused the people in collectives of being too process-oriented, too concerned with their development as collectives, and too unconcerned with their skills as lawyers. In turn, the collectivists told the traditionalists that they were guilty of the same types of oppression that they were fighting in the establishment. And there are also differences among radicals from different parts of the country.

People from the other sections of the people's law movement accuse radical lawyers of engaging in too much in-fighting, of being too emotional and flamboyant, of identifying with their clients so much that they lose their effectiveness as defense counsels within the courtroom. Second nation lawyers also accuse the radical lawyers of being parasites, of refusing to allow ethnic lawyers to participate in the cases of minority people, of building the collective ideology in such a way that it excludes second nation people who are not willing to accept that entire ideology. There is also a feeling that white radical lawyers and legal workers should be relating to the problems of whites, rather than trying, through political education and reading, to relate to the problems of minority groups.

As minority people in the United States are a second nation within the boundaries of the dominant white one, so second nation lawyers are a second nation within the people's law movement. The attorneys within this section range from liberal to revolutionary. In addition, there are differences among the Black, Chicano, Indian, and other ethnic attorneys based upon their ethnic identities.

Some second nation attorneys favor reform, while others favor revolution. Some believe in capitalism, others, in socialism. Some are concerned with the woman question; others feel that it is irrelevant to them. In other words, the only real bond between the attorneys here described as second nation is that they are all the victims of the dominant culture, and they are united in their opposition to that victimization of them, and of their people.

The older second nation organizations, such as the Inc. Fund, come under attack by both radical and other second nation lawyers because they are viewed as establishment-oriented, timid, and too cut-off from the people they purport to serve.

Some militant second nation attorneys are accused of the same things that white radical attorneys are—too much emotionalism and flamboyancy, and a high client identification that often cuts down their effectiveness in the courtroom. White radical lawyers also tend to accuse these attorneys of being impractical and, perhaps, immature in their demands that only third world lawyers serve third world groups at this time when the legal profession is still composed largely—over 95 percent—of white male attorneys.

There is also a lot of discussion among radical and second nation attorneys about the so-called "star" system whereby those lawyers who get most attention in the press become most in demand to handle "big" political cases. A lot of lawyers feel that this system is unjust both to the attorneys and to their clients. They feel that star lawyers usually begin to believe their own press reports, and thus increase their elitism and professionalism. They also feel that, by bringing big-name lawyers into different localities to handle cases, local legal talent is not given the chance to develop its skill in political cases. Clients often suffer because their causes are dimmed by the radiance of the "stars," and because the "star," already having a heavy case load, cannot give as much attention as he or she should to the case.

The solution most often proposed for this problem is developing community law firms that relate to all of the cases, big or small, coming out of their own communities. Acceptance of this solution seems to be spreading, and, in the next decade, many more community firms will probably come into existence.

Despite these differences, and internal criticisms, the lawyers who compose the people's law movement basically do support each other, and work together closely during times of stress, such as during the southern civil rights movement, the Attica Prison rebellion, or the Indian takeover of Wounded Knee, South Dakota, in 1973.

It is natural for the people in any movement for change to criticize and analyze themselves and each other. If they did not show this sensitivity to internal, as well as external, injustice and contradictions, they would not be involved in a movement for change. People's lawyers are trying to redefine their own internal roles while they are working for a change in the legal system and the country. They are trying to move the remnants of their own horse and buggy mentalities into the global village age, and this is a difficult, sometimes painful, process, yet one that is obviously important.

Over the next few years I expect that the people's law movement will continue to grow and evolve. Law school enrollment has more than doubled between 1961 and 1971, and even at that, law schools are able to accommodate fewer than one-half of those who want to enroll. By 1974, thirty thousand people will graduate from law school each year, and more than half of them won't be able to find conventional legal jobs.

In view of the political convictions of most college people less than twenty-five years old today, it seems safe to assume that a good percentage of law students over the next few years will be radical by the time they graduate, if not before. While many of the lawyers in this book had to struggle to become radicals, these new lawyers will be radical almost as a matter of course.

They won't have to search their souls to find reasons to oppose the dominant system since they will have been opposing it for years, and with good reasons. They know that with its outdated laws on the draft, politics, conspiracy, drugs, sex, etcetera, the system has made unnecessary criminals out of many of their friends. One out of two males born after World War II has been or will be arrested sometime during his life.

These new people's lawyers, like some of the younger ones discussed in this book, will have become lawyers specifically because they know a lawyer's education gives one outstanding tools for undermining, or, at least, stalemating the dominant system. With at least two lawyers to fill every available legal job opening through 1980, the chances of these new people's lawyers being bought off is minimal. Legal collectives or some form of public interest firm will be about the only employment alternative open to these lawyers.

As more people's lawyers come into the movement, and those already in it become more dedicated and proficient, it's likely that external repression of the movement and its lawyers will increase. With Nixon's re-election, and his administration's apparent attitude that every instance of opposition to its policies must be regarded as a test of strength, more repression is almost guaranteed. We can now only guess how much muscle the government will use to prove its strength, and how much muscle the movement has to show its opposition.

As long as the government chooses to show its strength by dragging people who oppose it into the courtroom, people's lawyers will stand ready to fight in that arena. And many are ready to help take the battles out of the courtroom if that becomes necessary.